A Fiery Gospel

A VOLUME IN THE SERIES

Religion and American Public Life

Edited by Darryl G. Hart and R. Laurence Moore

For a list of books in the series, visit our website at cornellpress.cornell.edu.

A Fiery Gospel

*The Battle Hymn of the Republic
and the Road to Righteous War*

Richard M. Gamble

Cornell University Press

Ithaca and London

First published 2019 by Cornell University Press

Printed in the United States of America

Library of Congress Cataloging-in-Publication Data

Names: Gamble, Richard M., author.
Title: A fiery gospel : the Battle hymn of the Republic and the road to righteous war / Richard M. Gamble.
Description: Ithaca [New York] : Cornell University Press, 2019. | Series: Religion and American public life | Includes bibliographical references and index.
Identifiers: LCCN 2018052746 (print) | LCCN 2018056017 (ebook) | ISBN 9781501736421 (pdf) | ISBN 9781501736438 (ret) | ISBN 9781501736414 | ISBN 9781501736414 (cloth; alk. paper)
Subjects: LCSH: Civil religion—United States—History—19th century. | Howe, Julia Ward, 1819-1910. Battle hymn of the Republic. | Battle hymn of the republic (Song) | United States—History—Civil War, 1861–1865—Religious aspects. | Nationalism—United States—History—19th century. | Nationalism—Religious aspects—Christianity.
Classification: LCC BL98.5 (ebook) | LCC BL98.5 .G36 2019 (print) | DDC 201/.720973—dc23
LC record available at https://lccn.loc.gov/2018052746

To the memory of my father

CONTENTS

THE BATTLE HYMN
OF THE REPUBLIC

As published in the *New-York Tribune*, January 14, 1862

Mine eyes have seen the glory of the coming of the Lord:
He is trampling out the vintage where the grapes of wrath are stored;
He hath loosed the fateful lightning of His terrible swift sword:
His truth is marching on.

I have seen him in the watch-fires of a hundred circling camps;
They have builded Him an altar in the evening dews and damps;
I have read his righteous sentence by the dim and flaring lamps:
His day is marching on.

I have read a fiery gospel writ in burnished rows of steel:
"As ye deal with my contemners, so with you my grace shall deal;
Let the Hero, born of woman, crush the serpent with his heel,
Since God is marching on."

He has sounded forth the trumpet that shall never call retreat;
He is sifting out the hearts of men before His judgment-seat:
Oh, be swift, my soul, to answer Him! be jubilant, my feet!
Our God is marching on.

In the beauty of the lilies Christ was born across the sea,
With a glory in his bosom that transfigures you and me:
As he died to make men holy, let us die to make men free,
While God is marching on.

A Fiery Gospel

PROLOGUE

President Lincoln arrived late. By the time he and the First Lady took their seats in the House chamber, they had missed the evening's convening prayer and Vice President Hannibal Hamlin's opening remarks. The Philadelphia merchant George Stuart was well into his speech when the audience spotted the Lincolns and greeted them with "a tempest of applause" followed by a standing ovation that brought the proceedings to a temporary halt.[1]

This was a rare public appearance for the president in 1864. He found it hard to take time away from his duties as commander in chief nearly three years into civil war. But he accepted Stuart's telegraphed invitation to join the other dignitaries that evening in early February. The celebration in the House of Representatives marked the second anniversary of the United States Christian Commission. The order of events differed little from a worship service. One DC newspaper described the crowd as "composed, in great part, of the religious element of the city."[2] They had come to reaffirm their faith in the Union war effort and renew their commitment to serve soldiers and their families. The wartime mix of state, church, and military was on full display. The audience heard not only from preachers and laymen active in founding and running the commission but also from the Speaker of the House Schuyler Colfax of Indiana, Senator John Sherman of Ohio, and Major General John Henry Martindale, the military governor of Washington, DC.[3]

The Christian Commission had been founded on November 16, 1861, by the Young Men's Christian Association (YMCA) at a convention in New York City. The commission's publicized aim was "to promote the spiritual and temporal welfare of the officers and men of the United States army and navy, in co-operation with chaplains and others"—in a way that "would be pleasing to the Master." For the sake of that high calling, the commission solicited donations of goods and money, distributed Bibles, books, and tracts by the tens of thousands, promoted temperance in the encampments, and recruited volunteer workers and ministers of the gospel from all Protestant denominations to care for the souls of men in uniform. Along with the parallel United States Sanitary Commission, it tended to the sick, wounded, and dying. Its tireless chairman was the successful entrepreneur Stuart, founder of the Philadelphia YMCA. Testimonials poured in praising the work of the commission.[4]

The highlight of the evening for Lincoln, and certainly for others in the House chamber, was a rendition of the "Battle Hymn of the Republic" by Chaplain Charles C. McCabe, a frequent speaker and fund-raiser for the Christian Commission. In 1862, while chaplain of the 122nd Ohio Infantry, McCabe had been captured by Confederate forces and taken to Libby Prison in Richmond. He was there on July 6, 1863, when news reached the inmates of the Union victory at Gettysburg. The soldiers burst into song—everything from "Yankee Doodle" to the "Doxology." But then McCabe led them in singing the words of a poem he had clipped from the *Atlantic Monthly* and memorized. He knew Julia Ward Howe's poem matched the cadences of "John Brown's Body," a favorite Union marching song, and the prisoners joined him in the chorus, singing, "Glory, glory, hallelujah!"

McCabe told this moving story of his prison experience, and then sang the "Battle Hymn" as a duet with an army colonel just released from Libby, asking the audience to join him in the chorus accompanied by a regimental brass band. According to the *Sunday School Times*, McCabe sang "with much sweetness and power." Swept up by the refrain, the audience's "enthusiasm was aroused to such a pitch, so that few scenes like it have ever been witnessed in a public gathering." "Applause greeted the ending of nearly every stanza," the account continued, "and in the last, before reaching the chorus, the pent up enthusiasm could be restrained no longer, but burst forth in a torrent of exultant shouts and cheers that made the Hall ring to the roof."[5] Soon, Lincoln shouted, "Sing it again!" and Vice President Hamlin announced that McCabe would repeat his performance. Before he did so, McCabe delivered a charge to the president from a fellow Libby prisoner "in the name of the martyrs of Liberty": "Tell the President not to back down an inch." Lincoln replied, "I won't back down." Shouts of "Amen!" came from the crowd. The uproar and the whole evening were unlike any spectacle most had ever witnessed.[6]

For the twenty-seven-year-old McCabe, this had been a thrilling commemoration at the Capitol. He was seated right in front of the Lincolns. He wrote to his wife before going to bed that night that during the speeches of two pastors he had seen "tears [roll] down the rugged cheeks" of the president. The press agreed that "there were few dry eyes in the hall" as the first pastor told gruesome and sentimental stories of caring for the wounded after Antietam and Gettysburg. The second said he repented of his pharisaical indifference at the outset of the war and now, conscience-stricken, rejoiced that he had come to understand that in order to be of real service "he had only [to] follow Christ's example, whose hands were as busy as his sympathies were unbounded." According to McCabe's diary, when the president saw him again at a White House reception two weeks later, "Mr. Lincoln recognized me as the man who sang the 'Battle Hymn of the Republic' at the Capitol and was kind enough to compliment both the song and the singing. My vanity was considerably delighted. Sure, and how could I help it?"[7]

From this point on, McCabe helped make the "Battle Hymn of the Republic" inseparable from the Union cause. At fund-raising events across the country for the duration of the war and for years afterward, the Methodist chaplain and later bishop would center Howe's poem in a decidedly evangelical setting—closer to the childhood she had left behind than to the world of liberal religion she promoted as an adult. He sang the anthem and told the story of Libby Prison for decades. As it spread, the "Battle Hymn" seemed unimpeded by any denominational boundaries or theological affirmations. Soon it was freed from historical and theological contexts altogether and was with ease turned to the purposes of other wars and reform causes at home and around the world—not only by Americans, but by the British Empire, other nation builders, and idealists everywhere.

Over the past century and a half, Americans of all sorts have used the "Battle Hymn of the Republic" to understand their nation's meaning, to define their enemies, to justify their wars, and to reaffirm God's special plan for the United States in world history. Howe's anthem seems ubiquitous on Memorial Day, the Fourth of July, at political conventions and funerals, and in Sunday morning worship. With the "Battle Hymn," Americans who glide easily among religion, politics, and war are able to honor their God and their nation at the same time. Or so it would seem. In one sense, the story of the "Battle Hymn of the Republic" falls under the rubric of "civil religion." If we define civil religion, in Ronald Beiner's handy formulation, as "the appropriation of religion by politics for its own purposes," then the "Battle Hymn" easily qualifies as part of this process and endures as one of the national faith's most successful products.[8] But it does so only indirectly, since Howe's poem itself appropriated Christianity (at least an abstract Christianity of philosophical idealism), followed by politicians who used its allusions to the Old and New Testaments to define a nation, promote domestic reform, and justify foreign wars. Howe's mobilized "Bible" became itself an American scripture ready to be appropriated for further service to the savior-nation.

In its origin and many of its subsequent uses, the "Battle Hymn" was not strictly a piece of civil religion along the lines of Beiner's definition. Terms like "civil religion" can obscure as much as they illuminate. When Howe appropriated scripture for a war poem in 1861, she did so as a private citizen who voluntarily devoted her religion to the Union cause, and beyond that to the redemption of humanity. When preachers and journalists and innumerable ordinary citizens and churchgoers quoted and sang the "Battle Hymn" to affirm their patriotism, mobilize the economy, explain why the South must be defeated, or simply support the Union troops, they too engaged in a voluntary act that knowingly or otherwise spiritualized America for the sake of winning the war and the peace to follow. What resulted was not necessarily the political appropriation of religion. Something larger was at work.

To be sure, there is a looser meaning for "civil religion" that might better capture the complex story of the "Battle Hymn" and its role in making America sacred. In his landmark essay in 1967, the sociologist Robert Bellah launched a whole field of scholarship when he looked at the way civil religion functioned in America, taking his cue from John F. Kennedy's use of religion in his inaugural address.[9] Kennedy's God-talk was generically theistic rather than recognizably Christian or doctrinally Roman Catholic. Bellah placed Kennedy within what he argued was an authentic American tradition of mixing religion in general with politics. Some of what counted as "religion"—what served, that is, to bind the nation together with a common affirmation of faith—was in fact not originally religious at all but rather a host of heroes, battles, founding myths, documents, and principles raised to the level of creed and ritual. A nation honors these memories and ideals, passes them on to younger generations, and elevates them into the unquestionable realm of a sacred deliverance to a people for their safekeeping. Memories can be faulty, ideals can be reinvented over time, and political propositions can become armed doctrines animated with missionary zeal—but civil religion continues to prove its durability in politics and war.

For some, "civil religion" has served as a fairly benign way of speaking of America's founding documents and principles *as if they were* religion and never goes beyond being *like* a religion to substitute for Christianity or another historic faith. But this tendency seems to be the exception rather than the rule. The civil religion on display at national holidays and presidential inaugurations looks and sounds like a national liturgy for a national worship service, as was clearly the case in the House chamber in 1864. The temptation to make something transcendent and metaphysical out of America's documents, ideals, and history has proven irresistible for many. This has been the case especially with the Declaration of Independence, or fragments of it. Even the sociologists, political theorists, and literature professors who write about American civil religion seem more often than not to be engaged in an act of reaffirmation of civil religion or even, in Bellah's case, to be adding another "I believe" to the nation's creed. The effort to make nations sacred was most evident in the romantic nationalism that shaped Europe and North and South America in the nineteenth century. *Altar, saint, apostle, martyr, temple, ark, creed*—all of these words were used to speak of the nation-state in wars for independence and wars for national consolidation. Greece, Poland, Hungary, Italy, Germany, Latin American republics, and the United States all spoke this way at midcentury and used this language to define themselves, their enemies, and their cause.

The "Battle Hymn of the Republic," its durability and success, makes the most sense in the context of romantic nationalism and the philosophical idealism that accompanied it. Julia Ward Howe brought these two worlds together as effectively as anyone of her generation. The way the poem was formulated, how it was put to work, how it was in turn appropriated for wars and reform crusades of all kinds is better described as religious nationalism—or nationalism *as* religion—than simply "civil religion," with its narrow concern with politics. The story of a "sacramental" poem as potent as the "Battle Hymn," its success as a means of grace to make and keep America holy and righteous, its use even by other nations to inspire America to take up its duty to the world—this whole story shows the analytical power available to students of the past when they think in terms of religious nationalism rather than merely civil religion. At the very least, "religious nationalism" more accurately names one aspect of the experience of religion in American life. Americans take pride in their institutional separation of church and state, no matter how much they might disagree about a "wall of separation" or whether the church is more a danger to the state or the state to the church. Innumerable books attempt to understand church and state in America. If, instead of church and state, officially separated for the sake of religious and civil liberty, we think of the relationship between *religion* and *nation*, a wider world of inquiry opens up before us. If Americans have honored and even strengthened the legal separation of church and state, they have rarely separated religion from nation. Americans on the whole have proven eager, on the one hand, to bring nationalism into their churches (witness flags at the front, the national anthem sung in worship, political sermons, and even the Pledge of Allegiance in the weekly order of service) and, on the other hand, to bring religion into their celebrations of the sacred nation called to do God's will in the world. Perhaps it is telling that academics publish

a *Journal of Church and State* but not a *Journal of Religion and Nation.*
The combination of religion and nation in American history might be
more important than the ostensible separation of church and state.

An examination of the role the "Battle Hymn of the Republic" played
in making America sacred offers an opportunity to broaden, deepen, and
enrich our understanding of the phenomenon of religious nationalism. It
may help us to see religious nationalism in unexpected places, being invoked by unlikely people, and happening early and in circumstances other
than what we expected. Religious nationalism uses the language of meta-
physics, transcendence, and redemption to extol the nation and its history and people. But Americans' tendency to speak in transcendent terms
about their nation has been anything but otherworldly; it has instead been
an exercise in radical immanence. Sacred nations drag the divine down to
earth. America's homegrown and imported romantic nationalism put God
in nature, God in history, and God in America. Since the United States
stood as the highest embodiment yet of God's will in the world, America
was the instrument of his plan. Other nations and people could either join
in that common cause or be treated as an obstacle to God's truth. In 1858,
a German immigrant who popularized Hegelianism in the United States
called America the "savior nation"—nothing less than the fulfillment of
Jesus's call to his disciples to be a "city on a hill."[10] In the Civil War that
soon followed, Julia Ward Howe wrote a poem that placed God inside
the war, inside the American nation, and inside the progress of humanity.
Whether Howe's song of divine immanence was used to announce God's
wrath, justice, redemption, or calling to future service—it always made
America sacred.

When Julia Ward Howe stayed in New York, she often attended the Unitarian All Souls Church to hear her friend Henry Whitney Bellows preach.
Bellows was Stuart's counterpart at the United States Sanitary Commission, a civilian agency founded in 1861 and authorized by the War Department to provide medical care and other relief to Union soldiers and
sailors and their families. The Crimean War in the 1850s had shown what
modern mechanized warfare would demand of support services charged
with preventing and treating disease in the camps, tending to the sick
and wounded, and caring for the dead. The Civil War soon outstripped

anything the Crimean War had prepared Americans to imagine happening on their own soil to their own sons.[11]

In many ways, the Sanitary Commission and the Christian Commission complemented each other, and they often joined forces in fund-raising campaigns. The two worlds of the more Unitarian and liberal Sanitary Commission and the more evangelical Christian Commission met personally in Julia Ward Howe's extended family. Her physician husband, Samuel Gridley Howe, worked closely with Bellows on the Sanitary Commission, and her uncle, a leading evangelical Protestant Episcopal rector in Brooklyn, was one of the original commissioners tapped by Stuart to organize the Christian Commission. In a sense, though, both benevolent organizations were evangelical. Both promoted an active Christian faith that spoke to the most pressing ethical, political, and economic troubles of the day. Both mobilized their churches for a nation at war. Both absorbed the sacred into the secular and the secular into the sacred.

Reviewing the Sanitary Commission's singular service to the nation in 1879, Bellows boasted that one of the organization's purposes had been to "help make America sacred in the eyes of the living children of her scattered States."[12] The "Battle Hymn of the Republic" was drawn into that effort. Each stanza united God's judgment and his highest purposes with the Union army and America's historic mission. From the moment of its composition, Howe's "Battle Hymn" has been used to sustain that effort to make America sacred—whether rallying troops, mobilizing the home front, reassuring doubters, or turning in judgment against a nation that has failed to live up to its meaning and aspirations. The "Battle Hymn of the Republic" proved to be an effective tool for making the nation and its wars holy and righteous. Politicians, diplomats, preachers, novelists, journalists, and others have kept the "Battle Hymn of the Republic" securely at the nexus between nationalism and religion. Indeed, following Bellows's lead, they have used it ever since the Civil War to preach nationalism as religion in times of crisis.

Abraham Lincoln did not forget the work of the Christian Commission and the Sanitary Commission in the months following the celebration in the House chamber with its tent-revival enthusiasm and personal rededication to the cause. Union victory seemed certain by the summer of 1864 but still slow in coming, and care for soldiers' bodies and souls would have to carry on to the end. At a joint fair held in Philadelphia, the president praised the efforts of both benevolent organizations for "giving proof that the national resources are not at all exhausted, and that the national patriotism will sustain us through all."[13] When Christian Commission chairman Stuart thanked the president for his kind remarks, he still had McCabe and the "Battle Hymn" on his mind. He reminded Lincoln that the "Battle Hymn" had been sung a second time that night at the president's request.[14] The Army of the Potomac under Ulysses S. Grant now bore down on Richmond, and Stuart pledged the unstinting efforts of his commission as the North pressed on to a decisive victory.

That army, under the prior command of George McClellan in 1861, had inspired Julia Ward Howe to write her religious-nationalist anthem. When the war ended in 1865, the role the "Battle Hymn" would play in national and world affairs had hardly begun. Howe's song quickly became a way to celebrate victory, honor Union veterans, memorialize the war dead, and mobilize Americans for new battles on the domestic front and in the Caribbean, the Pacific, Europe, Southeast Asia, and the Middle East. While many Americans sang the "Battle Hymn" ignorant of its author, origin, and meaning, they nevertheless sang words that summoned their nation to an apocalyptic holy war infused with divine wrath and a spirit of conquest aimed at remaking their nation and their world in ever-widening gyres.

The "Battle Hymn" began in 1861 as a song of judgment, as Howe's contribution to a beleaguered righteous nation fighting for unification and faced with troubling setbacks and confusion. With Union victory in 1865, the "Battle Hymn" rang out from pulpits and platforms as a song of triumph, and from black schoolchildren in Richmond, Virginia, as a song of deliverance. Thereafter, it helped sustain a culture of victory in the North while the South nursed a culture of defeat.[15] In America's subsequent wars, from the Spanish-American War in 1898 to the War on Terror after September 11, the "Battle Hymn" has served the nation as its song of destiny, a theme song to accompany American exceptionalism and the nation's benevolent global mission. Meanwhile, for an increasing number of Americans, the "Battle Hymn" reappeared as a song of judgment, calling the nation to repentance for sins past and present. That call went out in crusades as different as Billy Graham's and Martin Luther King Jr.'s. Upon

John F. Kennedy's assassination in 1963, the "Battle Hymn" began to take hold as the nation's song of mourning. It became an American requiem. Democrats and Republicans, famous and obscure, found in the "Battle Hymn" a way to honor the fallen. Only the "Battle Hymn" among the nation's anthems has had the power to combine religion, nationalism, and war in a way that has seemed as fitting for slain presidents as for victims of international terrorism.

1

THE BESIEGED CITY

Newspapers hardly noticed the band of Bostonians making their way by train to Washington, DC, in November 1861. If they happened to report on the visit at all, it was only to mark the comings and goings of the most famous members of the entourage.[1] Massachusetts governor John Albion Andrew and the philanthropist Samuel Gridley Howe were by far the most newsworthy of the group, closely connected as they were to the war effort now entering its eighth month. James Freeman Clarke was known in America and abroad as one of the nation's most progressive theologians, second only to the late Theodore Parker in pushing the boundaries of liberal Christianity. The rest of the travelers included the governor's wife and his chief of staff, the Reverend Clarke's wife, the literary critic Edwin P. Whipple and his wife, Charlotte, and the poet and abolitionist Julia Ward Howe. They were all friends and at one time or another all members of Clarke's church. Julia had not yet begun to keep the journal that would ultimately cover more than forty years. Later in life she would have to rely on others for some of the details of this week in

Washington. Surviving letters are few. Only in hindsight would Julia, her children, the American public, and the world at large make the abolitionist poet the centerpiece of this visit to Washington and turn the poem she wrote there into the most famous literary production of the Civil War.

The Julia who arrived in Washington in mid-November was forty-two years old, a wife and mother of six, and responsible not only for a large family and servants but for hosting an endless stream of guests at her home.[2] A full-length photograph taken about 1861 shows her dressed in black, with her hands crossed at the waist, the left hand grasping the wrist of the right. Her eyes seem unfocused, and the overall impression is somber if not melancholy. She suffered from depression her whole life, at times debilitating depression, and her marriage was never easy, teetering at one point on the brink of divorce.[3] In the autumn of 1861, her children ranged in age from seventeen to not quite two: Julia Romana (born in Rome in 1844), Florence "Flossy" Marion (born in 1845), Henry Marion (born in 1848), Laura Elizabeth (born in 1850), Maud (born in 1855), and Samuel "Sammy" Gridley Jr. (born in 1859).

Julia did not begin life as a Bostonian. She was born in New York City in 1819 at a time of explosive growth after the War of 1812. The postwar boom had drawn many New Englanders to Manhattan to seek their fortune. Her father became one of the wealthiest men in the city. Her lineage combined Puritan and Cavalier ancestry of distinguished pedigree. Julia's mother, Julia Rush Cutler, a published poet in her own right, had South Carolina roots that included the Revolutionary War hero Francis Marion. She was a pious woman, faithful in the work of the church, and her brother was a leading cleric in the evangelical movement within the Protestant Episcopal Church. She died after childbirth when her daughter Julia was only five.

Julia's widowed father, Samuel Ward, was a partner in the New York banking firm of Prime, Ward, and King. He helped the city weather the storm of Andrew Jackson's Bank War and the Panic of 1837. He worried constantly over the education and spiritual formation of his children. He reared them in the low-church Protestant Episcopal Church, which stood for orthodoxy in a city being infiltrated by New England Unitarianism, among other threats to fundamental doctrines of the faith. Samuel Ward descended from hearty New Englanders, including a refugee from Oliver Cromwell's army who had fled to Rhode Island. His grandfather served

Figure 1. Julia Ward Howe, ca. 1861. From Laura Richards, Maud Elliott, and Florence Hall, *Julia Ward Howe, 1819–1916* (Boston: Houghton Mifflin, 1916), 1:186.

as colonial governor of Rhode Island and in the Continental Congress. His father rose to the rank of lieutenant colonel in the Continental Army. Ward's philanthropy included membership in the American Bible Society and the New York Colonization Society, the presidency of the New-York City Temperance Society, and fund-raising for the construction of Episcopal churches and colleges in the expanding West and South.[4] He died in 1839, leaving Julia in the care of his brother.

Julia grew up in a world of privilege, of books, art, and music, good manners and witty banter, all tempered by evangelical piety. Ward at first sent Julia to private girls' schools in New York, but when she was in her late teens he hired the brilliant Joseph Green Cogswell as her tutor. Cogswell had pursued graduate studies in Germany, along with Edward Everett, George Ticknor, and George Bancroft—all among the first Americans to do so. With Bancroft, Cogswell founded the prestigious Round Hill School in Northampton, Massachusetts. Ward sent all three of his sons to Round Hill and helped keep the school afloat as Cogswell struggled on for several years after Bancroft departed. At Ward's insistence, Cogswell came to live with the family on Bond Street to supervise his three daughters' education.[5]

Julia's marriage to Samuel Gridley Howe in 1843 plunged her into the intellectual, religious, and reform world of Boston. This was the Boston of transcendentalism and Unitarianism, of nearby Brook Farm and Harvard Divinity School; of literary journals, denominational magazines, and publishing houses; of Ralph Waldo Emerson, Henry David Thoreau, Nathaniel Hawthorne, Margaret Fuller, and William Ellery Channing. Born in Boston in 1801, Samuel Howe was eighteen years Julia's senior, a physician and philanthropist of considerable social standing among the Boston Brahmin by the time he met Julia. He counted Henry Wadsworth Longfellow and Charles Sumner among his lifelong friends. Howe was a Whig in his politics and an abolitionist with a flair for the dramatic.[6]

Upon graduating from the Harvard Medical School in 1821, Howe had served as a surgeon in the Greek War of Independence. Edward Everett had called the Ottoman Empire's campaign to crush the Greek rebellion "a war of the crescent against the cross."[7] This modern crusade inspired romantic philhellenes like Howe. He publicized the Greek cause in the United States to raise money for this bid for liberty. In his portraits, whether painted in the uniform of a Greek soldier or as photographed in

Figure 2. Samuel Gridley Howe, 1860.
Courtesy of Perkins School for the Blind Archives, Watertown, MA.

1860 with his right armed tucked in his frock coat like some bourgeois Napoleon, Howe looked the part of the idealist he was. At home, his humanitarian causes included prison reform, public education, innovative techniques for teaching the blind, and the abolition of slavery. As director of the Perkins Institute for the Blind, Howe won international fame for his success in teaching the blind and deaf-blind. In 1842, just before Howe's marriage, Charles Dickens visited the institute and in his *American Notes* praised the young doctor's work. Through his activities in Kansas with the New England Emigrant Aid Society, Howe first met John Brown. His involvement with arming and funding Brown as part of the "Secret Six" became so deep that he had to flee to Canada after Brown's capture, fearing arrest on charges of treason and extradition to Virginia. While in Toronto he missed the birth of his sixth child and namesake, born a few weeks after Brown's execution and always associated in Julia's mind with the drama of those days.

Though as a child Julia strove to share the piety of her parents, her extended family, and her pastor, she came to resent what she called the "grim dogmas" of her father's Calvinism, even though she turned back to some version of these teachings briefly after his death in 1839. She also recoiled from the revivalism she flirted with in emotional despair after her brother Henry's death from typhoid in 1840. By 1844 she was warning her sister Annie not to let the Episcopal bishop or their uncle the rector force her to conform to their beliefs. "Tell them, and all others," she wrote, "that, even if you agree with them in doctrine, you think their notion of a religious life narrow, false, superficial."[8] Through the help of a family friend and her own reading of the Bible and from what she later referred to vaguely as other "studies and observations," she found her way to liberal Unitarianism.[9]

Her introduction to Unitarianism came in the early 1840s by way of William Ellery Channing, elder statesman of the liberal movement. New England Unitarianism, tracing its origins to England, was a self-consciously modern, enlightened, and benevolent reformulation of Christianity. It spoke for a "rational" faith, one purportedly nondogmatic, nonsectarian, and optimistic about man and his world. It rejected the doctrines of the Trinity and original sin, and emphasized ethics over creeds. Channing never wavered from his understanding of the Reformation's articulation of the right of private judgment, and he turned that freedom into the sine qua non of Christian liberty. No one had the right to claim that a conscientious seeker after God was not a true Christian no matter how deviant he or she might be in doctrine. At the time, the movement's radicalism went just so far. Most Unitarians continued to affirm the uniqueness of Jesus as God's agent for human redemption, the authority of the scriptures, and the necessity of miracles as testimony to the veracity of the Christian faith. Indeed, the plain text of scripture seemed to demand rejection of the doctrine of the Trinity for any honest student of God's word. No matter how far their innovations went, the old-school Unitarians retained their evangelical piety, participated in the wide-ranging Second Great Awakening, and fought to rid Christianity of the last vestiges of Romanism.[10]

Fear of Rome and the papacy, at a time of mass Irish and German Roman Catholic immigration to America, meant there were limits to the tolerance accorded to others by this liberal faith. Like many Americans in the 1840s, Julia and her circle inherited an instinctive anti-Catholicism from their Puritan ancestors, from the Revolutionary War's fear of papist plots, from Whig ideology on both sides of the Atlantic, and from American evangelicalism generally. Unitarians emphasized Catholicism's danger to human progress and freedom. Rome was the past. Priest and prince shackled the body and mind of men and women. Any teaching or practice of Protestantism that was still "too Catholic" had to be jettisoned on the march toward the autonomous individual's private judgment in all matters of faith and life. The Reformation would not be complete, indeed the American Revolution as an extension of that seamless story of liberty would not be complete, until every chain of oppression had been broken and every prison of the human soul had been flung wide open. The historic empires of Europe—Austria, Russia, and Ottoman Turkey—impeded the worldwide movement for human emancipation. If America ever acted like these atavistic regimes, it too would prove to be on the wrong side of history.

But the "right" side of history kept moving, and that posed a challenge to progressives determined to keep up with the times. When the younger generation of Unitarians took a radical turn guided by German innovations in theology and philosophy, the old-school Unitarians found themselves battling "the latest form of infidelity" just as much as any Princeton Presbyterian. Old adversaries found they now had common enemies among the young. Theodore Parker, Emerson, George Ripley, Channing's nephew William Henry Channing, Frederic Henry Hedge, and others historicized the Bible, denied the need for miracles to attest to Christian truth, and turned Jesus into simply the highest embodiment yet of God's ideal humanity. They exchanged a supernatural religion for a "spiritual" religion of idealism and reform. They plunged into social activism to a depth never before thought prudent, whether it took the form of Ripley's Brook Farm experiment or abolitionism.

When Julia married and moved to Boston, she and her husband attended Theodore Parker's church. They had socialized with Parker in Rome on their extended honeymoon, and there he had baptized their first child, Julia Romana.[11] Parker was one of the most important conduits of German higher criticism and philosophical idealism into the United States. He spoke of America itself as "Idea." He became so radical that few of his fellow Unitarians in and around Boston dared exchange pulpits with him for fear of being tainted by his reputation. Even to attend Parker's church was to make a public statement. Julia did not shy away from that statement. And Parker returned the compliment by quoting her poetry from the pulpit.[12] But after a decade at Parker's church, Samuel decided to move the family to James Freeman Clarke's congregation. Julia found the decision painful, but Samuel feared Parker's disorderly congregation would set a bad example for his older children now that they were old enough to attended Sunday services.[13] Julia later wrote of Parker's sermons that "they presaged and preceded grave crises on both sides of the Atlantic. In Europe was going on the ferment of ideas and theories which led to the Revolutions of 1848 and the temporary upturning of states and of governments. In the United States, the seed of thought sown by prophetic minds was ripening in the great field of public opinion."[14]

Julia found a permanent spiritual home at Clarke's Church of the Disciples. Her pastor's dedication, brilliance, and gentle spirit won many allies to his cause. In 1861, Clarke was fifty-one years old, with a full, graying beard and wire-rimmed reading glasses that made him look like the scholar he was. After graduating from Harvard Divinity School, Clarke served a Unitarian mission work in Louisville, Kentucky, and edited the *Western Messenger*, the voice of liberal Unitarianism on the expanding frontier. He also contributed to the transcendentalist *Dial*.[15] A prolific author with a long list of publications to his name, Clarke became a leading voice in liberal Unitarianism, rivaled only by his friend Theodore Parker. In 1841, he founded the progressive Church of the Disciples in Boston.

Governor Andrew described his pastor as "logical, sensible, earnest, pious, forcible, solemn, quiet and calm, in fine, my beau ideal of a pulpit orator and a private gentleman and christian [*sic*]." "This is high eulogy, but deserved," he insisted.[16]

Figure 3. James Freeman Clarke, cabinet photo, no date.

Courtesy of the Joel Myerson Collection of Nineteenth-Century American Literature, Irvin Department of Rare Books and Special Collections, University of South Carolina.

Clarke's experimental church served as a model for reform. In an 1845 sermon outlining the principles of the new congregation, he offered his vision of the ideal church: "The church for me is the church of the future, not the past; the church which seeks for unity not in dogma and form, but in faith and love. The true Holy, Apostolic and Catholic church is yet to come. It will not aim at union by crushing freedom, as the Roman church has always done—nor aim at freedom by relinquishing union, as the Protestant church has done—but it will combine freedom of thought and form with unity of the spirit and cooperation in all good labors."[17] This vision of the church of the future dedicated to freedom, unity, and social reform inspired Clarke's congregation, not least among them Julia.

Keeping the distractions of family and society at bay, Julia intended to make her mark as an author and public intellectual. Though her career was delayed, she would one day do just that. Julia's mastery of French as an adolescent led to her first significant publication. In 1836, at the age of only seventeen, she published an extended review of Alphonse de Lamartine's poem *Jocelyn* in the *Literary and Theological Review*. It featured her own translations from the French.[18] Cogswell had known Lamartine in France, and perhaps had suggested his young student write the review under his supervision. Julia excelled at German as much as at French. In 1839 the *New York Review*, edited by Cogswell, published her review of a recent translation into English of Goethe and Schiller by the transcendentalist and Brook Farm resident Dwight Sullivan.[19] Julia's proficiency in German also opened the world of idealist philosophy to her in the pages of Fichte, Herder, Kant, and Hegel. She always preferred Kant to Hegel. Like Emerson and other transcendentalists, she imbibed the mysticism of Swedenborg and the pantheism of Spinoza, whose *Ethics* comforted her in times of grief. By the 1860s, she had become as Europeanized as any intellectual in America.

Julia found critical success when she published a collection of poems she called *Passion-Flowers*. The book appeared anonymously in 1854, but her authorship was an open secret. Reviewers hailed it as the work of America's most promising woman poet. Nathaniel Hawthorne was impressed, though he worried privately that she had revealed too much about her stormy marriage.[20] Samuel thought some of its poems too erotic and unsuitable for a woman of Julia's social standing. He dreaded what his own daughters would think when they encountered these poems in later life.[21] Aside from marriage, the poems dealt with the Revolutions of 1848, the papacy and the prospects for reform in Italy, the moral complacency of the churches in America over the scandal of slavery, and the nature of Christ and redemption. These poems were rough-hewn but conveyed an intensity and depth rarely matched by her later productions. Their depictions of Christ would later illuminate whom she might have meant by the "Hero" in her most famous poem.

Leading publications accepted Julia's reviews, essays, and verse. Not long before her trip to Washington in 1861, the *Atlantic Monthly* carried a few of her poems and travel essays about Cuba. She had also begun writing dispatches for the *New-York Tribune*, and even though these long articles appeared anonymously, as did the submissions of many of the paper's contributors, her authorship was known to her husband, friends, and associates. Her latest installment for Horace Greeley's paper had appeared in October 1861, only weeks before her encounter with wartime Washington. As a whole, her publications in the *Atlantic* and the *Tribune* reveal how complex her attitudes toward race, slavery, and war were on the eve of writing the poem that would become the "Battle Hymn of the Republic."

The *Atlantic* carried her first submissions in 1859. The *Atlantic* was just two years old at the time and drew contributors mostly from Boston, such as Emerson, Thoreau, and John Greenleaf Whittier. It also featured the very popular Harriet Beecher Stowe, whose *Uncle Tom's Cabin* had made her an international celebrity in 1852 and whose novel *The Minister's Wooing* appeared serially in the *Atlantic* in 1859 alongside Howe's essays. Under the poet James Russell Lowell, the *Atlantic* became the premier high-toned monthly for the nation's antislavery writers and readers. Its masthead promised "A Magazine of Literature, Art, and Politics," and the front page featured an engraving of the Puritan governor of the Massachusetts Bay Colony, John Winthrop, which was soon replaced by an American flag for the duration of the war.

The first of six installments of Howe's travelogue *A Trip to Cuba* appeared in May 1859. Julia recounted the voyage she and her husband had made with Parker and his wife in February, for the sake of the minister's failing health.[22] Parker would travel on to Europe and die in Florence in 1860. These installments reveal that Julia's crusade against chattel slavery did not necessarily mean advanced views on race. She saw stark limits to blacks' capacities for improvement. Drawing out the lessons of her visit to the Bahamas and the spectacle of the "negroes" at work there, she offered her readers—as "orthodox" as herself on the question of slavery, she was sure—"one heretic whisper" to disturb their otherwise sound "confession of faith": the free black whom Northerners pictured was only "an ideal negro," that is, a type remote from the reality that confronted her in Nassau. This imaginary "negro," she wrote, "is refined by white culture, elevated by white blood, instructed even by white iniquity." But in his actual condition, he "is a coarse, grinning, flat-footed, thick-skulled creature, ugly as Caliban, lazy as the laziest of brutes, chiefly ambitious to be of no use to any in the world. View him as you will, his stock in trade is small;—he has but the tangible instincts of all creatures,—love of life, of ease, and of offspring." To rise above these elemental needs, this Caliban would have to rely on white civilization: "He must go to school to the white race, and his discipline to the white race must be long and laborious." And then she added darkly, "Nassau, and all that we saw of it, suggested to us the unwelcome question whether compulsory labor be not better than none."[23]

Just as revealing in these essays from 1859 was Howe's proposed solution to slavery in the United States. Growing frustrated, she asked for less speechmaking and less moral posturing. She trusted God to work his will through the dialectic of history. "We and they are two forces," she said of North and South, "pulling in opposite ways to preserve the equilibrium of a third point, which we do not see. We must keep to our pulling, they cannot relinquish theirs. The point of solution that shall reconcile and supersede the differences is not in sight, nor has the wisest of us known how to indicate it." She appealed to agitators for restraint despite her public and private stance on emancipation. Her expectations were circumscribed by the acknowledged difficulty of maintaining the Union. "Looking down from where I sit," she wrote from Boston, "I cannot curse the pleasant Southern land, nor those who dwell in it. Nor would I do so if I thought tenfold more ill of its consequences. Were half my body gangrened, I would not smite nor reproach it, but seek with patience an available remedy." "This is half of our body," she said of the slaveholding states, "and the moral blood which brings the evil runs as much in our veins as in theirs."[24] What she pictured as metaphorically true of the United States was, of course, literally true of the Puritan and Cavalier blood that ran through her own veins.

But Julia's moderation would not last the year. At the end of 1859, she grappled with the most stirring national event of that fateful year: John Brown's raid on Harpers Ferry. The veteran of guerilla warfare in the Kansas territory intended to carve out a refuge for runaway slaves in the East and spark a general slave rebellion. He was captured by United States Marines under the command of Colonel Robert E. Lee, tried by the Commonwealth of Virginia for treason, and executed in December. Julia had met Brown in her home in Boston when her husband worked with the "Secret Six" to aid Brown's efforts.[25]

Sometime between Brown's capture in October and his execution in December, she wrote a draft essay about the Bahamas she called "Since Then," perhaps intended for her *Atlantic* series but never published.[26] She sensed that war between North and South was now imminent, indeed that a war for abolition had now become a moral duty incumbent upon Americans. Brown's raid, though impetuous and devoid of "common sense," as almost every abolitionist said publicly, had "involved a principle, to wit, the right and duty of armed intervention in the abrogation and abolition of slavery." The institution of slavery had made America "two nations," and the boasting and posturing on both sides had now to give way to courageous deeds. The old federal republic was dead. It was time to remove the "mask" of the fated Union and replace it with another "idea"—that is, with another basis for a union threatened by mere "acquiescence" on one side (the North) and "inordinate ambition" on the other (the South).

Howe foresaw more violence to come as Brown awaited his martyrdom. His raid may have been foolhardy, but underneath lay "the spirit of the man" that demanded respect beyond words. The death "of the Just Man, sweeter than the life of the Conqueror, shall be his," she prophesied. "Soft fall the stroke of death upon that venerable head," she pleaded, waxing Shakespearean. "May angels wait around to ease the inevitable pangs, and aid the agony from which nature cannot be absolved. Yet surely those who judged him, did they know the truth, might envy him. And we who have tears to shed for him, let us consider these things in patience, understanding that such events have root in the past and a point in the future both of which are beyond our knowledge, but not beyond our faith."

Once the war began, Julia's contributions to the *Atlantic* became more prominent. Her friend James T. Fields had assumed the magazine's

Figure 4. John Brown, facing left, holding *New-York Tribune*, three-quarter-length portrait, ca. 1859.

Library of Congress, Prints and Photographs Division.

editorship in 1861. Her publishers, Ticknor and Fields, had bought the magazine in 1859. The first issue prepared under the new editor's direction appeared in July, and the first page featured a poem by Howe. The war had been underway two months by June as the new issue was being readied for the presses. Union and Confederate forces had engaged each other in eastern Virginia, with disastrous results for the Lincoln administration's war effort and hopes for a quick victory over the rebels. Howe's six-stanza "Our Orders" mourned the Northern battle-dead and called the nation away from frivolous pursuits. Musicians, poets, and all the arts had higher duties to serve in these difficult days, she wrote. By the final stanzas, Howe tied the war to the very destiny of humanity. The hour of peril demanded courage; nothing less than "God, and Truth, and Freedom" stood in the balance.[27] This poem marked only the beginning. The *Atlantic* proved a dependable outlet for Howe's work in the early months of the war.[28]

But an outlet with much wider readership also published Howe in these months. Horace Greeley's *New-York Tribune* ran her latest submission in October 1861, identifying it as a submission by the paper's "Boston Correspondent."[29] Her name did not appear with the long article, but it was common for the paper's special dispatches to be left unsigned. William Lloyd Garrison's *Liberator* named her as the author soon after.[30] The *Tribune* essay provides a detailed insight into Howe's conception of the war's purpose and politicians' failings immediately before her trip to Washington. Hidden behind anonymity and male pronouns, she let loose a barrage of angry denunciation against New Englanders who misconstrued the war's purpose. The *Tribune* gave her all the space she needed.

The annual agricultural fair at Barnstable, Massachusetts, provided Howe with the unlikely occasion for her essay. Among the dignitaries there was her friend Governor Andrew, who had been escorted to the fair the evening before with appropriate military fanfare. Barnstable, on Cape Cod, was one of the first towns settled by the Plymouth Colony. The "Boston Correspondent" played on this proud heritage and turned it against wartime complacency. Howe was always a Puritan confident in her chosen nation. Touring the Cape, Howe wondered, "What but religion could have built up such a Colony? The purpose of God lay deeply hid within the bud, and the thought of its mysterious unfolding filled the eyes with strange tears."

The main speaker at the fair angered her by his misunderstanding of the war. He dared limit it to a war to end the rebellion, saying nothing of a war to emancipate the slaves. In response, Howe wrote a speech she imagined herself giving in place of the morally obtuse one she had just endured. The war's "highest point of interest" could not be the selfishness of mere reunion and certainly not the grubbing materialism of account books scrutinized by creditors and debtors. Thinking themselves materially prosperous, they were morally bankrupt if they did not rise to the war's high idealism and the duties of "conscience." Self-interest had to yield to the cause of divine justice. Yes, the slaveholders had committed crimes against the North, but their real sin offended God himself, the "Master Creditor," who now demanded payment. The nation stood on the brink of insolvency.

Howe turned her fictional speech into a jeremiad. Like her Puritan ancestors, she exposed sin, condemned spiritual declension, and called her people to repentance. But when she came to the point of pronouncing judgment against these worldly descendants of the Fathers, she held back, confident they would remain true to their forebears and fight the good fight for freedom. "The Cape is the ground of conscience," she wrote. "Those who first cut down its forests and tilled its fields came here to worship God in purity and sincerity. Their pastors preached to them a thorny Gospel, full of self-sacrifice and crucifixion, and they were all able to receive, aye, and to thrive upon it." Thankfully, the "Puritan spirit" had not "died out from mankind." The innate goodness slumbering in the American soul would soon be roused by "the voice of exhortation and sympathy." The time for action had come, and Northerners could now fight to win the slave's liberty and preserve their own. God had always allied himself with "the poor and oppressed." Indeed, Christ had lived among humanity hidden in humility and weakness and on the cross had "died the death of a criminal." The ignominy of his life and death "taught us to look for the Divine in all disguises of humility and poverty." This is what fairgoers forgot. They expected the kind of pomp and glory that accompanied Governor Andrew, but God hid himself among them as the lowly slave. Today the slave demanded payment of the nation's great debt to him. He had presented his "writ of execution," and the debt would be settled.

Howe's "unspoken speech," as the *Liberator* called it, would soon speak openly, this time under her own name and in the form of a poem.[31]

The "Battle Hymn of the Republic" would capture the power of her ancestors' "thorny Gospel, full of self-sacrifice and crucifixion" quite unlike anything before or since. All she needed was the right inspiration.

Governor Andrew had enlisted Massachusetts in Lincoln's war for reunification without delay. In April 1861, three days after the Confederate bombardment of Fort Sumter, the president had issued a proclamation convening a special session of Congress and calling up 75,000 state militia. Their purpose was "to maintain the honor, the integrity, and the existence of our National Union, and the perpetuity of popular government."[32] He said nothing of slavery. Across the North, volunteers responded to the president's call while the states of Virginia, North Carolina, Tennessee, and Arkansas voted to secede from the Union, joining the seven states that had departed after Lincoln's election. By early May, the president had expanded the United States Army with the addition of some 42,000 volunteers. These recruits' primary task was to secure the capital, which was exposed to a Confederate attack from across the Potomac.

John Andrew was forty-three years old in November 1861, married, and the father of four.[33] Contemporary photographs show a short, stocky man, clean-shaven, with curly, tousled hair and dapper clothes. Unsurprisingly, he was often called "boyish." He was in his first term as governor and had just been reelected by a wide margin. Within four months of his inauguration in 1861 he faced the unprecedented task of mobilizing his state for the Union war effort. A graduate of Bowdoin College, Andrew read law with Henry Fuller, the uncle of the feminist and reformer Margaret Fuller, and became a prominent attorney in Boston. In 1848, he married Eliza Jane Hersey, who accompanied him to Washington in 1861.

Andrew's opposition to slavery had been evident since his college years, and the cause came to define his careers in law and politics, moving him from Conscience Whig to Free-Soiler and finally to radical Republican. He built a résumé of activism sure to attract attention from party organizers. He served as part of the defense counsel in the Anthony Burns case. He opposed the Kansas-Nebraska Act and the Supreme Court's 1857 *Dred Scott* decision. As a Republican state legislator, he supported enactment of personal liberty laws nullifying some of the enforcement provisions of the Fugitive Slave Act. Following John Brown's raid at Harpers Ferry, he mobilized a team of lawyers for the defense in Charlottesville, Virginia, to

Figure 5. Portrait of Gov. John Albion Andrew, ca. 1860.
The Miriam and Ira D. Wallach Division of Art, Prints and
Photographs: Photography Collection, The New York Public Library.

New York Public Library Digital Collections.

represent Brown at his trial. He solicited contributions among his Boston contacts to defray the attorneys' costs. When Andrew urged a plea of insanity, Brown refused.[34]

The governor paired radical politics with radical theology. By 1861, Andrew had been part of Clarke's Church of the Disciples for twenty years. When he first met Clarke, he was an idealistic young reformer. He soon became an active member, led a popular midweek Bible study, and wrote essays for the *Christian World*, edited by Clarke.[35] He also taught Sunday school and later served as Sunday school superintendent. Clarke said he "never knew a more pure, simple, straight-forward piety than his; faith without narrowness, piety so manly and cheerful."[36] Julia Ward Howe could be less generous. Exasperated with him the day before John Brown's execution, she exclaimed to her exiled husband somewhat tongue in cheek, "Never was a man so jolly in his piety—no idea of divine wrath—he don't [*sic*] know what it means."[37]

The Bay State's plans for mobilization had been mapped out over the three months since the new governor had taken office. He launched a reorganization of the state militia almost immediately after Fort Sumter. Some existing companies had to be augmented to make up the thousand soldiers necessary for each regiment. The Third and Fourth Regiments were soon ready to reinforce Fortress Monroe in Charleston Harbor, and the Sixth was destined for Washington to defend the capital. Others soon followed, joining early regiments from Pennsylvania, Rhode Island, and New York. In July, Union forces suffered an alarming defeat at Bull Run. In response, Massachusetts mustered several additional regiments to reinforce the Union army at Washington. Governor Andrew secured emergency funding from the state legislature and requisitioned uniforms, rifles, artillery, horses, and supplies. His office was flooded with requests for civilian and military appointments and for patronage through his political connections in Washington. An attack on the Sixth Regiment in Baltimore on its way to the capital claimed the first Massachusetts soldiers to die in the war. Clarke later declared that these simple farmers, weavers, mechanics, and shoemakers had won glory as they marched through Baltimore, "leaving Pilgrim blood on Catholic pavement."[38]

Andrew's duties as governor often took him to the nation's capital to visit these regiments and to consult with the Lincoln administration. One of these trips became the occasion for Julia's encounter with the besieged city. Visits to Washington brought opportunities for Andrew to stop in other cities along the way to meet with Massachusetts state agents and to join in the reviews of Bay State troops as they headed south. The governor helped boost the morale of soldiers, state bureaucrats, and patriotic organizations, among them New York City's Sons of Massachusetts, an organization similar to the New England Societies that the Yankee exodus had spread as far as San Francisco. Andrew's trip this time happened to coincide with a grand review planned for New York. The Massachusetts state office in New York seized the opportunity. Officials worked hard to guarantee the governor and his wife would linger long enough to review a parade of the Massachusetts Twenty-Third Regiment down Broadway. The soldiers would sing the John Brown song as they marched. Indeed, the New York office urged Andrew to "put a little Glory Hallelujah into your telegram" to the local Sons of Massachusetts by way of encouragement for their good efforts on behalf of the troops.[39] Julia's "Glory, hallelujah" would follow in a week.

Andrew had urged Clarke to make the long trip from Boston to the nation's capital. He knew Clarke wanted to see wartime Washington for himself. In a note to Clarke on November 7, Andrew told him the Howes, along with Mrs. Andrew, "will probably start for Washington next Tuesday." The members of the Sanitary Commission made it a point this time to include the "ladies," Andrew wrote. He urged Clarke and his wife to go along and "visit the camps, [and] hospitals."[40] The busy governor doubted he would be able to return to DC so soon after his October visit to the Massachusetts regiments. But in the end, the whole circle of Bostonians made the trip south.

This would not be Julia Ward Howe's first visit to Washington, but she was about to see the encampments and battlefields that until now she had only imagined from the safe distance of Boston and New York. She hoped to find some way to contribute to the cause. That cause was emancipation and not mere restoration of the Union. The war could not be righteous without the higher aim of freedom for the slaves. She had denounced human bondage for decades and in her wider vision of progress championed European wars of liberation and self-determination. Greece, Poland, Hungary, and Italy had won her admiration for their struggles against autocratic empires, which were holdovers of a barbaric age and soon to be toppled in the advancement of human liberty and civilization.

The chains of all sorts of captives were being loosed in her generation. The American slaves' moment had come.

The train ride to Washington had taken the better part of three days. In the rain and approaching dark of November 14, the Bostonians saw Union encampments along the last leg of their journey, guarding the thirty-eight-mile stretch from Baltimore to DC. These troops secured the passage of soldiers and supplies flowing from the north. Washington's depot had been unusually busy since the spring, pressed beyond its capacity by the war. The station struggled to accommodate the volume of traffic, and plans for expansion were underway, with a freight warehouse having just been completed. President-elect Abraham Lincoln had arrived at the station in disguise before his inauguration, delegates to an ill-fated convention had gathered in Washington in a desperate bid for peace, thousands of Northern militia and Union troops continued to descend on the city, and hordes of office seekers were in town, having jumped at the chance to advance their careers while serving their country.

The Willard Hotel became the base of operations for the Howes and Clarkes. The hotel was convenient to the White House and to the Treasury Department. The Treasury building had been the temporary headquarters of the Sanitary Commission before the move in October 1861 to its permanent offices in the "Adams House" on F Street. The Willard Hotel and its restaurant and bar hosted a large clientele of congressmen, military officers, cabinet members, diplomats, reporters, office seekers, and tourists.[41] From the Willard, Julia, Clarke, and the others set out on their excursions in and around the city. Over the next week, the group bustled about Washington calling on friends, meeting President Lincoln, visiting hospitals, attending services on Sunday, and more than once venturing across the Potomac to see Union fortifications and troops, especially their own Massachusetts regiments. The most anticipated event was the "grand review" of General George McClellan's Army of the Potomac at Bailey's Crossroads scheduled for November 20.

In one of the few surviving letters from the week, Samuel described to his daughter Laura how he and her mother spent their days in Washington: "Your Mamma is having a delightful time," busy every day in the weather that had turned fine, visiting encampments and "objects of curiosity." He seemed pleased that the Willard's patrons recognized Julia's musical gifts:

BALLOON VIEW OF WASHINGTON, May, 1861.

Figure 6. Balloon view of Washington, DC, with US Capitol in foreground, wood engraving in *Harper's Weekly*, July 27, 1861. Library of Congress, Prints and Photographs Division.

"In the evenings there are many people gathered in the saloon of the Hotel; and all the people who can appreciate talent and wit and conversational power are sure to be drawn about her." As for Dr. Howe, he went "about inspecting camps and hospitals and doing what I can to help the common cause of the country and of freedom." He reserved his only complaint for the "army of office seekers" besieging the city. He reassured his daughter they would "be home on Sunday or Monday" of the following week.[42]

The most detailed account of this week comes not from the Howes but from Clarke. The minister kept a journal about his visit, preached a sermon on his experiences immediately upon his return to Boston, and then published a revised version of the sermon in the *Monthly Journal* of the American Unitarian Association, a magazine he edited for the denomination.[43] Clarke never mentioned Julia's name. He referred to her only as the Boston correspondent of the *New-York Tribune*—a thinly veiled allusion that he might have meant more as an inside joke among Unitarians than an effort to hide her identity. Clarke's diary for these days became available only years later when his first biographer quoted fragments from it.[44] Julia consulted it once, but it seems to have vanished. The story about Washington the public heard and read in 1861 was Clarke's, not Julia's.

Immediately upon his arrival in the capital, Clarke met with William Henry Channing and Frederick Knapp, who were members of the Sanitary Commission. Knapp was Henry Bellows's cousin, a Unitarian minister and graduate of Harvard Divinity School, and a key agent for the organization. The commission carried out inspections, solicited and coordinated funding and supplies, published reports, and overall tried to keep pace with the demands of an army that in a matter of weeks had ballooned to more than ten times the size of the one Lincoln had called up in May. Dozens of associate members helped raise funds and spoke on behalf of the commission, including the prominent preachers Henry Ward Beecher and Phillips Brooke, in addition to Clarke and Channing. As a charitable organization, the commission received large donations of goods for the benefit of soldiers—bedding, clothes, books, magazines, homemade wine, brandy, tea, cocoa, preserves, and games.[45]

Clarke reported in the *Monthly Journal* that "all is war and warlike" in Washington. An experienced European traveler, Clarke contrasted the mobilized city with the capitals of autocratic Prussia, Austria, and Russia. Washington was indeed in some ways "like a city of Europe,—like Berlin or Vienna or St. Petersburg; but with a difference. For this [army] of ours is not a mere standing army, to be wielded blindly in the interests of despotism; but an intelligent army of freemen, come to protect liberty and law. It is the nation itself which has taken up arms, and come to Washington to defend its own life and the ideas of the fathers. It has come to defend the Declaration of Independence, and the Constitution, laws, and traditions of the land."[46]

The work of the Sanitary Commission still occupied Clarke the next day. After taking a tour of the renovations underway at the Capitol, he and his old friend Channing headed to the offices of the commission in the Adams House. Clarke marveled at what the Sanitary Commission had been able to accomplish in the few months since it was improvised in April. On November 16—the same day George Stuart and the YMCA met in New York to organize the Christian Commission—the Sanitary Commission issued a report on the status of the hospital supplies it had received and the scale of the problems facing an army they estimated now to number between 300,000 and 600,000 in Virginia and Maryland.[47] Between meetings, clerical work, and writing reports, Clarke and his colleagues made sure to experience this war firsthand.

Armed with passes issued by General McClellan, Clarke met up with Channing again on Saturday to visit several Massachusetts regiments in Virginia. Julia and Governor and Mrs. Andrew joined them. The group would have headed southwest by carriage out of Washington, using the Long Bridge over the Potomac, before continuing on to Fort Jackson, and then southwest to Fort Runyon and Fort Albany. This ring of forts made up an important part of the timber and earthen works hastily erected around DC. Forts Runyon and Albany were manned by the Massachusetts Fourteenth. The troops had departed Massachusetts in August singing "John Brown's Body." They sang it again as they passed through New York, Philadelphia, and Baltimore, and finally as they marched down Pennsylvania Avenue in the summer heat and driving rain, an event publicized by *Harper's Weekly* with a dramatic woodcut showing the men ankle-deep in water and armed with fixed bayonets illuminated by a jagged lightning bolt.[48]

At Fort Albany, Clarke, Julia, and the others visited the regimental commander, Colonel William Batchelder Greene, an important but little remembered transcendentalist philosopher.[49] The visit with Greene is

THE FOURTEENTH MASSACHUSETTS REGIMENT MARCHING UP PENNSYLVANIA AVENUE, WASHINGTON, IN A STORM.—[SEE PAGE 554.]

Figure 7. "The Fourteenth Massachusetts Regiment Marching Up Pennsylvania Avenue, Washington, In a Storm," illustration in *Harper's Weekly*, August 31, 1861, 549.
Author's collection.

notable in hindsight for bringing together Julia and the John Brown song perhaps for the first time. In the moment, however, Governor Andrew's wife seemed to draw more attention than Julia. According to Clarke's version of events, Colonel Greene "summoned his regiment together, and asked them to sing some of their songs and hymns for the party; introducing to them more particularly Mrs. John A. Andrew." "Among these songs," he explained to his readers, "the most conspicuous was the famous John Brown song:—'John Brown's body is mouldering in the grave; / His soul is marching on. / Glory, hallelujah!'" He and his companions heard the song several more times that week. The words seemed to have found their literal fulfillment. "John Brown's soul *is* marching on!" Clarke rejoiced. "For what is the soul of John Brown but his unconquerable hatred of slavery, and his fervent desire of seeing it abolished? And is not that desire and feeling MARCHING ON? Is not slavery recognized more and more as the cause of the war, the deadly foe of the Union, the poison in our cup, the enemy of true democracy and true Christianity, and something which must be destroyed, if the life of the nation is to be saved? Every day is adding to the strength and depth of these convictions; and John Brown's *soul* is yet to lead the armies of the nation to their destined work."[50] Clarke could not contain his enthusiasm for the tune and the words. John Brown's soul marched on in the army's living embodiment of "true democracy and true Christianity."

Stirred by the song, Clarke and his friends traveled on to Bailey's Crossroads, Munson's Hill, and Falls Church, and then crossed back into the city toward evening. "Washington is a beleaguered and defenced city," Clarke reported. "On every hill around are camps. As you ride into the city from any direction, these beautiful, spectral lines of tents gleam under the soft moonlight; their fires burn red among the trees. Sentinels stop your carriage, and demand your pass." That Saturday night was no

Figure 8. Winslow Homer, "Songs of the War," *Harper's Weekly*,
November 23, 1861.
Library of Congress, Prints and Photographs Collection.

exception. As Clarke and the others made their way to the Georgetown Ferry, they passed several camps and most likely Robert E. Lee's house at Arlington before they caught the striking vision of the setting sun illuminating the distant Capitol.[51]

Then as now, the Capitol dome dominated the city's skyline. In 1861, scaffolding and an iron skeleton sketched out the silhouette of the new dome. Construction continued at President Lincoln's insistence as a symbol of the Union's endurance and the North's resolve to persevere. To some, the edifice that Herman Melville called "the Iron Dome" suggested St. Paul's Cathedral in London; to others it evoked St. Peter's Basilica on the Tiber rather than Christopher Wren's masterpiece on the Thames. But with a difference. St. Peter's, especially after the disappointments of the Revolutions of 1848, was thought to symbolize political and religious tyranny, while the Capitol in Washington stood for liberty and self-government. But that symbol of freedom was precarious. Channing told a Boston audience in November that "he had seen the Capitol at Washington left unfinished, as it were prophetically asking the question of every beholder, whether it should become a ruin, or be finished amid universal peace and friendship."[52]

As for Clarke, he considered the Capitol's neoclassical edifice self-evidently superior to the neo-Gothic Houses of Parliament in Westminster. To him as to others, the impressive dome "constantly suggests St. Peter's."[53] Clarke meant the comparison as a compliment. But to Julia the new dome put St. Peter's to shame, not in its design but in its superiority to the reactionary despotism the Basilica continued to symbolize to her. In light of St. Peter's association with absolutism, she wrote in 1868, "I thought that its beauty did not so much signify." "We have a dome, too, in Washington," she reminded readers of one of her travel books. "The Genius of Liberty poises on its top; the pediment below is adorned with the emblems of honest thrift and civic prosperity. May that dome perish ere it be lit at the risk of human life, and lit, like [St. Peter's], to make the social darkness around it more evident by its momentary aureole."[54]

The interior of America's more splendid dome would soon be graced by a peculiar painting: *The Apotheosis of Washington*, an allegorical fresco completed in 1865 by the Italian artist Constantino Brumidi, a refugee from the failed Roman revolution. Crowning the dome after 1863 was the six-ton bronze statue Julia called "The Genius of Liberty." It was the figure "Freedom" created by her brother-in-law, the sculptor Thomas Crawford.[55] At the time of Howe's visit in 1861, the German immigrant Emanuel Luetze, most famous for his painting *Washington Crossing the Delaware*, had begun work in the House wing on his six-hundred-square-foot mural, *Westward the Course of Empire Takes Its Way*. The title came from the philosopher George Berkeley's eighteenth-century poem anticipating America's epic destiny as it followed history's heliotropic path toward empire. It was as if the savior-nation were busy defining itself in art and architecture at the moment of its greatest doubt.

Clarke received an invitation from Andrew upon his return to the city Saturday night. They were to visit President Lincoln. The hour was late. The commander in chief was busy with Secretary of State William H. Seward. The two callers had to wait. News of the *Trent* affair had just appeared in the city's papers, publicizing one of the administration's most serious diplomatic crises. The Confederate government had dispatched James Mason of Virginia and John Slidell of Louisiana to London and Paris. The two commissioners had sailed from Havana aboard the *Trent*, but on November 8 the British packet was stopped and boarded by the Union navy, and Mason and Slidell were arrested, forcibly removed, and taken as prisoners to Fort Warren in Boston Harbor. The British prime minister, Lord Palmerston, was outraged at America's audacity and prepared for possible war. Tempers cooled, diplomats soothed affronted dignities on both sides, and the crisis passed short of war. But for the moment, the diplomatic crisis added to the already high-stakes drama of politics and diplomacy agitating the capital that month.[56]

Clarke's and Andrew's patience paid off, and they finally met with Lincoln that evening. Clarke found him "an unassuming country gentleman, modest but self-possessed, with sagacity and full powers of observation, but without the least touch of political manoeuvring." "Mr. Lincoln is no politician," he conceded; "[he] does not pretend to be a great and accomplished statesman; but is an honest, candid, modest, sagacious American citizen, who means to do his duty as well as he can. He is not exactly the man for a leader in a great crisis like the present; yet where could we find a better?"[57]

On Sunday morning, Clarke and Andrew returned to the White House to see Lincoln again, this time accompanied by a much larger group that included Mrs. Andrew and Julia. Nearly fifty years later, Julia recalled

Andrew and Lincoln doing most of the talking. She was startled by the president's thick backwoods accent as he told one of his anecdotes. She left without gaining any insight into his statesmanship. Clarke, she remembered, remarked on Lincoln's "hopeless honesty." But Andrew remained confident in the president's capacity to lead.[58]

From the White House, Clarke and Julia headed to All Souls Unitarian Church to hear Channing preach at the eleven o'clock service. He had been with them at Fort Albany the day before. Channing had just been called to All Souls from a pastorate in Liverpool, England, and in a few weeks Bellows would preach his installation sermon. Clarke had known Channing since their days together at Boston Latin School, Harvard College, and Harvard Divinity School. Margaret Fuller had once referred to Channing, Emerson, and her hero, Giuseppi Mazzini, as men possessing "celestial fire" and "pure natures."[59] Channing described himself as owing his greatest intellectual debt to "Coleridge, Fenelon, Herder, Lessing, Carlyle, Cousin, Leroux, Swedenborg, and Fourier"—a list of English, German, French, and Scandinavian philosophers and mystics imbibed by New England transcendentalists and liberal Unitarians.[60]

Channing had worked as hard as anyone to advance religious nationalism. From the beginning of the war, he had been preaching sermons of righteous indignation against the "slaveholder's conspiracy" that had brought down such a catastrophe on the United States. He waged holy war from the pulpit. Judgment Day had come. "Terrible as appears to be this Civil War," he told his Liverpool congregation, "it is humbly welcomed, as the Providential method of National redemption. Monstrous has been the Nation's crime; total let the repentance be, and costly the sacrifice of atonement." Channing held nothing back. "Far and wide, among the People of the Free States, it is felt to be, and from pulpit and press it is declared to be,—a HOLY WAR,—because waged in defence of Loyalty against Treason, and of Liberty against Despotism; because entered upon from no selfish passions nor worldly ambition, but from stern sense of duty; because manifestly appointed by Providence, for the Salvation of the Republic from the sin and sorrow of Slavery."[61]

Channing's preaching continued to breath the fire of apocalyptic wrath and national purification. In his sermon notes for the fall of 1861, he put a star next to Revelation 19:6 ("And I heard as it were the voice of a great multitude, and as the voice of many waters, and as the voice of mighty

Figure 9. Portrait of William Henry Channing, ca. 1862–65.
From the Emily Howland photograph album.

Library of Congress, Prints and Photographs Division.

thunderings, saying, Alleluia: for the Lord God omnipotent reigneth").[62] He also listed Revelation 14:19 ("And the angel thrust in his sickle into the earth, and gathered the vine of the earth, and cast *it* into the great winepress of the wrath of God"). Julia would rely on these same verses for her "Battle Hymn." Channing liberally sprinkled his notebook with references to John Brown, the Italian revolutionary Giuseppe Garibaldi, Jean-Paul Marat's assassin Charlotte Corday, and the allegorical figures Greatheart and Apollyon from *Pilgrim's Progress*. He worried over the labor pains of a nation's "new birth." But he never wavered in these sermons from his faith in providential, cleansing, redemptive war. God himself would decide between slavery and freedom.[63]

This was the remarkable man Clarke and Julia heard on Sunday morning. One early historian of Unitarianism and transcendentalism described Channing's demeanor in the pulpit. He was a preacher who "burned with a pure enthusiasm that lifted souls into celestial air and made all possibilities of justice seem practicable. He did not argue or denounce; he prophesied. There was not a word of scorn or detestation; but there were passages of touching power, describing the influence of gentleness and the response that the hardest hearts would give to it, that shamed the listeners out of their vindictiveness. On the anti-slavery platform, his attitude was the same. There was no more persuasive speaker."[64]

Julia and Clarke heard a sermon Channing called "Religion for Our Age and Land." Given his extemporaneous pulpit style, a complete text does not survive. "I have usually planned only the *Skeleton* of my Sermons," he wrote on the inside front cover of his notebook, "trying to be filled with the *Spirit* of the Truth, to be taught, and leaving all expressions to the moment."[65] Clarke found Channing's performance that Sunday splendid. "I have seldom listened to a finer sermon than he gave the people this morning," Clarke wrote for the *Monthly Journal*. On the one hand, "it was in the best sense liberal" and, on the other hand, "in the best sense conservative." Channing "did full justice to all there is of truth in [Protestant] Orthodoxy, in the Roman-Catholic Church, and in Naturalism"—using Emerson for his example of naturalism, Henry Ward Beecher for evangelicalism, and the convert Orestes Brownson for Roman Catholicism. Clarke thought Channing's ecumenical breadth and generous spirit refreshing. Rarely do men do such justice to those with whom they disagree. The sermon's "impression on the congregation was very profound," Clarke remarked, no doubt including himself among those so moved.[66] Channing agreed: "My sermon was received with enthusiasm. I heard expression of Sympathy and admiration of all sides."[67]

Channing contributed to the war effort beyond his fiery preaching. He ministered to the sick and wounded in military hospitals in and around Washington.[68] He offered the use of All Souls as a military hospital, making it necessary for his congregation to gather for worship in the Capitol. In 1863 and again in 1864, Channing served as chaplain of the House of Representatives. Two Republican members reportedly considered him the minister "who best represents the antislavery policy of the Republican party in Washington." His duties as chaplain included presiding over the Sunday services held in the House chamber, in addition to those his own congregation held in the building. As chaplain, he made it a point to include ministers from many denominations and once a female Quaker preacher, and he invited a black minister and choir to lead services in the House for what some came to call the "People's Church."[69]

After worshipping at All Souls, Clarke filled his afternoon with a return visit to Colonel Greene and the Massachusetts Fourteenth. He preached to the soldiers, and despite the cold and wind, they welcomed Clarke's "interesting sermon" and assumed that such a famous preacher paid attention to them because of his connections to Governor Andrew, Colonel Greene, and their regiment's Unitarian chaplain.[70] After the sermon, Clarke watched the men on parade and then witnessed what he called the "cultus of the flag." This ceremony was unfamiliar enough that Clarke felt he had to explain the ritual to readers of the *Monthly Journal*: "The soldiers were drawn up around the flag-staff: the band saluted the flag; the men presented arms. Then the flag was lowered by four men, and carefully folded into triangular form; then carried by one of them in his arms tenderly, as though it were a baby, while the others walked beside him; and the soldiers formed an escort for it to head-quarters, where it was put away for the night on a shelf."[71] The sacred aura around the flag was unmistakable.

Julia's excursion on Monday did not go as smoothly as the visits over the weekend had, but its impact on her would be much greater. Military passes in hand, the Bostonians crossed the Potomac for a review of General Irvin McDowell's division of 10,000 troops. Julia and her companions rode the eight miles by carriage to Upton's Hill to visit General James

S. Wadsworth's headquarters. Upton's Hill lay between Falls Church and Bailey's Crossroads. During the review, General McDowell, who had been defeated at Bull Run in July, was alerted to a skirmish near Falls Church involving pickets of the Fourteenth Brooklyn Regiment and some Confederate cavalry. McDowell ordered the rest of the Fourteenth Brooklyn and Twenty-Fourth and Thirtieth New York to repel the attack.[72]

The review ended abruptly, but not the excitement for Julia and her friends. Clarke described the scene in detail in his sermon in Boston, often soaring to poetic heights. By the time he finished, Washington, DC, had become a holy city fighting a holy war, much in the spirit of Channing. His sermon manuscript seems hastily prepared, perhaps drafted on the train ride back to Boston: "Immediately the aids [*sic*] rode in all directions, and it was evident, that, if we were to get away with our carriage we must go before the masses of soldiers filled the road. So we drove rapidly back toward Wadsworth's Head Quarters, which was also in the direction of the skirmish. Soon we reached a hilltop, on which stood some soldiers who pointed out where, some two miles away, thin puffs of smoke came up from among the trees. 'There,' said they, 'the fighting is going on. Now we shall have some fun. I hope the general will send *us*.' "[73]

For Clarke, as for the soldiers, the drama of the moment only intensified: "The excitement to us was great, for we did not know, nor probably did the Generals, but that it might be the beginning of a great battle. We left our carriage and climbed on the ramparts of a fort near by, where we could see better. The firing continued in the distance for perhaps three fourths of an hour. At last it became pretty evident that the fight was nearly over and we turned our horses' heads homeward." Had Clarke's congregation ever heard a sermon of such drama and immediacy? "Soon we were surrounded by soldiers marching home from the review,—men of two Wisconsin regiments. They tramped before and behind and beside us, singing their songs, while occasionally a wild bugle note, or the drum and fife, woke the echoes of the forest. The day had been windy, but the night was calm. The evening star hung in the West, and the full moon rising in the East over the distant Capitol silvered the waters of the Potomac—our holy river, made sacred with patriot blood."[74]

Clarke noted Julia's reaction to the excitement. Clarke elaborated in the *Monthly Journal* that "one of our party (who had been very anxious to get nearer to the fight, and very reluctant to come away from it) sang for us and for the soldiers, songs appropriate to the hour." He then emphasized the poignancy of the moment: "The pathetic tones of her voice were in unison with the scene, to complete whose picturesque character came presently the addition of fires in the woods. Long streams of red flames ran over the hills, and followed the courses of dried-up streams, choked with sticks and leaves. So at last, passing the heavy gates of Fort Albany and Fort Runnion, we reached the Long bridge, and returned into Washington, bearers of the news of another skirmish."[75]

Having heard the John Brown song, having seen the soldiers' encampments in the twilight and their campfires dotting the scene, and having heard bugle calls piercing the air, Julia returned to the Willard and went to bed. By her own account, she woke before dawn the next morning. She often experienced half-waking, half-sleeping dreams or visions, at times in great detail, even prophetic utterances revealing her own purpose on earth. In one version of this experience, told to a friend soon after the war but not reported until after Howe's death, the poet spoke of a mystical encounter and of standing in "the Presence." Troubled and depressed by the state of the Union effort, she had looked out over the moonlit streets of Washington from her hotel room window (the moon had just passed full on November 18): "She told us that her mind was so burdened with sorrow for her country that she knew not whether she slept or not but finally a vision seemed to envelop all her faculties. . . . Slowly the vision, call it inspiration or revelation, as you will, was outside and beyond herself. It took form in prophetic words and lines of verse, till she could no longer remain quiet."[76]

In the dark, Julia groped around for a scrap of paper. She was in the habit of using any bit of paper, including the backs of envelopes and the reverse sides of letters, to jot down notes for lectures and essays or fragments of poetry as they came to her. To write out the poem that morning she used a piece of Sanitary Commission stationery with the words "Treasury Building" printed on it. Now that the commission had moved to the Adams House the letterhead could be used only as scrap or for informal family correspondence. The surviving manuscript includes six stanzas, with only four words crossed out and replaced.[77]

Mine eyes have seen the glory of the coming of the Lord
He is trampling [thru?] the wine press where the grapes of wrath are stored

He hath loosed the fateful lightnings of his terrible swift sword
His truth is marching on.

I have seen him in the watchfires of an hundred circling camps
They have builded him an altar in the evening dews and damps,
I can read his righteous sentence by the dim and flaring lamps
His day is marching on.

I have read a burning Gospel writ in fiery rows of steel
As ye deal with my contemners, so with you my grace shall deal
Let the hero, born of woman, crush the serpent with his heel
Our God is marching on.

He has sounded out the trumpet that shall never call retreat
He has waked the earth's dull bosom with a high ecstatic beat
Oh! be swift my soul to answer him, be jubilant my feet
Our God is marching on.

In the whiteness of the lilies he was born across the sea
With a glory in his bosom that shines out on you and me
As he died to make men holy, let us die to make men free
Our God is marching on.

He is coming like the glory of the morning on the wave
He is wisdom to the mighty, he is honour to the brave
So the world shall be his footstool, and the soul of [illegible] his slave
Our God is marching on.

Given what Julia had seen and heard from the moment her train approached Washington five days earlier—the encampments in Maryland and Virginia, the soldiers marching and singing, Channing's apocalyptic preaching—she had a wealth of images at her disposal, images of the "watchfires of an hundred circling camps," the "dim and flaring lamps," the "fiery rows of steel," and God's fearful yet glorious wrath—a world of sacred flags and sacred rivers, of holy cities and holy wars, of martyr heroes and atoning blood. Through her imagination, war, nation, and faith fused into the perfect poetic expression of the North's religious nationalism, an anthem worthy of the savior-nation in its hour of peril.

Monday's skirmish with the Confederates did not deter Julia from returning to the encampments. Wednesday promised to bring the highlight of the week. General McClellan and the Army of the Potomac were to

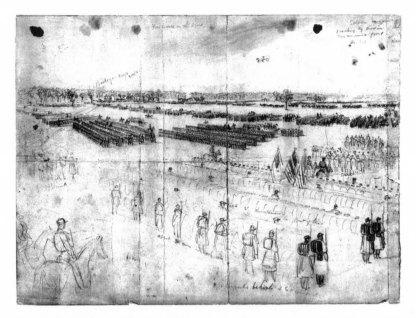

Figure 10. Alfred R. Waud, [McClellan reviewing his troops near Baileys Crossroads], drawing, November 20, 1861. Morgan Collection of Civil War Drawings. Library of Congress, Prints and Photographs Division.

stage a spectacular "grand review" for President Lincoln. Just two weeks earlier, word had spread among the soldiers and through the press that the infirm General Winfield Scott had retired as head of the Union army, and Lincoln had replaced him with George McClellan. The newly appointed McClellan had every reason to ensure his men put on a good show for the politicians and their guests. Julia and Clarke and their party joined the throng determined to witness McClellan's grand review. As many as 20,000 spectators, including President Lincoln and his cabinet, converged on the fields between Bailey's Crossroads and Munson's Hill.

Military passes were not required that day. The roads became so congested that simply reaching the parade ground from the city took half the day. When Julia and her friends finally arrived, they saw thousands of infantrymen joined by cavalry regiments, military bands, artillery salutes, and McClellan and his staff on horseback reveling in it all with Lincoln and his cabinet. It was the largest military review ever staged in North America. It took three and a half hours for the regiments to pass by. Clarke's diary recorded a figure of 53,000 soldiers. The Washington *Evening Star* gave the number as 75,000. Whatever the number, this at last appeared to be a fighting force ready for action, irresistible in its magnitude and skill, the hope of the besieged city and fractured nation.

The next day, Julia boarded the train back to Boston. On Massachusetts's calendar, it was Thanksgiving Day, moved up a week so it would coincide with the date of the signing of the Mayflower Compact. Governor Andrew's proclamation invoked Psalms 66 and 81 and called on the citizens of Massachusetts to observe the anniversary of the compact "with devout and religious joy." He offered consolation to the women of the state whose loved ones' "heroic blood has made sacred the soil of Virginia, and mingling with the waters of the Potomac has made the river now and forever ours." He ended with Psalm 59:11: "Scatter them by Thy power, and bring them down, O Lord, our shield."[78] Julia later claimed that on the trip back to Boston she read Clarke her yet unnamed poem.

2

A RICH CRIMSON

Clarke had considered getting another minister to fill his Boston pulpit on November 24, but he decided to hurry home to preach that Sunday. He had much to say. A large congregation turned out to hear his report from the front. William Lloyd Garrison's *Liberator* carried a story about the sermon.[1] According to the abolitionist paper, the service opened with a hymn of Sir Walter Scott's, beginning, "When Israel, of the Lord beloved, / Out from the land of bondage came." God's new Israel sought its own deliverance in 1861, and holy war was on full display at the Church of the Disciples.

Clarke chose the morning's scripture reading from the first chapter of Isaiah, verses about the city of Jerusalem. Every word in the text seemed to evoke the Civil War and echoed the poem Howe had read to him—a vineyard, a besieged city, divine judgment, rebellious princes, and a coming purge:

Your country is desolate, your cities are burned with fire: your land, strangers devour it in your presence, and it is desolate, as overthrown by strangers.

And the daughter of Zion is left as a cottage in a vineyard, as a lodge in a garden of cucumbers, as a besieged city. How is the faithful city become an harlot! it was full of judgment; righteousness lodged in it; but now murderers. . . . Thy princes are rebellious, and companions of thieves: every one loveth gifts, and followeth after rewards: they judge not the fatherless, neither doth the cause of the widow come unto them. Therefore saith the LORD, the LORD of hosts, the mighty One of Israel, Ah, I will ease me of mine adversaries, and avenge me of mine enemies: and I will turn my hand upon thee, and purely purge away thy dross, and take away all thy sin: and I will restore thy judges as at the first, and thy counsellors as at the beginning: afterward thou shalt be called, The city of righteousness, the faithful city.

Clarke meant the parallels between Jerusalem and Washington to be obvious. The dire condition of Judah's capital was the dire condition of America's capital. Washington, a city "besieged" and "defenced," was exactly what Clarke and a handful of his congregants had just seen. "At last," Clarke rejoiced, "Massachusetts blood had made sacred Virginia soil, and made [the] Potomac our holy river with its great sacrifice. I do not despair of seeing Washington made also our Holy city!"[2] In contrast to the "miserable place" of "hypocrisy" he had seen on a visit in 1851 when the capital groaned under the "Slave Power" and when the Free-Soil movement "was a mockery," now "Washington seems to me much purer to-day, in the midst of war, than it did then in apparent peace and prosperity. We have an immense and difficult task to perform. War is a terrible evil. . . . War is bad; but is it not better than to see the heart of the nation corrupted? Is it not a glorious thing to see men sacrificing all on the altar of their country?"[3] There was no doubt that the Union's capital was a city being purged of its sin and being renewed into a faithful city of righteousness.

According to a report in the *Christian Inquirer*, Clarke urged his congregation to embrace the John Brown song as the national anthem. He had been stirred by hearing the soldiers sing it in Virginia. Many had attempted to write a made-to-order song suitable for a nation at arms fighting the Lord's battles. Every attempt to date had failed. But why look any further? "Has not the John Brown Army Hymn met and supplied the need?" Repeating the chorus, Clarke called on his parishioners to see the truth that "the soul of John Brown" was nothing "but an earnest hatred of slavery." With the coming of this war upon the nation, "the work has been taken out of the hands of the Abolitionists, and is now wholly in the hands of God."[4] Julia was there to hear these words and to hear again the refrain "His soul is marching on." Her visit to Washington and the battlefields of northern Virginia, and the soldiers' rendition of the John Brown song, had inspired her to write her own war anthem. But as Boston prepared to celebrate the first Christmas of the war, victory for the Union and emancipation for the slaves remained elusive goals no matter how confident the poet was that her eyes had seen the glory of the Lord. Whether the poem would be published depended on her editor at the *Atlantic Monthly*.

Confident enough, Julia wrote to James T. Fields a week after Clarke's sermon. She had revised her first draft somewhat, changing a number of words and dropping the sixth verse entirely. It was Fields who added the title "Battle Hymn of the Republic." She set his expectations low and adopted a world-weary tone. "Fields!" she began. "Do you want this, and do you like it, and have you any room for it in [the] January number?" "I am sad and spleeny," she added, "and begin to have fears that I may not be, after all, the greatest woman alive. Isn't this a melancholy view of things? but it is a vale, you know. When will the world come to [an] end?"[5]

Fields bought the poem and featured it on the front page of the *Atlantic Monthly*'s February 1862 issue, ready for sale by mid-January. As was typical of the magazine at the time, Howe's name did not appear as the author, leaving that to the index. The press, however, knew from the beginning that she was the author and gave her credit. Newspapers across the North and West, having received advance copies of the February issue, wrote notices, ran advertisements, and reprinted the "Battle Hymn."[6] The *New York Times* on January 27 praised the new issue of the *Atlantic* with its "Battle Hymn." "True to the instincts which have led [the *Atlantic*] to reflect the color of the day," the *Times* wrote, "a 'Battle Hymn of the Republic' leads off the well-ordered columns. Despite the refrain of 'Marching on'—which seems to have been suggested by the song we have all heard the Massachusetts regiments sing, as they marched with bristling bayonets down Broadway—we like this lyric much. If poetry can be said to have color—and it is contended that music has—we fancy that this would reveal itself to the subtle sense in a rich crimson, warming and nerving the soldier's soul like the notes of a trumpet."[7] And while each stanza did indeed include Howe's one-line refrain, the "Glory, hallelujah" from the John Brown song was not printed with the "Battle Hymn." Publishers would soon combine the two in sheet music for soldiers, soloists, choirs, and congregations.

Howe later downplayed her expectations for the poem. If the *Atlantic Monthly* had been the primary way the "Battle Hymn" reached the public, she might have had reasons for low expectations. While the *Atlantic's* combined sales in the United States and England reached a respectable 32,000 during the war, that figure could not match the biggest newspapers.[8] Fortunately for Howe's poem, the full text of the "Battle Hymn" appeared on the front page of Horace Greeley's *New-York Tribune* on January 14, with proper credit given to the *Atlantic* and to Julia Ward Howe, the paper's anonymous Boston correspondent. Greeley, the Whig reformer, disciple of Fourier, and enterprising editor, always had his eye out for talent. He had hired Margaret Fuller as a correspondent to cover the Revolutions of 1848, recruited Karl Marx to write dispatches from Europe, and cultivated a disillusioned George Ripley following Brook Farm's collapse to become one of the nation's leading literary critics.[9] Greeley built the *Tribune* into the largest circulation newspaper in the nation, perhaps the world; its combined editions approached a quarter million, and the daily edition alone sold 45,000 in 1860 and 90,000 in 1865.[10]

Greeley's was only the first of dozens of newspapers to run the "Battle Hymn," typically on the front page.[11] Within months, far more households in the North and West had heard of Julia Ward Howe and had read her poetry than ever before. When readers picked up the *New-York Tribune* on January 14, these are the five stanzas they saw, perhaps not realizing they were meant as new words to the John Brown tune:

Mine eyes have seen the glory of the coming of the Lord:
He is trampling out the vintage where the grapes of wrath are stored;
He hath loosed the fateful lightning of His terrible swift sword:
His truth is marching on.

I have seen him in the watch-fires of a hundred circling camps;
They have builded Him an altar in the evening dews and damps;
I have read his righteous sentence by the dim and flaring lamps:
His day is marching on.

I have read a fiery gospel writ in burnished rows of steel:
"As ye deal with my contemners, so with you my grace shall deal;
Let the Hero, born of woman, crush the serpent with his heel,
        Since God is marching on."

He has sounded forth the trumpet that shall never call retreat;
He is sifting out the hearts of men before His judgment-seat:
Oh, be swift, my soul, to answer Him! be jubilant, my feet!
        Our God is marching on.

In the beauty of the lilies Christ was born across the sea,
With a glory in his bosom that transfigures you and me:
As he died to make men holy, let us die to make men free,
        While God is marching on.

Howe's language evoked the book of Genesis, the Psalms, the prophet Isaiah, and the apocalypse of Saint John. Its most vivid imagery came from Isaiah 63 and Revelation 14 and 19. The poem sounded thoroughly biblical. Its debt to the Old and New Testaments made it a poetic sermon or even a poetic prophecy easily added to the canon of American scripture alongside the Declaration of Independence, Washington's Farewell Address, and soon Lincoln's Gettysburg Address. The blending of the Bible with war and politics was nothing new in 1861. Preachers and politicians had been reading American history through the lenses of ancient Israel and the church since colonial times. The Puritans who came to the New World had been confident that they witnessed all around them events they called "speaking providences"—manifest affirmations from God that he was among them, approved of the work they had undertaken, and would bless them for their faithfulness, while at the same time threatening judgment for unfaithfulness to the modern covenant. Good harvest or bad, peace or war with the Native American tribes and predatory European empires, sound health or devastating plagues—all were readable signs of God's relationship with his chosen people. From the beginning, war proved to be the most fertile ground for producing this hybrid between the Bible and national history. The God of battles heard the prayers of his people in the colonial wars with France, in the War of Independence, the War of 1812, and now in the Civil War. This war would continue to stock the warehouse of metaphors and symbols for the nation's political religion.

Protestant Americans, and Christians in general, would have understood Howe's "coming of the Lord" to mean the Second Coming of Christ. The more orthodox their theology, the more literal this coming in glory would be to them. Whether postmillennialist, premillennialist, or amillennialist, liberal or conservative, they would have imagined Christ the Lord returning to judge the world in righteousness. Howe's debt to Old Testament images of Gideon's Army of the Lord and to the prophet's visions was real and important and noted by many at the time and since. The figure who appears in the triumphant first line of the "Battle Hymn" is not the God of the Old Testament but the victorious Christ of the New. More particularly, this is the Christ of Revelation 19, which in turn was indebted to Isaiah 63. Isaiah 63 paints a picture of a warrior, his robe red with the blood of his enemies, stained like the garments of a man treading grapes in a winepress. Revelation 19 depicts an angel of God sent with a sickle to reap the harvest of judgment on the earth. Another angel tells him to "thrust in thy sharp sickle, and gather the clusters of the vine of the earth; for her grapes are fully ripe." Picking up these images, Catholic and Lutheran art depicted Jesus himself standing in the winepress, trampling the grapes, and bearing the wrath of God himself, at times with the press shown in the form of his cross of crucifixion. Militant Unitarians like Clarke, Channing, and Howe may have rejected Jesus's literal blood atonement for sin, but they rushed to make the soldiers' blood redemptive for the nation.

It did not take the massive bloodletting of Gettysburg or other epic battles to make the Civil War sacred. That had happened long before, even in anticipation of the suffering and dying ahead. No one had to revert to Calvinism to invoke the God of battles and the Final Judgment. Indeed, there appeared to be fewer theological constraints on Unitarians and low-church evangelicals than on confessional Protestants worried about the consequences of confusing worldly warfare against political enemies with spiritual warfare against sin and the devil. Howe and other Unitarians, along with countless other activist Christians, were never squeamish about literal wars for righteousness. They preached peace—ultimate peace—but in the meantime waged violent war to get there. Soldiers fought, suffered, and died doing the Lord's work. Their sacrifices brought them apotheosis. It seemed obvious that the flag should join the altar in the nave and fly atop church spires. And this was true of all denominations, and true to

Torcular calcaui solus, et de gentibus non est vir mecum . Esaie 63 .

Hieronymus Wierx fecit et excud . Cum Gratia et Priuilegio . Buschere .

Figure 11. Hieronymus (Jerome) Wierix (Netherlandish, ca. 1553–1619, Antwerp), *Christ in the Winepress*, engraving, before 1619. Harris Brisbane Dick Fund, 1953.

Metropolitan Museum of Art.

some extent of both sides. North and South proclaimed fast days to call their peoples to repentance and thanksgiving and renewed fidelity to God and to the cause. Pacifism in the churches was rare, and the more confessional churches had a hard time keeping politics and war out of their pulpits and out of their denominational assemblies.

Given her education, favorite authors, and theology, Julia could have written a truly radical poem that pushed the boundaries of war and religion, but she did not. She could have written a distinctively Unitarian poem that overtly denied the divinity of Christ, but she did not. She could have written a transcendentalist poem imbued with German idealism, but she did not. She wrote a poem that sounded like America because it sounded so much like the Bible.

But what exactly was a "battle hymn"? How would readers in 1861 have understood the title Fields chose? The *New York Times*, after all, had welcomed *a* "Battle Hymn of the Republic," not *the* "Battle Hymn of the Republic." It took time for it to become that. One minster had already published his own "Battle Hymn" in *The Soldier's Companion*, published by Clarke's *Monthly Journal*.[12] The poetic genre of battle hymn seems to have come most directly from the psalm-singing Calvinists of the sixteenth century, a tradition brought by English Puritans and others to the American colonies in the seventeenth century. Psalm singing spread wherever Reformed Protestantism spread, in France, Hungary, England, Scotland, the Netherlands, Geneva, and beyond. Encouraged and instructed by Calvin himself, Calvinists built their identity and unity in part by singing the psalter in metrical versions in their own languages and together as congregations. They sang psalms in corporate worship, under persecution, as martyrs heading to scaffold and stake, and in battle during the Wars of Religion. The psalms served them most commonly in prayers and praise to God and in their battle with the world, the flesh, and the devil, but also on the literal battlefield in earthly warfare against their enemies. Soldiers kept up their morale, faced hardship and the terrors of death and injury, and celebrated victories with favorite psalms.[13]

This is not to say that battle hymns had to be inspired directly by the Psalms or that they were unique to Calvinists in Europe, England, Scotland, Northern Ireland, or America. The German romantic poet, soldier, and nationalist Karl Theodor Körner wrote a celebrated "Battle Hymn" translated into English and popular in America by the 1830s. This voice of "Young

Germany" became one of the best-known Teutonic poets in the United States, just behind Goethe, Schiller, and Richter.[14] Körner had enlisted in the German resistance against Napoleon and became a romantic hero to many in Europe and America. German immigrants to the United States kept his fame and poetry alive, especially among their settlements in the Midwest. His most popular verses included the "Sword Song" and the "Battle Hymn," although a number of his poems were thought of as battle hymns.

For years to come, Howe and the "Battle Hymn of the Republic" were mentioned in the same breath as Körner and his war poems. The first lines of his "Battle Hymn" make clear why this was the case: "Father of earth and heaven! I call thy name! / Round me the smoke and shout of battle roll; / My eyes are dazzled with the rustling flame; / Father! Sustain an untried soldier's soul." In the last lines, Körner made his plea for righteous warfare emphatic: "Earth cries for blood! In thunder on them wheel! / This hour to Europe's fate shall set the triumph seal!"[15]

Regardless of Körner's popularity, a more likely source for the public's idea of a battle hymn was the English Civil Wars of the seventeenth century, at least the way the Puritan wars were depicted in the literature and history of the nineteenth century. In the 1820s, the celebrated English historian Thomas Babington Macaulay had already used Isaiah 63 in a poem for his "Songs of the Civil War." The parallel to Howe's poem of forty years later stands out in Macaulay's first two stanzas alone, complete with grapes, a vintage, and a winepress:

> Oh! wherefore come ye forth, in triumph from the North,
> With your hands, and your feet, and your raiment all red?
> And wherefore doth your rout send forth a joyous shout?
> And whence be the grapes of the wine-press which ye tread?

> Oh evil was the root, and bitter was the fruit,
> And crimson was the juice of the vintage that we trod;
> For we trampled on the throng of the haughty and the strong,
> Who sate in the high places, and slew the saints of God.[16]

For others, the idea of a battle hymn called up associations with Martin Luther's "A Mighty Fortress Is Our God." Luther's hymn appeared in an English translation by Thomas Carlyle in 1831.[17] Frederick Henry Hedge, the American transcendentalist, Unitarian minister, and friend of Julia's, published his own English version, known as "Luther's Psalm," in his 1853 collection, *Hymns for the Church of Christ*—the English translation that still appears in most American hymnbooks despite its Unitarian pedigree.[18]

Additional help in understanding Howe's contribution to the battle hymn genre comes from the "war hymns" already published in the North in 1861. Many of these were written by Howe's friends and acquaintances. Clarke's Harvard classmate Oliver Wendell Holmes Sr. published his "Army Hymn" in *Chimes of Freedom and Union: A Collection of Poems for the Times* (1861). This book also included John Greenleaf Whittier's "Ein feste Burg ist unser Gott"—not a translation of Luther's hymn but an original work set to Luther's tune ("We wait beneath the furnace-blast / The pangs of transformation: / Not painlessly doth God recast / And mould anew the nation")—and Harriett Beecher Stowe's "The Holy War" based on Revelation 19, complete with a victorious Christ on horseback, trumpet calls, a heavenly army robed in white, and a "sacred war" ("To the last battle set, throughout the earth! / Not for vile lust of plunder or of power, / The hosts of justice and eternal right / Unfurl their banner in this solemn hour").[19] The savior-nation found poets eager to present the prophet's outcry of rebellion, judgment, and redemption.

Holmes's hymn appeared in newspapers in the summer of 1861 under the title "The Battle Hymn."[20] He drew on the Old Testament's imagery for Israel. Holmes addressed God as the "LORD of Hosts," invoked the pillar of fire and the pillar of cloud that guided the Hebrews by night and day through the wilderness, and affirmed an intimate bond between America and her covenantal God. He emphasized the God of battles, the public's "sacrifice," the "holy faith" of their forebears, the Lord's providential care for the nation, and a war fought in his name for his cause. Indeed, "to die for [America] is serving Thee."

O LORD of Hosts! Almighty King!
Behold the sacrifice we bring!
To every arm Thy strength impart,
Thy spirit shed through every heart!

Wake in our breasts the living fires,
The holy faith that warmed our sires;
Thy hand hath made our Nation free;
To die for her is serving Thee.

Be Thou a pillared flame to show
The midnight snare, the silent foe;
And when the battle thunders loud,
Still guide us in its moving cloud.

God of all Nations! Sovereign Lord!
In thy dread name we draw the sword,
We lift the starry flag on high,
That fills with light our stormy sky.

From treason's rent, from murder's stain,
Guard Thou its folds till Peace shall reign—
Till fort and field, till shore and sea
Join our loud anthem, PRAISE TO THEE!

Despite Holmes's stature as a poet, the way remained open for Howe's poem to fill the void as the nation's "Marseillaise," the French Revolutionary anthem to which it was often compared. Her words managed to strike the right tone, with the right intensity, imbued with prophetic Biblicism. Her timing was fortuitous, and she found her audience eager for her message. At one level, Howe's "Battle Hymn" is direct and unambiguous: it expresses an abolitionist's dramatic encounter with the Union army in northern Virginia in late 1861. It reflects her efforts to capture that experience in symbols, to memorialize self-sacrifice in a way appropriate to the nation's depth of suffering, and to evoke the war's meaning with a visceral intensity not possible in another literary form. But at another level, the poem is open to a more complex theological, literary, and historical reading, one that can go a long way toward understanding Howe's purposes in choosing the words and images she did. Howe ranged widely across the Old and New Testaments, but her way of handling Christ and the gospel reveals most clearly what she achieved in her anthem and what she added to America's religious nationalism.

Like Lincoln in the Gettysburg Address in 1863, Howe left the North and the South unnamed in the "Battle Hymn." She never identified a battlefield or general or politician by name—and she had seen all these in the days before and after drafting her poem. She never even mentioned slavery as such. Her poem is much less explicit than the overt "holy war" verses of Holmes, Whittier, and Stowe. Nevertheless, Howe helped make

the war sacred, and America sacred, by infusing her poem with biblical quotations, allusions, and images of apocalypse, judgment, redemption, and victory. The sheer violence of her poem escapes most Americans
today, but this was not violence for the sake of violence but for the sake of
national redemption. Even the poem's vineyard imagery emphasizes both
the judgment that fell on Christ and the ultimate judgment of God upon
all his enemies. Howe reached back to Isaiah 63, as had Macaulay, and to
Revelation 19, as so many did in the midst of the Civil War. Revelation 19
features a repeated chorus of "Alleluia," praising God for his righteous
justice against the Whore of Babylon, as well as the Marriage Supper of
the Lamb and Christ leading the armies of heaven to victory astride his
white horse, his clothes dripping with blood, and a sword coming from his
mouth to "smite the nations."

This is the Christ who treads the grapes in the winepress of God's wrath.
Howe's poem brought the Christ of judgment to earth and into the here
and now. This was "the Hero, born of woman," who would "crush the serpent with his heel," the one "born across the sea" who "died to make men
holy" and called his followers to "die to make men free." The first of these
phrases echoes the language of the third chapter of Genesis, often referred
to by Christian theologians as the *protoevangelium*, the first announcement
of the gospel. (In Genesis 3:15, the Lord says to the Serpent, "And I will put
enmity between thee and the woman, and between thy seed and her seed;
it shall bruise [or crush] thy head, and thou shalt bruise its heel"). Howe's
invocation of the gospel made it easy for American evangelicals (and later
Catholics and Mormons) to sing her verses about Christ as if the stanzas
spoke for their own theology. But Howe's Christology came from other
sources: a mix of mysticism, liberal Unitarianism, and her own poetic imagination. It is not too much to say that humanity itself became her Christ.

The mystical dimension of Howe's Christ derived from the eighteenth-
century Swedish eccentric Emanuel Swedenborg. The founder of the
Church of the New Jerusalem won admirers among a number of transcendentalists, including Emerson, George Ripley, and William James Sr. Boston was the site of the first Swedenborg congregation in Massachusetts,
originally known as the Boston Society of the New Jerusalem and today
as the Church on the Hill. Howe singled out Swedenborg's "theory of the
divine man" for the way it shaped her conception of Christ, and his essays

"Heaven and Hell," "Divine Love and Wisdom," and "Conjugal Love" as the "writings which interested [her] most." She credited Swedenborg with formulating the doctrine of Christ she still adhered to in 1899. Jesus was "the heavenly Being whose presence was beneficence, whose word was judgment[,] whose brief career on earth ended in a sacrifice, whose purity and pathos have had much to do with the redemption of the human race from barbarism and the rule of the animal passions."[21]

By 1861, Howe had been wrestling with Christ's identity in her published and unpublished poems for more than a decade. Some of these poems appeared in her 1854 *Passion-Flowers*. Even the title pointed to Christ and his suffering. The passion-flower vine, first encountered by Spanish explorers in the Americas in the sixteenth century, was popular in Victorian Britain and America. An Italian monk early in the seventeenth century had published a description of the flower's complex structure and its supposed symbolic connections to the wounds of Christ, including the crown of thorns. In the title of her collection, then, Howe invoked powerful Christological symbolism.

The poem "Whit-Sunday in the Church" illuminates the nature of Howe's Christ.[22] Whitsunday is another name for Pentecost in the liturgical year. It falls seven weeks after Easter and celebrates the gift of the Holy Spirit and the apostolic miracle of tongues. Howe identified the miracle of Pentecost in this poem as the binding of humankind back together through the recovery of man's "lost ancestral tongue," a reversal, that is, of the curse of Babel in the book of Genesis that divided human language. Out of divided "Men" would one day come the ideal "Man." In contrast to the vibrant church at the time of its birth, the modern church earns Howe's rebuke for its "flimsy" preaching, "dead Bible," and ritual of "song and prayer"—a common charge from conservative and liberal evangelicals alike against forms, creeds, confessions, and sectarianism. In his anemic sermon, the pastor merely admonishes the congregation to pray, to attend services, to take the sacrament, and wait for the work of the Holy Spirit. This was God's "appointed way," he tells them.

But the poet proclaims that none of this cold indifference to the state of the world could prevent the true message of Christ from breaking through dead formality, biblical literalism, and the "cold abstraction" of orthodoxy. It was "doctrine" that killed Christ. The living Christ of an active faith appears among the complacent worshippers:

> And Christ, my Christ, by doctrine slain,
> By ritual buried, from his ashes
> Breathed out the fervor of his soul,
> And swept the aisles, and shook the sashes;
>
> And turned us to the simpler truth
> He taught, beside the sea's wild splendor,
> And showed the meaning of his life
> With urgings passionate and tender:
>
> "For song and prayer, the old time had
> The Hebrew and the classic Muses;
> I left a rule of work and life,
> A work of love, a life of uses."

Jews and Greeks had given former ages their forms for contemplation, but this is the Christ of action who "stood [as] God's champion" and waged "war for all who wrought you wrong," who treated women with justice, interposed on behalf of the slave, and cleansed the temple of the money changers. This Jesus now worked in solidarity with peasant and factory worker, with the liberal theologians who "free the truth" from "dead symbols," with the victims of Russian despotism and the Lombards in chains in Austria's prisons, and with the beaten slave. Howe's Christ chastised Christians in their comfortable churches for their "dead worship," and asked in astonishment:

> "Think ye, in these portentous times
> Of wrath, and hate, and wild distraction,
> Christ dwells within a church that rests
> A comfortable, cold abstraction?
> . . . .
>
> "He cries: 'On, brethren, draw the sword,
> Loose the bold tongue and pen, unfearing,
> The weakness of our human flesh
> Is ransomed by your persevering.'"

In 1861, Howe loosed her bold pen. In the "Battle Hymn," this figure became the Christ who once "died to make men holy," the Christ who called his brethren to "die to make men free," the theologically modernized Jesus, the zealous reformer.

During the war, Howe meditated further on Christ and his work in several poems published in *Later Lyrics* (1866). These poems followed the "Battle Hymn" but trace the consistent thread of her thought. This was Christ as the exemplary, self-sacrificial teacher who had attained the highest expression yet of the divine ideal on earth. "Requital" works out Howe's conception of Christ and the relationship between his suffering and the North's blood. The powerful scene she conjures up is Christ's examination by Pontius Pilate and his flogging by the Roman guard. The next to last stanza reads: "Sweet Christ, with flagellations brought / To thine immortal martyrdom, / Cancel the bitter treasons wrought / By men who bid thy kingdom come." Witnessing Christ's torture, the poet appears to desire self-sacrifice more than vengeance, although the two are not incompatible, as the "Battle Hymn" itself shows: "Their sinful blood we may not urge / While Mercy stays thy righteous hand; / But take all ours, if that should purge / The wicked patience of the land."[23] In "The Battle-Eucharist," an appeal to Christ to sustain the war's weary with wine and bread in "our sacrament of woe," Howe connects the wounds Christ suffered on the cross to the "pangs" endured by those who fight for earthly victory: "And open wide the gates of thought, / That, sitting at this feast divine, / Our faith may see deliverance wrought / By pangs that bear the mark of thine."[24] This is what the *imitatio Christi* had come to mean for Howe in time of war.

Some in Howe's circle claimed all along that the "Hero" of the "Battle Hymn" was in fact not Jesus but John Brown. Christ and Brown merged in her mind as they had for other New Englanders and for reformers in Europe. Victor Hugo told a friend in December 1859 that "slavery must disappear even if it should mean that the American republic be split in two," a tragedy that might delay the world's "Progress" "for fifty years to come," he wrote. "John Brown has torn the veil," he continued, showing that "the American question has now become as important as the European question." He sketched a drawing of Brown hanging from the scaffold, intending it as a symbol of a new crucifixion. To Hugo, "his gallows [was] a cross." Below the picture, he wrote in Latin, *"Pro Christo, sicut Christus"*—for Christ, as Christ.[25]

Julia's thoughts paralleled Victor Hugo's. Brown became the equal at least of the martyrs of the early church. On the day of Brown's execution, she wrote her husband in Toronto about the abolitionist's impending death and exaltation. "This is a day of mourning to all of us," she acknowledged. "If there be such a thing as religion, John Brown must have it's [*sic*] support today, and God can give him a peace, a rapture in dying which you and I might envy. I do believe that he will be lifted above the brief pangs of his death, and see, like Stephen of old, the heavens open, and the Christ of consolation waiting to receive him." That same peace did not await Governor Henry Wise of Virginia. He "will not pass so tranquilly, after all, from time to eternity, as his noble victim. We must think of this, and believe in the support that conscience and Faith can give."[26]

Howe captured her grief over Brown in a wartime poem she called "The First Martyr." It suggests close connections in her mind between Brown and Christ's sacrifice (i.e., "Then shall his form be lifted high" at his execution). But the poem's reference to John's Apocalypse at the end may provide a better clue to its meaning. The poet, trying to explain to her five-year-old daughter why she is grieving over this man's imprisonment and impending death, warns future generations of their fate should they not end chattel slavery. That future may have narrowly meant the child (Sammy) she carried in 1859, but she clearly intended to alert America as a whole: "O babe unborn! O future race! / Heir of our glory and disgrace, / We cannot see thy veiléd face; / But shouldst thou keep our crime, / No new Apocalypse need say / In what wild woe shall pass away / The falsehood of the time."[27]

Frank Sanborn, a member of the Secret Six and a friend of the Howes', had no doubt years later about John Brown's identity as the "Hero" of the "Battle Hymn." In 1910, not long after Julia's death and therefore immune to contradiction, Sanborn answered a Civil War veteran who asked for his interpretation of the third stanza of the "Battle Hymn." Sanborn obliged with an amplified paraphrase and detailed exegesis:

I have read in the weapons of this holy war against slavery and for the Union (the muskets and bayonets carried by our soldiers) a gospel as in words of fire thus: "As ye deal with those who despise me their God, in despising my black children, buying and selling God's images carved in ebony, even so my grace shall deal with you, giving you the victory if you fight for me and my poor black children." Hearing this I said or sung: "Let the hero born of the line of Mother Eve, who was told to bruise the head of the old Serpent, Satan, now crush this child of that serpent with his iron heel,—that is, put down the champions of slavery; and do this because God is marching on to the emancipation of all slaves; that is, he is the God of the living and not of the dead,—and slavery is a live issue."

"Is this intelligible?" Sanborn asked readers of the *Springfield Republican*. He thought so. "If [Howe] had any one hero in mind, probably it was John Brown."[28]

Regardless of Howe's precise intention, her use of the Hero and Christ helped to make American religious nationalism more Christocentric and thereby more redemptive. She paired New Testament motifs of vicarious atonement through self-sacrifice and death with Old Testament motifs of the chosen nation and covenantal blessings and curses. The Christ-nation identity had been present in America for generations, certainly in the Revolution, but the scale of suffering and bloodshed from 1861 to 1865 conjured up images of the cross as never before. So much death had to be justified. God's ways had to be vindicated. To be sure, Howe used fierce language of vengeance from the Hebrew scriptures. But just as significantly she invoked the symbolism of Christ's exemplary sacrifice to inspire men and women of conscience to lay down their lives for humanity.

Lincoln used a similar strategy in his Gettysburg Address in 1863. Lincoln, however, left behind Old Testament imagery completely, though he would return to it later, most famously in his second inaugural address. The Boston poet Robert Lowell, writing in the 1960s at the time of the Civil War centennial, credited Lincoln at Gettysburg with infusing the born-again United States with its identity as the Christ-nation. "For us and our country," Lowell wrote, "he left Jefferson's ideals of freedom and equality joined to the Christian sacrificial act of death and rebirth."[29] Lincoln moved from conception to birth to death to rebirth to life everlasting. Howe produced a similar fusion of America and war with Christian sacrifice, death, and rebirth. Howe invoked the "Hero, born of woman," who will crush the serpent's head, the Christ who, "in the beauty of the lilies," was "born across the sea." The God of battles offers "grace" to warriors who fight on his side, and Christ "transfigures" his followers with his "glory" as they offer themselves as willing sacrifices on the altar of human freedom. This was Howe's "Battle Hymn" gospel.

For others, the "Battle Hymn" was no gospel. It was blasphemy. From May to July 1863, New York City briefly became a battleground over the school system's right to use the "Battle Hymn" to enforce public orthodoxy in its classrooms. Civil religion met stiff resistance. Under state law and in line with court rulings, instruction in the city's schools was permitted to be generally religious while not being narrowly sectarian. Even simple Bible reading had been banned as too sectarian and divisive. The state's Supreme Court had ruled as recently as 1851 that public schools must be nonsectarian and had denied public funding to a Catholic orphanage in Brooklyn.[30] But the war proved that another kind of sectarianism could find its way into public school classrooms in the form of a civil religion at odds with religious conscience and entangled with bitter politics.

In May 1863, a teacher named Lizzie Cavanaugh had a student suspended from Grammar School 16 in the city's Ninth Ward for refusing to sing the chorus of the "Battle Hymn of the Republic." According to press reports, the student, Catharine (Kate) McGean, the daughter of the prominent Irish-Catholic Democrat Hugh McGean, "objected to the mention of the Deity, deeming it irreverent and blasphemous." At its June 3 meeting, the city's Board of Education heard an appeal from Mr. McGean asking that his daughter be reinstated. What the press described as "a lively debate" followed a motion to ask the trustees of the Ninth Ward to reconsider the suspension. One board member identified the "Battle Hymn" as "an abolition song" and defended Kate's liberty of conscience not to be forced to sing it. Some members were unfamiliar enough with the hymn that the board ended up discussing whether the hymn had been written by Harriett Beecher Stowe or Julia Ward Howe.[31]

Following a time-honored bureaucratic strategy, the school board appointed a special committee to investigate, taking care to balance its membership politically. At its June 17 meeting, the board passed three resolutions by a wide margin of 23 to 3 exonerating Kate of the charge of insubordination and ordering the Ninth Ward to return her to her class with the full "rights and privileges" of the other students. The trustees of the Ninth Ward flatly refused, though at least one of the trustees supported the order to rescind and defended Kate's "sacred obligations to her conscience and to her God." The trustees had even removed the "Battle Hymn" from the curriculum in the meantime, so why punish Kate, he asked.

The Board of Education was not happy with the stubborn ward trustees and was not so easily thwarted. On July 1, the board ordered salaries

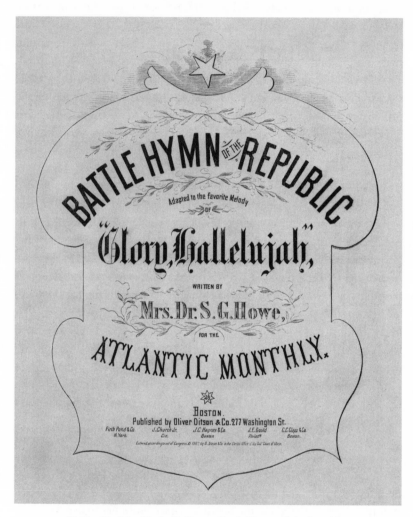

Figure 12. Mrs. Dr. S. G. Howe, *Battle Hymn of the Republic* (Boston: Oliver Ditson & Co., 1862), notated music. https://www.loc.gov/item/ihas.200000858/.

Library of Congress, Music Division.

to be withheld in the Ninth Ward until the trustees "compl[ied] with the resolutions" and reinstated Kate at Grammar School 16. A controversy ensued over the ambiguous wording of the board's directive, and at its July 8 meeting, the board rescinded its flawed resolution and did not pass a substitute. An explanation for the board's hasty retreat is not hard to find. Between its principled stand in favor of Kate on July 1 and its sheepish retreat on July 8 the Battle of Gettysburg had bloodied Pennsylvania. Union victory at such staggering cost made criticism of the "Battle Hymn" and defense of the right of conscience seem in bad taste if not outright treasonous. Moreover, New York City had been plunged into the violence of the Draft Riots that pitted Irish against free blacks. When McGean tried to have the state Supreme Court issue a writ of mandamus to review the board's decision, he was denied. Kate's plight became relevant only later in flag salute cases in the twentieth century.[32]

Whatever controversy the "Battle Hymn" might stir up in Howe's hometown, it would not be long before her anthem became a standard part of school curricula and pageants. Immediately in 1862, the "Battle Hymn" appeared as sheet music from the Boston firm Oliver Ditson. That same year, it appeared in hymnbooks for the first time. Since the Civil War, editors have included the "Battle Hymn" in over 470 hymnbooks, gospel songbooks, Sunday School supplements, and patriotic collections for the use of churches. Baptists, Methodists, Congregationalists, Presbyterians, Pentecostals, Mormons, and many others have sung it since 1862. The "Battle Hymn" rallied the faithful for evangelism and revival meetings, antisaloon crusades, and political campaigns. In the twentieth century it was sung as easily by fundamentalists as by modernists. Before long, it was translated into Armenian, Portuguese, Spanish, French, Italian, and Sanskrit.[33] Howe's hopes for her poem may have been modest when she submitted it to the *Atlantic*. She may not have ever known how widely it was reprinted in the national press in 1862. Some may have thought Harriett Beecher Stowe or Chaplain McCabe wrote it. But soon her identity became inseparable from the "Battle Hymn" and through the "Battle Hymn" inseparable from the Civil War and the reunified nation.

3

"The Glorious Freedom of His Gospel"

In March 1862, Samuel sent Julia news from Washington: "One of the best men in the world told me to day [sic] that his sister (who is better even than he) wrote to him that she should be prouder of the authorship of the Battle Hymn, than of winning a victory." Samuel agreed. "It was a great service, as I too, feel."[1]

But perhaps there was more his wife could do. He wondered whether she might come stay in Washington for a while, long enough to insinuate herself into the corridors of power, gather information, and expose the corruption in Congress impeding the war effort. Maybe with her *New-York Tribune* essays in mind, he proposed that she "could do a great service by an anonymous revelation and 'depictment' of the same." Julia considered the idea. A week later she responded, saying, "I should like to render that service you spoke of . . . getting behind the scenes, etc." She thought she might stay with the Channings. She knew how much she had accomplished on the last visit: "I could not have written my Battle Hymn, if I had not gone to Washington. I consider it the most important thing my pen has done."[2]

That early impression would only grow in time. Between 1862 and her death in 1910, Howe told and retold the story of her visit to Washington and the inspiration for her "Battle Hymn." She recalled it as nothing less than a vision from God. For decades to come, she remembered the war through the lens of her poem. Early on, breezy associations between her and the poem annoyed her. One woman in DC in 1864 "tormented" her "by introducing me everywhere as Mrs. Howe, the author of the 'Hymn', which she always misquoted."[3] But more appropriate accolades always pleased her. For forty years, she recited the "Battle Hymn" at gatherings large and small, in public and private, thanked choirs and soloists for singing it in her honor, lectured about the moment of its creation, answered requests for autograph copies, and wrote about it in popular magazines for adults and children. She found all the attention quite touching. She helped create the poem's deep, mythic resonance with the Civil War. At times, she might regret that this single poem eclipsed her wide-ranging achievements, but she also learned to enjoy the celebrity it brought her, and even to profit from it.

As was true of any part of the America's national religion, Howe's "Battle Hymn" became public property subject to all the blessings and curses of fame. Through it all, Howe always thought of the "Battle Hymn" in personal terms. In her journal, she invariably called it "my Battle Hymn" or simply "my Hymn." But the American public—or rather large segments of it in the North—appropriated the "Battle Hymn" as their own gospel of righteous nationalism. They did so quickly. They did so with little or no direct knowledge of what Howe herself meant by her poem's apocalyptic and redemptive images. The public did not become the sole proprietors of the "Battle Hymn" until after Howe's death, but even then Howe's daughters protected the family's interest in their mother's poem and tried to control what it symbolized and the causes for which it stood. Maud, Laura, and Florence—all of whom became successful writers— projected the "Battle Hymn" beyond America's borders in three wars. And others proved eager to help them. No domestic or foreign conflict seemed incompatible with the "Battle Hymn." From the moment Americans first read the "Battle Hymn" in print in the winter of 1862, they turned it to political, religious, and military purposes. It nearly became the national anthem. Admirers deployed it to define the Civil War and its legacy, interpret the American experience during the Gilded Age, and anticipate a glorious future for their empire of liberty. The "Battle Hymn" Howe made for America became America's affirmation of faith in itself.

Union soldiers may have been among the most reluctant to adopt Howe's poem, especially as doing so meant giving up their beloved "John Brown's Body." They sang this favorite while marching in parade, passing time in the camps, or distracting themselves as they faced the terror of battle. Clarke had seen no reason to give up the words to the John Brown song when he and Julia heard the soldiers sing it in Virginia in 1861. Despite Chaplain McCabe's emotional rendition of the "Battle Hymn" at the anniversary celebration of the Christian Commission in 1864, and Lincoln's tearful call for an encore, these brothers-in-arms would be slow to embrace the "Battle Hymn," and there is some evidence that veterans remembered singing it more often than they actually did. Thomas Wentworth Higginson, the veteran colonel of the all-black First South Carolina Volunteers and a friend and associate of the Howes, remarked in 1907 that "even this poem . . . was not (although many supposed otherwise) a song sung by all the soldiers. The resounding lyric of 'John Brown's Body' reached them much more readily, but the 'Battle Hymn' will doubtless survive all the rest of the rather disappointing metrical products of the war." Higginson turned out to be right, but while he predicted a bright future for the "Battle Hymn" in the nation's affections, he doubted Howe's poetic achievement as a whole. "For the rest of her poems," he wrote, "they are rarely quite enough concentrated; they reach our ears attractively but not with positive mastery."[4] Some veterans and others old enough to remember the war insisted that soldiers would never have steeled themselves for battle and faced death singing Howe's mystical vision of grapes, altars, and lilies. Others were eager to claim that they had been part of its inspiration.

As for McCabe, he made the most of the "Battle Hymn." A paper in Topeka, Kansas, once tried to correct a public speaker who had allegedly robbed McCabe of the credit by attributing the poem to "a Boston lady."[5] A pious evangelical Methodist, McCabe never shrank from combining the Unitarian Howe's poem with a presentation of the gospel. McCabe

Figure 13. Portrait of Bishop Charles Cardwell McCabe, ca. 1905.
American University Library University Archives.

was back on active duty in the fall of 1864 as a chaplain with the troops in Virginia. On one occasion, when asked to speak to a group of several hundred soldiers, he said he "talked to them in a patriotic strain for some time, I sang for them 'The Battle Hymn of the Republic,' and then I talked to them of Jesus and His dying love. Oh, it was a magnificent opportunity!"[6] After Lincoln's assassination a few months later, McCabe honored the slain president with the "Battle Hymn," linking Howe's poem to a new martyr, a connection politicians would soon perpetuate. At Bryan Hall in Chicago, at a Sunday memorial service for Lincoln the day before his body arrived in the city, McCabe was asked to sing the "Battle Hymn." "I did so," he wrote in his diary. "It did not seem appropriate to me at first, but, as we sang on, it was the natural expression of our gloomy joy." He sang it twice again in Springfield as Lincoln's body lay in the Illinois Statehouse before the funeral.[7]

In the months and years ahead, McCabe continued to raise funds for the Christian Commission on the lecture circuit, often with a distinctly evangelical emphasis on the religious revival that had swept Libby Prison.[8] His sentimental lecture, the "Bright Side of Libby Prison," became the "Singing Chaplain's" signature performance for decades. He might adapt the story to his audience, the occasion, and events of the day, but he always sang the "Battle Hymn of the Republic." In the only surviving transcript of a late version of McCabe's popular lecture, he thrilled at the memory of how he and his fellow prisoners "made the welkin ring with its chorus of 'Glory, Glory, Hallelujah!' The rebel guard came up and compelled us to stop, but the song was out and it still echoes over the city [of Richmond]."[9] McCabe's early biographer claimed that the chaplain deserved credit second only to Howe for giving America the gift of the "Battle Hymn": "He with his glorious voice introduced it to the country and made it popular with the people." Howe herself heard McCabe sing it, and she told him the story of how she wrote it.[10] In 1904 Howe sent the now-bishop McCabe a handwritten copy of the "Battle Hymn." A grateful McCabe wrote back explaining how he had taught it to the other prisoners at Libby: "No hymn has ever stirred the nation's heart like 'The Battle Hymn of the Republic.'"[11]

McCabe's efforts on behalf of the Christian Commission, the temperance movement, and other reform causes did not directly aim to make America sacred. His use of the "Battle Hymn" may have encouraged audiences to think of their nation, especially after the Union victory and political reunification, as specially chosen by God for a purpose of transcendent significance, but that assumption had been present in American culture for generations. His audiences were prepared to hear the "Battle Hymn" as yet one more affirmation of what they already believed about America's holy mission, though perhaps now with a more explicit messianic emphasis and blood-bought sacrifice. The "Battle Hymn" blended easily with the "city on a hill," which had just recently been added to America's stock of metaphors by the historian George Bancroft.[12] The real work of fitting the "Battle Hymn" into a liturgy for postwar civil religion and religious nationalism was undertaken by Radical Republicans and militant preachers. Howe's poem offered striking words and images for making the Civil War sacred in American memory. Indeed, the poem itself showed politicians and preachers how to do it. However much the "Battle Hymn" might become a cliché in the future, in 1865 its use in speeches and sermons was a creative act, rhetorically new and fresh.

Among the earliest of the early adopters of the "Battle Hymn" were preachers in the North. Congregationalist, Universalists, and Unitarians proved as ready as McCabe to use the poem. The first republication of the "Battle Hymn" aside from newspapers seems to have been in a sermon pamphlet printed even before the poem ran in the *Atlantic.* Congregationalist William C. Whitcomb preached a Thanksgiving sermon in the towns of Lynnfield Center and Stoneham, Massachusetts, on November 21, 1861, the same day the Howes, Andrews, Clarkes, and Whipples were traveling back to Boston from Washington by train. Whitcomb seasoned his sermon with an excerpt from the Mayflower Compact, references to Plymouth Rock, and praise for Governor Andrew and the Bay State's troops battling in the South to bring down the "Moloch of Slavery." The preacher entitled his sermon "Praising God in Troublous Times." He ended with "Hallelujah! Hallelujah forever!" The inside back cover of the published version featured the full text of the "Battle Hymn." While the pamphlet carries a confusing publication date of 1861, and the dedication is dated January 1862, it could not have appeared before mid-January, when the new issue of the *Atlantic* became available and the poem appeared in newspapers. Julia later saw this pamphlet and in 1881 inscribed the last stanza on a copy.[13]

Whitcomb may have been the first minister to connect the "Battle Hymn" to a sermon, but he was not the last. On June 6, 1864, the Reverend Thomas Baldwin Thayer, pastor of Boston's Shawmut Avenue Church, preached the anniversary sermon for Boston's Ancient and Honorable Artillery Company, founded in 1638 by the Massachusetts Bay Colony. Thayer, a leading Universalist, told his audience that the golden age did not lie behind the nation in some distant mythic epoch. No, "the golden age, the age of universal freedom, justice, righteousness and peace is in the future, not in the past." He drew on the record of colonial jeremiads to prove that their fathers had not thought of their own time as Edenic but as an age of sin, self-seeking, luxury, and corruption. The same laments issued from pulpits during the Revolution, he noted. There had even been sectional jealousy and rivalry.

But, Thayer continued, the North's conduct in the current trial, the people's generosity and sacrifice for victory, proved that the current generation was "worthy of the best days of our national history." The age of heroes had not faded but flourished "in the very noon of its glory." Impressed by the Union's astonishing mobilization on land and sea, Thayer concluded, "*This* is our golden age; or, at least, it is the dawn of it. It is the commencement of the most magnificent future that ever yet opened on a nation." Ahead for the nation in 1864 lay emancipation, elevation of the poor white laborer, and the North's freedom from economic and political vassalage to the South. The slave power would be gone once and for all. America's Lucifer would be cast down from his attempt to usurp the throne of God. The evidence of God's hand in the war was unmistakable. "And in faith," Thayer proclaimed, "I take up the words of that 'Battle Hymn of the Republic.'" He read four of the five verses, sighing, "Yes, God's day is coming on, and it brings with it universal freedom." With slavery out of the way, the nation would see the fruit of its regeneration and rise to "wealth, and power, and happiness." The United States, filling the continent from ocean to ocean, would soon grasp "in its hands the destinies of the world!" At the dinner that followed, asked to propose a toast, Thayer raised a glass to "the State, the Military, and the Clergy.—In all the troubles of our country, may this trinity be an undivided unity."[14] Only four months earlier, this had been the holy trinity present in the House chamber when McCabe sang and Lincoln wept, the trinity that formed the core of religious nationalism.

Given Clarke's close association with Howe and the events that inspired her poem, it is unsurprising that he, too, incorporated the "Battle Hymn" into his wartime preaching. As the war entered its final months, he delivered a patriotic Christmas address at the Church of the Disciples in 1864. The preceding week, Boston had celebrated the return of the state's battle flags. At the State House Governor Andrew welcomed the returning regiments of soldiers, artillery, and cavalry, and accepted their tattered banners. Three brutal years had passed since their departure. This emotional ritual, witnessed by many of Clarke's parishioners, and the way in which it signified the great work nearly completed for the nation and for the slave, brought to Clarke's mind the Gospel of Luke's account of the birth of Jesus and the angelic announcement to the shepherds. The link between American politics and Christ's new advent seemed obvious to him: "John Quincy Adams, Theodore Parker, [Joshua] Giddings, and the old Puritan chief John Brown, may well be conceived of as looking through the veil, and singing 'Glory to God in the Highest, and on earth peace, good will to men.'" He had never thought that the United States would be rid of slavery in his lifetime: "But God who makes the wrath of man to praise Him, rather restrains the remainder of that wrath—allowed the wrath of the Slaveholder to destroy Slavery, when it could not have been destroyed, as far as we can see, in any other way."

Clarke then turned more directly to the ceremony he had seen on December 22. The day was "full of Christmas meaning," he thought. "Who that saw the war worn battalions of veteran soldiers, the remains of five Regiments of cavalry, 16 batteries of artillery, and 53 Regiments of Infantry—men, many of whom had seen more battles than any Field Officer in any European army—men who left home and comfort and safety, to risk all for the nation—who that saw them pass, but must have felt that it was the most solemn procession eye would ever look upon." Their eager self-sacrifice had proven that the Commonwealth of Massachusetts was composed of more than vulgar materialists preoccupied with moneymaking: "These men were to my eye and heart, sacred and holy. They filed before the State House, compassed about by a cloud of witnesses, the brave crusaders who never returned, victims of death on many a Southern battle field, prison and hospital. Who that saw that forest of battle flags, torn, defiled, begrimed, and besmoked, with the fire and fury of the great struggle, but could understand something of the Idolatry which bows before such relics of heroic days." Clarke's sermon performed a rhetorical "cultus of the flag" as real as the one he witnessed Greene's regiment perform at Fort Albany. Everything this war touched became holy.

Clarke moved toward the "Battle Hymn," combining the first and fifth stanzas: "As that procession marched through our streets, the Lord God of battles, was marching before them, even as He marched before them during all their years—a cloud and a fire—a cloud in the day of victory to temper the exaltation—a fire in the night of disaster, to light up a new hope. Yes, today, at this blessed Christmas time, we can say, better than ever before—amid all these omens and hopes

> Mine eyes have seen the glory of the coming of the Lord
> > Our god is marching on
>
> In the beauty of the lilies Christ was born across the sea
> With a glory in his bosom which transfigures you and me
> As he died to make men holy, let us die to make men free
> > While God is marching on.

Thrilled by events of that Advent season, Clarke reached back to the ancient Israelites and their deliverance from bondage in Egypt. By the hand of Moses, God had guided them day and night through the wilderness. Clarke, a student of higher criticism and liberal theology, did not need to believe that any of these stories in the Bible actually happened. As symbols, they were even more adaptable to current politics and war. These were images with deep resonances. They served Clarke as a means to help his congregation understand the impending Union victory. Victory meant deliverance for God's American Israel. Victory meant the advent of new hope. Victory meant the coming of the Lord. As Clarke compressed Howe's verses for his sermon's peroration, he sharpened their focus on Christ's first and second comings and on the war of emancipation that was soon to end. Clarke left no doubt what it meant to "die to make men free." Clarke urged his congregation, with hearts filled with gratitude to God at the Christmas season, to "remember that Freedom's battle has to be fought again and again, and that its price is perpetual vigilance."[15]

Politicians followed right behind the preachers, using the "Battle Hymn" as a tool to appropriate the Bible for the purposes of party politics and the nation-state. In October 1865, just six months after Appomattox, a Republican congressman from Ohio, John A. Bingham, gave a fiery speech in Wheeling, the first capital of the new state of West Virginia. Bingham's star was rising among the Radical Republicans. His speech's main target was the proposed "reorganization" of the Democratic Party in West Virginia, but he ended with an apotheosis of Abraham Lincoln and the "Battle Hymn of the Republic." It was not surprising that the Ohio congressman should do so. An antislavery lawyer and politician, fierce opponent of Ohio Copperheads, and veteran of many party struggles in the House, Bingham had been appointed a judge advocate by Lincoln in 1864 and then served in the sensational prosecution of the Lincoln assassination co-conspirators. He would later draft the language of the proposed Fourteenth Amendment, serve on the House committee that drew up articles of impeachment against Andrew Johnson, and then help argue the case before the Senate.[16]

In his Wheeling speech, Bingham praised the Union war dead for their "beautiful" self-sacrifice. Now that victory over the rebels was threatened by seditious Democrats, no voter in West Virginia should for a moment entertain the idea of putting traitors in office no matter what their campaign promises on reconstruction, race, or tax policy. Moreover, the Democratic Party was simply gone, annihilated by its own complicity in secession and war and beyond anyone's power to reorganize it. "Yes," he assured his audience, "it perished with the rebellion. It went down when Sheridan and Grant thundered through the streets of Richmond at the head of their victorious legions."

In his vision of a nation transformed, Bingham soared to dizzying heights beyond partisan politics. His scope was global. He saw an America reborn, a nation whose victory over its internal enemies now made reactionary tyrants abroad tremble: "The nation is triumphant; and to-day there is not a power in the Old World but feels it. There is not a throne in the Old World, or despotism, but trembled when the shout went out across the waters: The Republic still lives, saved by the virtue and valor of her children! The oppressed of all lands lifted up their hands and shouted aloud for joy. The crowned democrat of Europe, Garibaldi, bowed his head in thanksgiving to God that the Republic, the last refuge of afflicted humanity on earth had survived this terrible ordeal."

Drawing on biblical language in ways familiar to an audience reared on the scriptures but also as intensified by his generation's romantic nationalism, he spoke of the "ark of the covenant" carried by the fathers in the Revolution; of the Union cause as "sacred" and the Democratic Party as "devilish"; and of the recent war as a "holy war for the Union." Let patriotic Americans "declare that henceforth the unity of the Republic shall be sacred—that the men of the republic will stand by it and defend it with the same zealous care with which they stand by and defend the altar of their God." To thunderous applause, he closed with an account of Lincoln's martyrdom and the inspiring power of the "Battle Hymn."

"I have but recently come down from your capitol where your good president lay in his bloody shroud," Bingham said, "fallen by an assassin's hand, not for any want of fidelity to his oath, but because he was faithful to the end, and, under God, saved to you and all the people their imperilled country, its government and laws. . . ." The South had failed to carry out its treason, but it took its "infernal" revenge by killing the president. Lincoln embodied the aspirations and institutions of the common people: "Sprung from the bosom of the millions who earn their bread in the sweat of their face, and are not afraid of honest toil, he fell at his post with the harness on, but not, thank God, until his work was done and God had permitted him to see the salvation of his country." "In his fall," the congressman continued, "[Lincoln] but taught the world how beautiful is death when crowned by virtue, invoking as his spirit went up to God, 'charity for all,' and uttering in his great soul the battle hymn of the Republic, the requiem which th[r]ough all the great struggle for the nation's life its heroic defenders had unconsciously borne upon their bayonets." Finally, tying together Lincoln, the Union army, and the call to self-sacrifice, Bingham quoted the "Battle Hymn": "In the beauty of the lilies, Christ was born across the sea, / With a glory in his bosom that transfigures you and me: / As He died to make men holy, let us die to make men free."[17]

Howe did not have to rely on preachers and politicians or others' memories to popularize her "Battle Hymn." She had at her disposal lecture halls, pulpits, and leading periodicals for children and adults. Especially after Samuel's death in 1876, Howe needed to stay busy to support herself. She toured the nation for decades, a client first of James Redpath's Boston Lyceum Bureau and then of James B. Pond's successor firm in New

York. Redpath has rightly been called a "forgotten firebrand."[18] Born in England in 1833, he emigrated to the United States with his family in 1848. He wandered the Midwest working for printers, and then took a series of jobs with Horace Greeley's *New-York Tribune*, William Lloyd Garrison's New York *Anti-Slavery Standard*, and a Republican paper with the unlikely name the *Missouri Democrat*. He became active in the Free-Soil movement in Kansas and then was a staunch defender of John Brown, writing a biography of the abolitionist and editing a well-known collection of speeches and letters in defense of Brown (*Echoes of Harper's Ferry*). During the Civil War, Redpath traveled with Sherman's army as a reporter for Greeley's *Tribune*. With a partner, he founded his lyceum agency in 1868 and launched the modern booking and agency system for America's disorganized lyceum circuit.

Redpath's firm employed Major James B. Pond, a veteran of John Brown's army in Kansas armed with a "Beecher's Bible," and a Medal of Honor winner. Five years Redpath's junior, Pond had gotten his start as a publicity agent by representing Ann Eliza Young, Brigham Young's nineteenth wife, who left Mormonism eager to tell her story. Pond ended up buying out Redpath in 1875 and within a few years started a new firm in New York that he called the Pond Bureau. The enterprising Pond cultivated a large clientele in the United States and Britain. His agency represented Charles Sumner, Frederick Douglass, Mark Twain, Henry Ward Beecher, Lyman Abbott, Susan B. Anthony, Arthur Conan Doyle, and dozens of other celebrities, including a young Winston Churchill desperate for cash in 1900.[19] In a letter to his mother, Churchill complained of Pond's "grasping" terms and incompetence and thought him "a vulgar Yankee impresario."[20]

The "Battle Hymn" became Howe's tagline on the lyceum circuit. Redpath advertised Howe as the "author of the Battle Hymn of the Republic, and of many other well-known poems." His client was available for serious lectures on social issues and discourses on philosophy as well as "comic entertainments." She would even fill the pulpit for "Sunday services when desired."[21] She lectured widely in the 1870s, the decade Pond recalled as the height of the lyceum years, when he could not meet demand for speakers generated by over 500 local lyceums in the United States. He compared Howe's success to that of the equal rights activist Mary A. Livermore, who "had over eight hundred applications for a single season," he boasted. Howe lectured not only in the United States but also in Paris, Athens, and Vienna. She would make extensive speaking tours into the 1890s and agreed to public appearances nearly to the day of her death.[22]

Howe's first publicized account of how she wrote the "Battle Hymn" took place in Detroit in February 1871.[23] Advertisements in the *Detroit Free Press* promoted her lecture on "The New World." Reporters turned out for the well-attended event at the city's opera house and helped publicize the story of the making of the "Battle Hymn." Her recollections that Sunday night amounted to only a few sentences: "I was on a visit to Washington, during the first winter of the war, with Gov. Andrew, and other Massachusetts friends," she explained. "We had been spending the day in the soldiers' camps on the Potomac, and I heard the 'John Brown Hymn' sung and played so often that its strains were constantly sounding in my ears." She was bothered by the soldiers' doggerel and thought it unsuited to the tune. She hoped she could do better. "I wished very much for an inspiration which would provide a fitting rendition of so beautiful a theme." Her muse kept her waiting. But "early in the morning, before daybreak, I awoke, and my mind in a half dreaming state began at once to run upon the rhythm of the 'John Brown Hymn.'" The muse had struck. "Very soon the words commenced fitting themselves to its measures, and the lines spun off without further effort. I said to myself, 'now I shall lose all this unless I get it down in black and white.' I arose, groped about in the dark, collected such stationery as may be found in the room of a Washington hotel, sat down and wrote, as I frequently do without lighting a lamp, the poem called the 'Battle Hymn of the Republic.'"[24]

More than lecture halls provided venues for Howe to secure the place of the "Battle Hymn" in America. She also turned to churches, including her own Boston congregation. In June of 1886, Howe lectured at the "Memorial Sunday" at the Church of the Disciples. The day honored the memories of Lincoln and Governor Andrew twenty years after their deaths. The aging Clarke preached in the morning on "the lessons of the war." It had been a war for freedom and union, he told his congregation, and both North and South had been liberated from the burden of slavery. The afternoon children's meeting heard from a Union veteran and then from Mrs. Howe. She gave her familiar account of November 1861, but then added new details about the train ride home to Boston. She had shared a car with Clarke and recited her new poem to him. She quoted the first line for her audience and then added an interpretive gloss: "Although that great military display was very impressive and magnificent to see, and although the manoeuvres were great and grand, the glory of the coming of the Lord which I saw was not in these things; it was not in the fact of war. The glory was this: we had found ourselves obliged either to give up the truth, the cause of right, of God's justice on earth, or to fight for it. We had chosen to fight for it; and that was the glory."[25] In her diary, she recorded that she told the children "that whenever they would stand up for the right in any struggle, contest or trial, they would see [God's] glory."[26]

Howe had been filling pulpits since at least the 1870s.[27] Churches would often ask her to come to the dais and recite her "Battle Hymn," organists would play and choirs and congregations would sing her anthem, and pastors would invite her to pray. On April 28, 1889, on a speaking tour through the West, she preached at the Unity Church in Chicago. She recited her "Battle Hymn" at the end of her sermon, telling the story of its composition, followed by the congregation singing it "with an intensity of feeling that is rarely witnessed in a Sunday morning service." In the words of a reporter for the Chicago *Herald*, Howe in 1861 "saw by prevision" in the ranks of Union soldiers and "in the outbursts of patriotic fires all over the land . . . the dawn of true liberty, the breaking of the shackles of slavery—a people altogether free." "Glowingly she eulogized the heroes of that war and the whole army of men who in the time that tried men's souls labored or fought to found and perpetuate true liberty upon these shores." Then, "turning to the great ensigns of our country which decorated the galleries of Unity Church, Mrs. Howe said it did her heart good to see patriotism associated with the temple." She remained confident in God's providential care for the nation. "As he is with his people in their affairs of government," she concluded, "it is right and proper that the country should be brought into the place of his worship, and there the young and old be taught that the Christian's duty is to be filled with patriotism."[28] Howe could hardly have spelled out more plainly the ideal union of religion and nationalism, altar and flag.

In addition to appearances in lecture halls and church sanctuaries, Howe continued to publish accounts for popular audiences. In 1884, the *Youth's Companion* featured one of the most detailed versions of the poem's creation she ever wrote.[29] The circulation of the *Youth's Companion's* reached an astonishing 442,000 in 1890. Between 1881 and 1909, Howe wrote sixteen essays as well as a number of poems for the *Companion*.[30] In the 1884 account, she listed few of her companions, perhaps because their names would have meant little or nothing to her young audience. She described wartime Washington in grim detail, including the embalming business near the Willard Hotel. When she heard the soldiers singing the John Brown song, she "remarked to a friend that [she] had always wished to write some verses which might be sung to that tune." She described waking early the next morning with the poem taking shape in her head. She claimed to have had few hopes for its popularity until she heard about Chaplain McCabe and the Union soldiers at Libby Prison. She gave thanks that since the war, across the country, the "battle-hymn has been sung by the lovers of God and men."

The "Battle Hymn" grew in Howe's memory and imagination as she beheld words that "scarcely seemed [hers]." She began to reflect more philosophically on the origins of her ideas, and she used her own words from the "Battle Hymn" to explain her thought. In an 1889 essay for *Cosmopolitan*, entitled "Recollections of the Antislavery Struggle," Howe can be caught in the act of interpreting herself through the lens of her own poetry. Poet and poem merged. Hymn writer and hymn fused in the national religion she helped create. Closing her narrative with a rush of memories of Lee's surrender in 1865 and of the celebrations in the streets of Boston followed by the tragic "heart-break" of the news of Lincoln's assassination, Howe summed up what the abolitionist crusade and the war had meant to her and her generation as they reached old age (she was now seventy): "When the war broke out, the passion of patriotism lent its color to the religion of humanity in my own mind, as in many others, and a moment came in which I could say: 'Mine eyes have seen the glory of the coming of the Lord!'—and the echo which my words awoke in many hearts made me sure that many other people had seen it also."[31] This sentence highlights the union of two ideas central to the "Battle Hymn" and to the religious nationalism it invoked: the "passion of patriotism" and the "religion of humanity." Sacred and secular combined as easily here as they would shortly at the Unity Church in Chicago.

Howe reached an even larger audience at the end of the nineteenth century thanks once again to the *Atlantic Monthly* and to publication of her memoirs. Howe's *Reminiscences* gave her the chance at the age of eighty to place the story of the hymn's creation in the larger context of her long and full life.[32] Her publisher, Houghton Mifflin, had bought out Ticknor and Fields and took over managing the *Atlantic Monthly*. In 1898, Julia made slow progress on her handwritten manuscript for the book as it lengthened into hundreds of pages. To give her achievable goals and some advance publicity, her editor, Walter Hines Page, worked with her to publish six excerpts in the *Atlantic*. The May 1899 issue carried the story of the "Battle Hymn of the Republic." Page suggested that the series be extended while Howe continued to write, delaying the book's publication until the spring and then the fall of 1899.[33]

When her memoirs appeared, the book included a facsimile of what was purportedly Howe's original draft of the "Battle Hymn" as written on US Sanitary Commission stationery. The manuscript belonged to Charlotte Whipple. Houghton Mifflin had to persuade Howe to let them publish it with the orphaned sixth verse included, making public for the first time lines she had cut in 1861. The challenge was to track down the original. "Houghton & Mifflin desire to print the rough draft of my Battle Hymn," she explained to Laura, "which they borrowed, with some difficulty, from Charlotte Whipple, who begged it of me, years ago. I hesitate to allow it, because it contains a verse which I discarded, as not up to the rest of the poem." Ultimately, she granted her publisher's request, perhaps thinking of the poem's literary and historical value as an artifact and as a way to boost sales: "It will undoubtedly be an additional attraction for the volume."[34]

Any reader hoping for new information about the creative act was disappointed. While Howe's 1899 version of the story added nothing new, it became even vaguer about the timing of the trip to Washington, saying simply that it was the "late autumn of 1861" despite what she had learned from Clarke's diary. Perhaps she was unwilling to contradict what she had already published elsewhere. There was much she left out. Some found the book frustrating. Higginson regretted that in Howe's "hurried grasp [the autobiography] is squeezed into one volume, where groups of delightful interviews with heroes at home and abroad are crowded into some single sentences."[35] It was no masterpiece of the genre.

Nathaniel Hawthorne's son Julian wrote a leisurely review of Howe's memoirs. His reaction showed how much times had changed since the antebellum epoch his father had known. Julian wrote about Boston transcendentalism as if the movement were some oddity from the remote past that made Julia and her circle part of a quaint, vanished America. His sense of the absurd was not far from Henry James's 1886 novel, *The Bostonians*, or from his own father's *Blithedale Romance*, which had satirized Brook Farm. Hawthorne wrote of Julia's "bout" with popular ideologies, as he called the affliction, as if she and her husband had suffered from a chronic illness. The couple had returned to the city from abroad in 1844 and came down with a case of "Transcendentalism and the other isms, which lasted during the major part of our heroine's life." "The epoch, as we know," he continued, in much the same vein, "had many interesting as well as inadvertently amusing features; but, upon the whole, the feelings of the actors were too 'strenuous' to make the record of the drama entertaining reading. The devotees of abolition were too serious to admit of ordinary human intercourse with them, and for fifteen years everybody seemed to be more or less angry with somebody or something."

Amused by Howe's "transcendental way" of reasoning, Hawthorne quoted as an example her recollection of South Carolinian Preston Brooks's attack on Charles Sumner in the Senate in 1856: "Sumner had won the crown of martyrdom, and his person thenceforth became sacred, even to his enemies." Sacred even to his enemies? Perplexed, Hawthorne wondered if "it might prove difficult for her to explain just what these words mean, but they at least have the virtue of showing what strange things they said, and thought they thought, in those days." Hawthorne sensed a chasm separated the 1840s and 1850s from the present. For him, antebellum America had become a distant, somewhat comical world. It was if Howe had outlived the world that had made her. While he acknowledged the "Battle Hymn" had "perhaps more than any other lyric of the war touched the heart and stimulated the aspirations of the people," this concession was ambiguous. Had Howe touched America's heart for good or evil?[36]

While Howe's *Reminiscences* simply continued a long and repetitive series of public reflections on the "Battle Hymn," in private she also thought about her poem and what it signified. Her interior world proved far more revealing. More than once she conjured up the vision that had come to her in the predawn hours in Washington in 1861. On a lecture tour in Saint Paul, Minnesota, in the spring of 1900, she wrote out notes one morning about the vision of her "Battle Hymn."[37] It is a passage remarkable for its detail. By the time of this trip, she had been thinking about her poem and the Civil War for nearly forty years. Using the words "I have seen" and

Figure 14. Julia Ward Howe, seated, facing left, half-length portrait,
ca. April 27, 1908.

Library of Congress, Prints and Photographs Division.

"I have heard," she repeated her own poem's emphasis on bearing witness
to these events and what they signified.

"I have seen what I therein described," she began, referring to her
"Battle Hymn"; "I have seen God in the circling camps, in the great

assemblage of men, all disciplined into a beautiful unity of impulse and restraint. I have heard him in the voice of the trumpet that shall never call Retreat. The mighty God of battles, present to Hebrew prophet and psalmist. I have seen how he lifts his hand, and how the armies of the earth rise up at his bidding, and lie down when he whispers, 'Peace, it is enough.'" But the work of that army was not confined to the battle-fields of northern Virginia: "While my woman's heart rose up and swelled within me at the sight of human courage and daring which could affront the terrors of death without flinching, a deeper chord was touched within my bosom."

Her mind traveled across the sea to Bethlehem as a witness alongside the shepherds and magi to the birth of Christ: "I saw, in a far distant land, a babe cradled in a manger, his guardian a sinless mother. I saw the pilgrims of the ancient wisdom rise up to do him honor. I heard the silver trump of an archangel proclaim that here was born the true Savior of mankind, the wonderful Being whose life, doctrine, and death, should lift all peoples out of self and savagery into sanctification and blessedness. I saw the career of that anointed child, how his whole soul was devoted to God's truth, his whole heart, to the succor of mankind." Immediately, the work of Christ and the work of the Union Army fused in her mind. "I could not refrain from crying out: 'As he died to make men holy, let us die to make men free!'" Like the persecution and martyrdom of the first generation of Christians, the urgent call to follow Christ endured: "Let that same holi-ness of redemption shine thro' our own dear land," she prayed, "and, if it must be so, let any of us who are called thereto become its martyrs, dying as he died to make men free with the glorious freedom of his gospel."[38]

As a record of the poet's retrospective interpretation of her poem, this journal entry is without parallel in Howe's other public or private utter-ances. Still pulsing in her mind in 1900 was the Union army, the trum-pet call, the Hebrew prophet and psalmist, the Old Testament "God of battles," God's sovereign rule over history, Jesus's advent in Palestine an-nounced by an archangel, "sinless" Mary, Christ's death (but no resur-rection), and finally the call to national holiness through the devotion of new martyrs willing to die for man's freedom. This was still her "Battle Hymn" gospel.

Nearing the end of this moment of transfiguration, she added simply: "God has given me this message, this day—May 14th, 1900."[39] Copying these words out again six weeks later at her summer home in Newport, Rhode Island, she did not find them unusual. "It is a rhapsody, which might help a sermon. I hope it will." These were private reflections, a "rhapsody," she called them, put to paper four decades after the events they described. How much had her memory clarified the significance of that moment at the Willard Hotel in 1861? How much had her memory been affected by the way others had interpreted her "Battle Hymn" and used it to define the Civil War and the American identity? At the very least, Howe helped to enhance and perpetuate the mythic and symbolic power she and others had bestowed on her "Battle Hymn," and there is no reason to think she was not a sincere believer in what her hymn had accomplished for the American people and their sense of purpose in re-demptive history. She was always in earnest.

Publicly, Howe continued to recite the "Battle Hymn" whenever she was asked, sometimes twice in one day. She told the story of its creation again and again. She heard it sung by soloists and children's choirs in her honor, and sang it with friends at home on Sunday afternoons. She wrote out lines of it for admirers and autograph seekers. She heard her new pastor, Charles Gordon Ames, who followed Clarke at the Church of the Disciples, quote it in a sermon, an experience "which moved me very much," she wrote in her diary.[40] When an aspiring young novelist named Upton Sinclair, "rather bumptious but very candid and genuine," told her of his intention to write a multivolume epic about the Civil War, she was pleased and noted his admiration for her hymn.[41]

One dilemma Howe faced by saying so much about the "Battle Hymn" and reciting it so often was how to take full advantage of her fame resting on one poem without reinforcing her reputation as a "monopoet." She was elevated to national and international stature by the "Battle Hymn" but at the same time reduced to its few stanzas, and sometimes to only fragments of these. The *Boston Transcript* coined the word "monopoet" in 1874 to describe a whole category of doomed poets, including Francis Scott Key and the authors of "God Save the King" and the "Marseil-laise." Already, a mere decade after the war, Howe had joined their un-lucky ranks. "Mrs. Julia Ward Howe's 'Battle Hymn of the Republic,' that soul-stirring strain, is the only one of her poems which even now can be called to mind," the paper claimed.[42] Thomas Wentworth Hig-ginson acknowledged the problem in 1907, more than thirty years after the original slight tendered by the Boston paper. "Mrs. Howe, like her friend Dr. Holmes," he wrote for the *Outlook*, "has perhaps had the disappointing experience of concentrating her sure prospects of fame on a single poem. What the 'Chambered Nautilus' represents in his published volumes, the 'Battle Hymn of the Republic' represents for her. In each case the poet was happy enough to secure, through influences impenetrable, one golden moment."[43] Howe savored that "one golden moment" even if she did not concede that there had been only one.

No clear line separated Howe's memories and use of the "Battle Hymn" from the public's memories and use of it. Howe's recorded memories shaped other's memories, and perhaps vice versa. This tendency is most obvious in the way people discovered many years after the war that they had been with Howe at the moment of the poem's inspiration—or so they believed. When they read one of Howe's magazine articles or her *Reminiscences*, they were sure they recognized the places and events she described. Among them, veterans published accounts of being present, if not exactly at the moment of creation, then as close as they could possibly place themselves to the events of November 1861. Who and what had mattered most in 1861 had changed in hindsight. The visit to Washington, if remembered by anyone outside of Howe's immediate circle, was no longer a story about a famous war governor or a famous liberal theologian or philanthropist and their entourage but now a widely known story about the famous Julia Ward Howe and her famous "Battle Hymn." Howe had been transformed into a central figure in the Civil War, a maker and molder of the nation's civic piety, and one of the chief interpreters of the meaning of America. By the turn of the century, Howe and her poem had been turned into monuments enshrining America's faith in America.

Captain Rufus R. Dawes of the Sixth Wisconsin Infantry was sure he had been one of the Union officers near Howe's carriage as she and her friends fled back to DC from the disbanded military parade on November 18, the day before she wrote the "Battle Hymn." Having read one of her published accounts, Dawes matched his memories of the divisional review to the words of the "Battle Hymn." He included all five verses and seemed delighted to find himself and his companions in almost every word Howe had written. Dawes's memories were vivid. He recalled singing the John Brown song and knew he and his men had been the ones who inspired Howe. "With our column rode a lady visitor; my authority is her own account," he wrote, keeping her identity for the moment unnamed. "As we marched, the 'evening dews and damps' gathered, and our leading singer, Sergeant John Ticknor, as he was wont to do on such occasions, led out with his strong, clear and beautiful tenor voice, 'Hang Jeff. Davis on a sour apple tree.' The whole regiment joined the grand chorus, 'Glory, glory hallelujah, as we go marching on.'" And that refrain had ignited the spark. "To our visitor appeared the 'Glory of the coming of the Lord,' in our 'burnished rows of steel' and in the 'hundred circling camps' on Arlington, which were before her." He had Howe's word for it, he thought, and now named her: "Julia Ward Howe, our visitor, has said that the singing of the John Brown song by the soldiers on that march, and the scenes of that day and evening inspired her to the composition of the Battle Hymn of the Republic. We at least helped to swell the chorus."[44] When a newspaper editor wrote to Howe in the summer of 1900 to confirm that the Sixth Wisconsin had indeed been with her that day, she answered that, regrettably, she could not provide the proof he sought.[45]

Examples of these encounters are plentiful in soldiers' memoirs and continued for years. In a history published during the First World War, veterans of the Massachusetts Fourteenth Regiment (renamed the First Massachusetts Heavy Artillery Regiment later in the war) matched their own records and memories with Howe's *Reminiscences*. They recalled the Andrews and Clarkes and Mrs. Howe visiting them, Howe saying a few words to them, and the regiment singing the John Brown song. Impressed by what she had seen and heard, early the next morning Howe wrote the "Battle Hymn of the Republic" "just as America sings it today"—an indication of the renewed popularity of the "Battle Hymn" during the First World War. Almost every detail of this story comes from Howe's 1899 memoirs. The aging veterans got everything right except the fact that they had not been with her on the day she described. They had met her on November 16, not November 18.[46]

No one could really blame these veterans. Howe herself had become increasingly vague about the details of her trip to Washington, even to the point of not remembering whether she had been there in November or December. In 1892, she wrote in her journal that she discovered in Clarke's "diary that my Battle Hymn must have been written on November 19th, in the year 1861. He mentions a review and distant skirmish, which

I saw with him. This was on the 18th; early the next morning I wrote the hymn."[47] She sounded as though she had finally resolved a question that had long nagged her.

While some of the facts might grow dim, Howe's conception of the significance of her "Battle Hymn" and what exactly she had experienced on her visit to Washington grew clearer and more dramatic over time. While others incorporated her poem into their speeches and sermons, Howe promoted the "Battle Hymn" on her own terms. She needed no one to show her how to secure its place in the nation's literary canon, or center it at the core of righteous nationalism. She took the "Battle Hymn" herself into the churches as a way to fuse nationalism and religion. But the poet's vision had always been wider than American redemption. Redemption for the nation ultimately meant redemption for the world.

4

RIGHTEOUS WAR AND HOLY PEACE

Julia Ward Howe arrived in Istanbul, capital of the troubled Ottoman Empire, in January 1879. She was nearly sixty. The recently widowed Julia and her daughter Maud were on a long journey through Europe and the Levant that they had begun in the spring of 1877. Robert College, the American institution founded by Protestant missionaries on the cliffs above the Bosporus near the fortress of Mehmed the Conqueror, hosted a luncheon in Howe's honor.[1] Afterward, she was told to listen carefully as she made her way down the steep hill back to her boat. She heard Bulgarian and Armenian students singing, "Mine eyes have seen the glory of the coming of the Lord." Relating this story in the *Youth's Companion*, she pointed out the moral for young readers: "We might see this glory oftener if we would look for it, and most of all where faithful souls are working together for the good of humanity."[2] In a later lecture she exclaimed, "Surely I had seen something of that glory when I beheld an American institution of liberal learning standing on the very ground where the old civilization had gone down before the youthful vigor of barbarism. . . . It seemed to me the dawn of the resurrection morning, and I would gladly have answered back the first strophe of the hymn with another line: 'He hath sounded forth the trumpet that shall never sound retreat.'"[3]

Howe's "resurrection morning" had not arrived all at once with Union victory in 1865. Nor had it been confined to the United States. It came in wave upon wave of progressive new births as civilization vanquished barbarism. Turkish barbarism may have overwhelmed the last remnant of the Roman Empire in the fifteenth century, but now the Ottoman's "youthful vigor" gave way to successor nations reborn, whether Greece in 1830 or Bulgaria, just liberated in the Russo-Turkish War of 1877–78. Wars of independence and national unification and campaigns for humanitarian relief all fit within the wide embrace of the "Battle Hymn." Howe, her family, and many others used the "Battle Hymn" to extol wars of liberation as selfless, uncomplicated acts of sacrifice for the good of humanity, wars without irony or unintended consequences. These wars added new chapters to history's unified story.

But the violent origins of the "Battle Hymn" posed a problem. Howe faced charges of hypocrisy when she insisted that her true hope for humanity lay in international peace and brotherhood. In 1870, when she denounced the bloodshed of the Franco-Prussian War, critics were quick to pounce on the seeming contradiction. How could the poet who had so recently roused Union forces for a relentless bloody war now call for peace? Not long after the outbreak of the Franco-Prussian War, Howe issued "An Appeal to Womanhood throughout the World." She condemned both Napoleon III and autocratic Prussia. Warfare affronted humanity's moral sense in "this day of progress, in this century of light," she wrote. War was a filthy and degrading thing, and women worldwide had to keep it from corrupting their husbands and sons. To that end, she called for an international conference of women dedicated to ending war as a way of settling disputes. "Let [women] meet first, as women, to bewail and commemorate the dead," she pleaded. "Let them solemnly take counsel with each other as to the means whereby the great human family can live in peace, man as the brother of man, each bearing after his own kind the sacred impress, not of Caesar, but of God."[4]

A skeptic wrote to the *New-York Tribune*, the first paper to publish the "Battle Hymn" eight years earlier, and ventured to pose "a question for Mrs. Howe." Signing himself "German Unity," he juxtaposed Howe's appeal for peace and the most militant lines of the "Battle Hymn": "Let me simply ask whether Mrs. Howe permits to the women of another country the same spirit of patriotic faith and readiness for sacrifice, which she has here expressed with such vigor as a loyal American woman? Or, has she now repented of her faith in the 'fiery gospel' and is ready to retract the truest and most living lines she has ever written?"[5] Picking up the story, a Nashville paper took undisguised delight in seeing Mrs. Howe exposed in this way.[6] But in 1875, the Universal Peace Society defended Howe's changed attitude, if indeed it was a change. The organization's *Voice of Peace* offered a way to resolve the apparent conflict: "As to Mrs. Julia Ward Howe, she has since explained at our meetings that the 'Battle Hymn of the Republic' was written under the old dispensation, and that now she was writing and speaking under the new."[7]

Not every war troubled Howe's conscience or clouded her vision of world peace. Redemptive war was always an exception, especially under the new dispensation. In 1870, her beloved Italy completed its national unification. With the conquest of the Papal States in 1870, Rome now served as the capital of a free, united Italy. The pope's temporal power was reduced to a tiny territory on the Tiber. The Vatican Council had just met in Rome, and the enunciation of papal infallibility seemed badly timed at best, mocked by the hand of history at worst. A large meeting in New York City on January 12, 1871, celebrated Italy's triumph. On February 23, the citizens of Boston held their own meeting to congratulate the Italian people now at last united as one in hope and destiny and pledged to human equality in the sight of God. The speakers included two of Howe's friends, James Freeman Clarke and Edwin P. Whipple, both of whom had been her companions in Washington a decade before.[8]

Howe wrote a commemorative poem that was read and distributed at the Boston meeting and printed at the end of the published proceedings of the New York meeting. "A Hymn for the Celebration of Italian Unity" matched the meter of the "Battle Hymn" and included the "Glory, glory, hallelujah" refrain. In these stanzas, Howe made two appeals to "mother" or "mothers," reflecting her current peace campaign, and included the line "sound the trumpet of resurrection." Howe saved her most striking claim for the third stanza. Italian unification did not mark the achievement of war or wrath or blood. No. Rather, "in the garden of Christ's passion did it slowly bloom and bud, / The love that makes men one." These lines refer to Christ's prayer in the Garden of Gethsemane, on the eve of his crucifixion (John 17:21), in which he asks the Father to grant unity to his followers so that "they all may be one." Italy was now gathered into one nation, a foretaste of the unity of humanity, thought Howe. If any Catholics were present at Boston's Music Hall, they might have found it strange that Christ's prayer for unity had at last been fulfilled as Italian armies "liberated" Rome, disrupted the Vatican Council, put the bishops to flight, and left Pope Pius IX holed up in the Vatican hurling excommunications at his enemies.[9] To these progressive Bostonians and New Yorkers, however, Italian unification marked an epoch in the march of civil and religious liberty, the triumphant export of American principles, and the vindication of the world-historical role Mazzini and others had always assigned to the United States of America.

Howe's 1871 adaptation of her "Battle Hymn" for the cause of Italian nationalism shows perhaps more clearly than any other evidence the scope of her vision, the breadth of what it could mean to "die to make men free." Howe never did anything by halves, and her involvement in international affairs proved no exception. Already in the antebellum period she had admired her husband's devotion to Greek independence, had added her voice to the uprisings in Poland and Kossuth's struggle in Hungary, and had sympathized with early efforts at Italian unification under Garibaldi and Mazzini. After the war, she joined her husband's controversial humanitarian intervention in Santo Domingo, initiated by the Grant administration with an eye toward annexation.[10] She regularly preached sermons there. In 1893, she protested autocratic Russia's oppression of political dissidents and signed the original petition to found an American branch of the Friends of Russian Freedom.[11] Other petitioners included Mark Twain, Lowell, Higginson, Whittier, and Garrison.[12] Also beginning in the 1890s, Howe used the pages of the *Woman's Journal* to publicize the suffering of Armenians in the Ottoman Empire.

The reorientation of US foreign policy evident in the Spanish-American War in 1898 led Howe to conclude that American victory marked nothing less than the nation's transition from an "Old Testament" in its history to a "New Testament." At a meeting of the Massachusetts Press Club in January 1899, Howe offered a few remarks that emphasized the split between the old and new dispensations. "On the spur of the moment," she posed the kind of question many Americans were asking as the United States stunned the world with easy conquests in the Pacific: "Why should we fear to pass from the Old Testament of our own liberties, to the New Testament of liberty for all the world?"[13] Undoubtedly, the United States now heard the call to spread to others the liberty it had secured for itself at such high cost. This is what it meant to "die to make men free" in the new epoch. A strong continuity bound together the Civil War and the Spanish-American war, and both of these to liberation movements and wars for national unification that did not directly involve the United States.

Howe experienced the war of 1898 from the city of Rome. Despite her age and bouts of depression, she seemed to have unbounded enthusiasm for extended overseas travel. She and Maud were staying in the Eternal City in February 1898 when the battleship USS *Maine* exploded in Havana Harbor. Hearing news of the disaster in Cuba, Maud was sure "there's malice in it." She wrote again in April regarding the declaration of war, concerned that America's military response seemed disproportionately large to the easy task of defeating Spain. "It may be necessary for our lusty youth of a nation to put its heel on the neck of a broken and aged nation," she conceded, "but it should be done in the spirit I feel in McKinley, sternly and firmly and without fireworks or bunkum. This may sound like treason at home, but it looks so to every Roman American I have talked with. It's awful; I wish I were at home and not away from it all and out of the magnetic current, for it is not likely that I can ever enter into what seems to be the national spirit at home." And she was unsettled in other ways: "[Florence's] letters in abuse of McKinley remind me of the Chinese who flog their gods when things do not suit them."[14]

Whatever Maud's reservations, Florence got busy explaining the war via the stanzas of the "Battle Hymn." She helped turn the poem into part of the "fireworks or bunkum" her sister hoped to avoid. The United States fought Spain over Cuba in a selfless humanitarian act—a noble war waged for liberation and not for anything as mundane as long-standing strategic interests. Politicians, preachers, and a host of journalists, editors, and schoolteachers inspired by America's crusade used the "Battle Hymn" to mobilize the nation for war and widened the poem's already ample scope. The same range of voices that had popularized the "Battle Hymn" in the 1860s now sent it abroad as US soldiers and sailors, from the North and South, died to make men free in Cuba, Puerto Rico, and the Philippines.

Prior to late March 1898, the text of the "Battle Hymn of the Republic" had appeared only sporadically in the US press after the Civil War. But the impending crisis with Spain changed that. Across the country, newspapers published Howe's war anthem in full and without comment, as if its suitability to the present war required no explanation.[15] President William McKinley sent his war message to Congress on April 11, the day after Easter. The House and Senate voted for war on April 18, and McKinley signed the declaration two days later. As it debated intervention, Congress needed no coaching about what to do with the "Battle Hymn." The *Boston Daily Advertiser*, covering the vote in the House, reported how the members spent their time in the Capitol while they awaited reconciliation of the House and Senate war resolutions: "Half a hundred representatives gathered in the lobby in the rear of the hall and awoke the echoes with patriotic songs." Among these were the "Battle Hymn of the Republic" led by the Iowa congressman, Union officer, and future Speaker of the House David Henderson, paired with the ecumenical gesture of " 'Dixie' . . . led by some of the ex-confederates." The climax came with a loud "improvisation" on the Union soldiers' favorite, "John Brown's Body," featuring a new villain in place of Jeff Davis: "Hang Gen. Weyler on the sour apple tree, as we go marching on."[16]

At the close of the war Florence wrote a set of articles for the *Independent* entitled "The Building of a Nation's War Hymn."[17] Starting with this title, Florence transposed the "Battle Hymn" from its context in the Civil War, turning it into a "war hymn" for the nation more generally and, over the series of articles, into a hymn for humanity. One striking feature of her articles (and of national religion in general by 1898) was her constant affirmation of how good America is. Florence thought it more than appropriate that the "Battle Hymn" should be revived during the war with Spain. She commended it for the way it blended religion and war, calling it "that splendid outburst of patriotic fervor, half religious, half martial, a fit war-song for the descendants of the Puritans, for a nation of freemen." Indeed, she continued, "its solemn invocation of the Almighty bears witness that we are a truly religious people, tho the name of God is not mentioned in our Constitution."[18]

Florence rehearsed the familiar story of the inspiration for the "Battle Hymn," drawing heavily from her mother's 1887 *Century* article, including the incorrect month of December 1861. But she set out to do more

Figure 15. Florence Howe Hall, 1903. From Laura Richards, Maud Elliott,
and Florence Hall, *Julia Ward Howe, 1819–1916*
(Boston: Houghton Mifflin, 1916), 2:46.

than tell yet again a tale her mother had told so often and was preparing to tell again in the *Atlantic* and her *Reminiscences*. Florence offered what she called the "last word" on the "Battle Hymn"; it belonged to the American nation and, more, it belonged to freedom fighters everywhere. Even her mother's identity as author was absorbed into American nationality: "The last word about the 'Battle-Hymn of the Republic' must be that it was the work not of an individual, but of a nation. The soul of the vast army of the American people struggling for utterance in the greatest crisis of its existence, at last found a voice to express its meaning and its aspiration, the voice of a woman; and when the message came to her she cried out in the watches of the night: 'Mine eyes have seen the glory of the coming of the Lord.'" Her mother's poem had captured that glory and enabled others to share her vision. The soldiers welcomed it, "and mighty hosts chanted the refrain: 'As he died to make men holy, let us die to make men free, While God is marching on.'" Now in 1898, this summons sounded again the nation's "watchword" for the hour. "May our great republic ever remain true to the high ideal of these lines!" Florence praised the "*universal* quality" of the "Battle Hymn," which made it "a hymn for men of every clime who love liberty and are willing to lay down their lives for its sake."[19]

Florence highlighted the story of Senator John M. Thurston and his "noble appeal for the freedom of Cuba" on the floor of the Senate, a speech that had culminated with the last verse of the "Battle Hymn." Much as Bingham had in 1865, Thurston used the "Battle Hymn" as a tool for civil religion. Thurston delivered his plea for military intervention before a packed chamber on March 24, 1898. The Nebraska Republican had just returned from the work of the New York *Journal*'s Congressional Cuban Commission with his wife and a small delegation of senators and representatives. The trip had been paid for by William Randolph Hearst, owner of the *Journal*, and perhaps owner for a time of Howe's original draft of the "Battle Hymn." He provided his largest press boat for the mission to Cuba. Tragically, Thurston's wife died of a heart attack on the visit to the island, and the distraught senator, shocked by the conditions he had witnessed there, pleaded for humanitarian intervention and Cuba's independence. Spain had lost any claim to sovereignty over Cuba, he vowed. The decrepit empire now waged a brutal war of "selfish" oppression. Spain needed to be removed from the New World as the last vestige of Old World tyranny. Such a war was a "holy cause," and only the callow "money changers" opposed intervention, to protect their own narrow business interests. Thurston ended his speech with a grand retelling of the past 700 years of history. This was Whig history pushed to the point of farce.

Thurston strung together every uprising in history into one long crusade for freedom that justified force at every step, from Runnymede to Appomattox to Cuba: "Force compelled the signature of unwilling royalty to the great Magna Charta," he insisted; "force put life into the Declaration of Independence and made effective the Emancipation Proclamation; force beat with naked hands upon the iron gateway of the Bastille and made reprisal in one awful hour for centuries of kingly crime; force waved the flag of revolution over Bunker Hill and marked the snows of Valley Forge with blood-stained feet; force held the broken line at Shiloh, climbed the flame-swept hill at Chattanooga, and stormed the clouds on Lookout heights; force marched with Sherman to the sea, rode with Sheridan in the valley of the Shenandoah, and gave Grant victory at Appomattox; force saved the Union, kept the stars in the flag; made 'niggers' men." This was "God's force," and the war with Spain was manifestly the next step in the march of progress. The "Battle Hymn" still summoned God's righteous people: "Let the impassioned lips of American patriots once more take up the song"—and here followed the fifth verse of the "Battle Hymn":

In the beauty of the lilies Christ was born across the sea,
With a glory in his bosom that transfigures you and me,
As He died to make men holy, let us die to make men free,
For God is marching on.

Thurston hoped that, having lost his wife, he would now meet death "calmly and fearlessly, as did my beloved, in the cause of humanity, under the American flag."[20] To Florence the moral of the story was obvious: in 1898, her mother's war hymn was "as appropriate at the present moment as it was thirty-six years ago, and we all rejoice that it is *now* the song of a united nation."[21]

Preachers were just as quick as the press, family members, and politicians to interpret the war of 1898 through the lens of the "Battle Hymn." Examples can be drawn from any number of pastors. Edward Lindsay

Powell, pastor of First Christian Church (Disciples of Christ) in Louisville, Kentucky, seized on the showdown with Spain as a battle between light and dark. The Virginia-born Powell framed the war of 1898 in Manichaean terms as "humanity against cruelty . . . liberty against oppression. If ever there was a righteous war, we are now entering upon it. If ever the sword should be unsheathed—this is the time; this, the very hour."[22]

As if on cue, Powell's confidence in righteous war led him immediately to the "Battle Hymn." To him, it "express[ed] the spirit of a Christian nation in waging a war of conscience and conviction." These were sacred words for sacred war. "Its solemn tones—deep as the bass of the ocean and religious as the prayer of a saint—give forth no uncertain call to the Christian manhood of America. The hymn is permeated with scripture teaching and needs no text to emphasize its summons to service and to death—if so costly a sacrifice should be demanded. It is a classic in literature. It was struck off when the soul was at white heat, and its mighty force will not be abated until every fetter has been broken and God and truth shall be supreme over human life."

Thinking of Howe's first stanza, Powell recognized that "the coming of the Lord" could be envisioned either as Christ's personal return at the end of history or more generally as his temporal judgment within history. It was the second interpretation that interested Powell, the kind of judgment in history he saw demonstrated in John the Baptist's rebuke of the Sadducees and Pharisees and his warning that the Messiah would judge them with fire and "burn up the chaff" (Matthew 4:11–12). Powell's further example came from Jewish history. God's judgment had come against that nation when the emperor Titus's Roman legions marched on Jerusalem in the first century. The same "coming" of the Lord continued whenever Christ's "spirit and life" advanced in the world. Now in 1898, at this epochal moment in history, the war with Spain manifested the Lord's "coming in judgment—in the overthrow of oppression, in the punishment of inhumanity, in the vindication of the inalienable rights of man to liberty, and the pursuit of happiness." Evidently, the Declaration of Independence had been the work of the Lord in history. It was now America's "high privilege" to witness God wielding "His terrible, swift sword"—"to gaze with awe and submission upon the divine presence as He marches on to the fulfilment [sic] of His purpose."[23]

Powell continued his exegesis of the "Battle Hymn" as if it were holy scripture. The will of God was transparent in history, and the "Battle Hymn" helped clarify events as if the poem were a prophetic utterance. Powell applied line after line to the war with Spain. He even managed to make the war more than a biblical epic of redemption; it was Arthurian to boot. If Senator Thurston got a running start with the Magna Carta, Powell did him one better by going back to Camelot: "God has placed Excalibur in our hands. On the one side is graven, 'Take me,' on the other 'Cast me away.'" In the spirit that marks any war for righteousness, and in twenty years' time would mark progressive America's global war for righteousness, the United States waged war for the sake of permanent peace, which has the rhetorical advantage of war not really being war at all. The American King Arthur would put Excalibur away in the new dispensation: "God grant that it may be sheathed forever, and that Peace may be the guardian saint of our republic."[24] Sacred nations always wage wars for peace.

The war of 1898 prompted another minister of the gospel to review the broad history of battle hymns over the past few centuries. The Congregationalist James H. Ross, in the essay "War and Peace in Hymnology," surveyed "martial hymns" from Luther's time down through the American Civil War. Ross served several congregations in New England and was active in the evangelical American Board of Commissioners for Foreign Missions and the American Bible Society. After an overview of the war poetry of Oliver Wendell Holmes Sr., John Greenleaf Whittier, and the Church of England's *Hymns Ancient and Modern* (1861), Ross turned to the "Battle Hymn of the Republic" and its author's "vision of war and of the God of war, of Human slavery and freedom, of soldierly courage, suffering, and endurance." Regrettably, he acknowledged, "some of the war songs and ballads contain reminiscences that revive unpleasant sentiments and facts that we would gladly forget." But other songs brought the nation together: "The hymns of war and peace, of Christ and the church, of the home and the Sabbath-school, of the battlefield and the hospital may well be revived, for they will do us good. . . . They are not divisive, but unifying. In the last analysis they are the hymns of eternal life."[25] Ross jumbled together war, nationalism, the church, and eternal life into a unified faith. And he seemed to know just how much forgetting of the messy past religious nationalism required. Undergirding this grand amalgamation lay Ross's dubious assumption that war and national religion (or the religious nationalism produced by war and embraced by the church) served as a means to unite Americans, ignoring war's and religious nationalism's ugly record of factionalism and alienation. For Thurston, Powell, and Ross, history in their hands told a story of addition and multiplication, never one of subtraction and division. It never failed to deliver a happy ending.

Back in the United States after the war, Howe continued to think of the "Battle Hymn" in global terms. On September 8, 1900, she drew a large crowd of admirers as the guest of honor at a reunion in Brooklyn, New York, of the Legion of the Congressional Medal of Honor. The Stars and Stripes decked the interior of the Academy of Music. The capacity crowd of 2,500 guests and 150 Legion members were entertained by a regimental band, the singing of "America," and the inevitable "Battle Hymn of the Republic" performed by a 300-voice chorus from a local girls high school. In his welcome, the editor of the *Brooklyn Daily Eagle* boasted of his city's record of patriotism and faith in America. Brooklyn, he said, stood out as "a community which believes in the Republic, which honors the Army and the Navy of that Republic," and noted that "the sword of the Republic has never been drawn, and is not drawn now, in an unworthy cause." But once committed to an honorable cause, that sword "will not be sheathed . . . until the cause in which it has been drawn has been vindicated by results commendable to conscience, compatible with liberty, agreeable to law, and certain to make the bounds of freedom wider yet." Wherever the American flag went in the world, so too would go "equality and justice, Christianity and commerce, and order and law."[26]

As part of that mission to the world, United States Marines occupied Beijing in a multinational force dispatched during the Boxer Rebellion to rescue diplomats besieged in their embassies. Speakers at the Academy of Music drew straight lines from Lexington and Concord to the Civil War, from Manila Bay and Santiago to Beijing. The mission in China was "a great work for God and humanity." After the singing of the "Battle Hymn," Brooklyn attorney James McKean, a leader of the New England Society of Brooklyn, introduced Howe as "the lady who was inspired to write this noble hymn to the tune of which the armies of the Republic have marched in the past and will march forever to victory and success." He then presented Howe with a large basket of lilies, invoking her hymn's last stanza: "Their beauty is temporal, their fragrance is ephemeral, but be sure, in presenting them to you, it is a token of our everlasting gratitude for what you have done and an appreciation that you are able to be here to-night."[27]

Howe thanked the distinguished veterans for their service to the nation, especially for passing on the legacy of their patriotism. She recalled that she had been "one of the women who wept and prayed for the soldiers in the field" during the Civil War. America had remained true to its calling ever since. "Our flag," she said, "shall go nowhere except on errands of justice and mercy. Where it has once gone, on no consideration shall it be recalled until it shall have accomplished what it has set itself to do. God grant that this pledge be never violated."[28] Howe's agent, Major J. B. Pond, considered this event important enough to include in his autobiography, along with a record of McKean's and Howe's remarks.[29] Howe's "New Testament" of American liberty for others, announced just a year before, faced an impending referendum on empire in the final weeks of the presidential contest between William McKinley and William Jennings Bryan. Bryan opposed acquisition of distant subject peoples, though he had donned a uniform for the humanitarian war for Cuba's freedom. A battle hymn that had once celebrated the North's triumph over the South, disunion, and slavery, and articulated a national theology of glory, now helped justify US intervention and new wars for justice and mercy. Perhaps it was the poet Richard Watson Gilder who best understood what Howe and her poem managed to combine at the turn of the century. He called her the "Priestess of righteous war and holy peace."[30]

Vestiges of the age of despotism continued to obstruct liberty's march in the new dispensation. The crisis of "cross and crescent"—as Edward Everett had called the Greek War of Independence and as many, including Howe, still characterized the turmoil tearing apart the Ottoman Empire— continued to trouble Howe up to the time of her death in 1910. She resorted to the strongest moralizing language to condemn Ottoman misrule: crusades, Europe's negligence, America's global duty to life, liberty, and the pursuit of happiness, the need to rid the world of the Turkish menace, and condemnations of Mohammad and Islam. In August 1909, just over a year before her death, Howe wrote an open letter intended for the *Boston Evening Transcript* but published ultimately in a New York newspaper. Here she returned to the problem of Crete. She pleaded that the island not be betrayed into the hands of the Ottoman Empire, now under the unstable rule of the revolutionary Young Turks. Howe had worried about Crete's fate for at least forty years. She had visited the island with her husband in 1867, only a year after Crete had risen against Ottoman rule and sought unification with Greece. Julia even lobbied President Andrew Johnson to appoint her husband foreign minister to Greece, the site of his first crusade in the 1820s, and Samuel raised funds to purchase guns for the Cretans and their guerrilla war while mobilizing care for Cretan refugees in Athens.[31] War between Greece and Turkey came in 1897, but British diplomatic pressure compelled the victorious Turks not to occupy Crete, while allowing them to retain formal sovereignty over the island. Now, in 1909, with Greece looking like it might claim Crete and with Turkey prepared to intervene militarily to hold the island, Howe took up her pen once again.

Howe's reaction to these events says a great deal about how, at the age of ninety and more than forty years after the Civil War, she still understood history, religion, war, and human progress. She claimed solidarity with the suffering Cretans and condemned Europe's great powers for not having the fortitude of their medieval ancestors to mount a modern crusade against a corrupt Islam. "For the moment," she wrote, "I am with the Cretan peasants in the fortress which gathers them around their flag, around the emblem of their national life, of their religious faith, of all that is more dear and sacred to them. . . . The old dreadful rule is to come back[:] the ruthless tax, the harem fed with Christian women, the crescent enthroned above the Cross." The civilized world's inaction left her in disbelief. "It is truly incredible this new crusade! When Europe was still half barbaric a body of its bravest warriors arose as one man and went forth to rescue the sepulchre of Christ from Pagan profanation. Today her strongest peoples are setting sail with an opposite intent. Let them acknowledge to themselves what they are doing, let them know what they are about. Let them tear down the Greek flag, with its cross upon it, but let them not set in its place the crucifix, the Christ martyred afresh in a Christian people."

Howe assured the public that she was no religious bigot. "I do not invoke this sacred emblem [of the cross] in any intolerant temper or intention. Too often has the cross been lifted in the cause of bloodshed and arbitrary conquest. I think now of all that it represents as peacefully and naturally within the rights of all men, to wit life, liberty and the pursuit of happiness." And then she turned more directly to the Declaration of Independence and its affirmation of universal principles. She demanded joint intervention by the European powers and the United States to secure those rights on behalf of others. It was a matter of duty. "We Americans once held Nature's title to these [rights] to be self evident. Have we seen reason to change our minds? Have we of these United States stood before all the world as the asserters and champions of these rights, and have we claimed them for our own people only?"

She insisted she was "conscious of no disrespect towards the Turks as a race or towards Islam as a religion." She opposed Islam only "in its perverted form, when it decrees persecution and death to the followers of another world religion [Christianity], dear and vital to a civilization broader, deeper, and more fruitful of good than that of the pr[o]phet Mohammed." At such a time, under such a threat, "civilization should stand by civilization, Christendom should stand by Christendom, and the new order which has won its way from the chaos of despotism at such illustrious and splendid cost must not be compelled to bow down before the symbols of that chaotic condition." Drawing an analogy to a clock face, she reached her summation of what was at stake: "Upon the dial plate of the world's history the nations supply the hands that mark the progress of civilization. Should any or all of them elect to point to midnight when the hour is really midday, the hand of divine justice must challenge the false record and set the true one in its place." Extending her clock metaphor, she pleaded, "Strike, strike oh heavenly Timepiece, for life, light, and liberty. National life, rational light, and Christian freedom."[32]

For Howe all of these efforts, spanning the course of half a century—whether for the American Union, Italy, Greece, or Crete—were subsumed under a mystical reverie of millennial peace. During a summer stay in Newport in 1908, she experienced a vision similar to what had happened to her in Saint Paul in 1900 and in Washington in 1861. Evidently, she mentioned this experience in remarks at a meeting of the Free Religious Association at the Parker Memorial Church in Newport. In her diary, she noted that she had "tried to say that prophetic souls really see visions of the good things that they foretell. Isaiah saw the millennium, though not indeed as we see it."[33] Her own vision of the millennium had been vivid. A reporter for the *Boston Sunday American* interviewed her about this

experience of the "veil" being lifted between this world and the coming millennium. Her mind did not focus on the earthly "Battle Hymn"
as it might be sung by actual soldiers fighting and dying on some future
battlefield, but on a global scale "in the world-wide battle with evil" to
inaugurate the millennial age: "There seemed to be a new, a wondrous
ever-permeating light," Howe told the reporter, "the glory of which I cannot attempt to put in human words—the light of the new-born hope and
sympathy blazing."[34]

Howe saw a throng of men and women sharing "in the world-wide
battle with evil." They stripped away "the mask from error, crime, su-
perstition, greed," and worked "to discover and apply the remedy." No
longer adversaries, men and women united in a single cause, "a common,
lofty, and indomitable purpose lighting every face with a glory not of this
earth." "All," she stressed, "all were advancing with one end in view, one
foe to trample, one everlasting good to gain. I saw them advancing like
a mighty army, laden with the fruits of their research, their study, their
endeavor, in this battle with the powers of darkness and ready to tear
vice from the earth, to strip away all of selfishness, of greed, of rapine."
They were eager to serve humanity with this knowledge that had purged
the earth. She alluded to language from John's Apocalypse depicting the
church triumphant: "I seemed to see them stoop down to their fellows
and to lift them higher, higher, and yet higher. Men and women, a vast
host whom none could number, working unitedly, equally, with superhu-
man energy, all for the extirpation of the blackness of vice and for the
weal of the race. And then I saw the victory! All of evil was gone from the
earth. Misery was blotted out. Mankind was emancipated and ready to
march forward in a new era of human understanding, all-encompassing
sympathy, and ever-present help. The era of perfect love, of peace passing
understanding."[35] More than fifty newspapers carried this story.

Howe mentioned her "Midnight Vision" again that summer during
the Biennial Convention of the General Federation of Women's Clubs in
Boston. She joined the audience, as she had done so often before, in singing her "Battle Hymn." But as she did so, the need for self-examination
struck her. She wondered, "Am I in Thy army, Jesus?" Doubt crossed her
mind: "Truly I hope so, but wish I were assured of it."[36] More than four
decades had passed since the Civil War, but Howe still yearned to march
in the army of the Lord. Appomattox had not ended her battle. As she

marched, she continued to rely on the book of Revelation to express her abiding hope in the coming Day of the Lord. That glorious return was imminent, though not literal. Victory over oppression, union of a divided humanity, and the consummation of the ages were at hand. The signs were everywhere. At the age of nearly ninety, the poet's eyes still saw the glory. If anything, her poem's apocalyptic intensity had only strengthened with the years.

Peace hymn, war hymn, or both, the "Battle Hymn" proved its usefulness to projecting America's power in the world. At the same time, the "Battle Hymn" also tightened the bonds of affection necessary to a national community, as the Reverend Ross and others hoped it would. The war with Spain was thought by many to symbolize and secure the final reunification of North and South. Politically, the two had been reintegrated into one Union by the end of Reconstruction. Cultural, economic, and racial divisions remained, but the "New South" supposedly worked out an accommodation that left the fate of blacks to the South, called a truce in the culture wars that accepted both Lincoln and Lee as heroes, and opened the region to northern investment, industrialization, and exploitation of raw materials for a national and global economy. All had been brave, all had been honorable, all had been chivalrous. In Cuba and the Philippines, sons of Yankees and Confederates fought side by side in the nation's and humanity's service. Battle dead from both sides rested in Arlington National Cemetery.

Late in life, Howe rejoiced in the public demonstrations of unity that appeared to mark once and for all the end of the Civil War and its animosities. An emotional celebration of this reconciliation came at a meeting of the Grand Army of the Republic (GAR) in Boston in 1899. The Memorial Day observance featured an address for the first time before the GAR by an ex-Confederate officer. General Joseph Wheeler, an ex-Confederate of Connecticut stock, who served in the Spanish-American War and soon headed back to fight in the Philippine-American War, spoke of national unity as the key to international military victory. His two daughters rode to the event in the company of Howe, one of the honored guests. Naturally, a soloist and choir sang her "Battle Hymn." Touched by the experience, she saved a clipping about the service in her journal. The soloist bowed to Howe's box. The crowd erupted into ecstatic shouts. She and the audience joined in singing about dying to make men free. And at once "the whole vast audience was on its feet, sobbing and singing at the top of its thousands of lungs." "If volunteers were really needed for the Philippines," one reporter rejoiced, "McKinley could have had us all right there."[37]

But could the "Battle Hymn" do more? Could it become the nation's official anthem? In 1903 Massachusetts senator George F. Hoar exclaimed, "We waited eighty years for our American National Anthem. At last God inspired an illustrious and noble woman to utter in undying verse the thought which we hope is forever to animate the soldier of the Republic." In this letter to women's rights activist Lucy Stone, Hoar then quoted the entire fifth verse ("In the beauty of the lilies . . ."). "Julia Ward Howe," as a woman, "cannot yet vote in America," he lamented. "But her words will be an inspiration to the youth of America on many a hard-fought field for liberty many a century after her successors will vote."[38] That expectation was soon fulfilled on battlefields around the world.

Until 1931, the United States had no national anthem sanctioned by Congress, though not for lack of contenders. Among these were "America" and "The Star-Spangled Banner." The "Battle Hymn" found its greatest champion in President Theodore Roosevelt, and its supporters were still active in 1931 when Congress and President Hoover chose Francis Scott Key's poem about the War of 1812. An insider's view of how Teddy Roosevelt hit on the idea of making the "Battle Hymn" the national anthem comes from his military aide Archibald "Archie" Butt. Archie Butt was born in Georgia just months after the Civil War ended. He worked briefly as a journalist before joining the US embassy staff in Mexico City and then serving in the Pacific during the Philippine-American War. He worked as military aide to both Roosevelt and Taft. He died aboard the HMS *Titanic* in 1912. With obvious pride in his new post, Butt wrote to his mother in Georgia about social events at the busy Roosevelt White House. On a Saturday afternoon in June 1908, the 150-voice Arion Chorus performed at an informal gathering. Among the guests was Admiral Dewey's wife. The president asked the male chorus to sing "Dixie," "My Old Kentucky Home," and "Suwannee River."[39]

As planned, the choir finished in time for the president, Archie, and Fitzhugh Lee (Robert E. Lee's son) to head out for an afternoon of horseback riding. Roosevelt was eager to try out his new horse, purchased for him by a nervous Archie Butt. The trio began to talk about "Dixie." "That is our only piece of martial music," TR told the two Southerners. "It is the best battle music in the world, even more than the Marseillaise, for it goes with more of a jump and dash. It does not fit to voices well, and the words are inadequate, but for a bit of martial music there is nothing finer." Butt agreed, but thought the United States did not possess a truly suitable marching song. Nevertheless, the Georgian proposed that the "Battle Hymn of the Republic" become the national anthem, "the grandest one ever written." He knew his Confederate mother disagreed and that she held a grudge against Roosevelt for inviting Booker T. Washington to the White House. But this son of the New South held out the "hope that some day it might supplant all the other non-descript national anthems which we now have."[40]

Butt reported Roosevelt's response as ecstatic. The president agreed with Butt's claim that "there is not a sectional line in the whole hymn. The line 'as he died to make men holy, let us die to make men free' is universal, catholic, as true a hundred years ago as it is now, equally true of Anglo Saxon or Hindu." The only question in the president's mind was how to get the "Battle Hymn" adopted. The two men started reciting the entire poem, helping each other if one forgot a line. The president was so touched by the episode that he started calling Archie by his first name. TR "seemed possessed with a desire to do something at once," Archie explained. Roosevelt added that the "Battle Hymn" had always been his "favorite short poem."[41]

During this lively exchange, Roosevelt decided to write to his friend Joel Chandler Harris, Southern editor, publisher, and author of the popular "Uncle Remus" stories. He hoped that Harris, though in failing health, would mobilize his *Atlanta Constitution* behind the campaign. Roosevelt and his family loved Harris's stories of Br'er Rabbit, Br'er Fox, and the Tar-Baby. The president often read them aloud to his children. Harris had been a guest at the White House for dinner in November 1907 and was a great favorite with the children.[42] Roosevelt's June 15 letter to Harris's *Home Magazine* appeared in the September 1908 issue and was reprinted in the *New York Times* and elsewhere. Roosevelt told Harris he thought the "Battle Hymn" "ought to be a great National treasure, something that all Americans would grow to know intimately, so that in any audience anywhere in the land when the tune was started most of the audience should be able to join in singing the words." Perhaps the *Home Magazine* could help stir up "popular feeling" behind making Mrs. Howe's hymn the nation's official anthem.[43]

Harris, in what the magazine called "perhaps the last article to come from his pen"—he died the first week of July—summarized TR's point for his readers. The president, Harris explained, "puts this idea before the country, and before the South first. Will Southerners be inclined to forget the partisan genesis of 'The Battle Hymn of the Republic' as completely as Northerners have forgotten that of 'Dixie'? Acquiescence in President Roosevelt's proposition would mark to a greater degree than almost anything else could the fact that this is indeed a united country. . . . We should like to hear from our readers with regard to this. What do you think about it?"[44]

Roosevelt still had the "Battle Hymn" on his mind in November. He wrestled with the problem of how to promote a national anthem without commissioning something made to order. Surely such a production would strike a false note and not emerge, as it must, from the nation's experience. Twenty years earlier, his friend Brander Matthews had already worried over the problem. "A national hymn is one thing that cannot be made to order," Matthews warned in 1887. Like the "Marseillaise," such songs were rarely the work of distinguished poets. They emerged spontaneously from the experience of the nation. Matthews was no doubt right that a national hymn cannot "be accomplished by taking thought," but it would be a mistake to extend the point to the cultural and political appropriation of a song like the "Battle Hymn of the Republic" once it becomes popular. Subsequent uses often were "made to order."[45]

Returning to this point, Roosevelt wrote to the poet Richard Watson Gilder on November 19, 1908—coincidentally the anniversary of Howe's first draft of the "Battle Hymn." Roosevelt had been reading the new edition of George Otto Trevelyan's *Life and Letters of Lord Macaulay.* Macaulay was Trevelyan's uncle and the historian who had used Isaiah 63 for his poem about the English Civil Wars. TR took Macaulay's point to heart that, given the organic nature of language, it would be impossible to produce a national literature by committee and on demand. "Don't you think that this applies to the excellent people who would try to get up somebody to write a national anthem to order?" he asked rhetorically. "Julia Ward Howe's 'Battle Hymn of the Republic' is an inspiration of genius. No other nation has so fine a poem for its national anthem, and there is a first-class tune for it—a great popular tune." "There really is not a word of sectionalism in the poem," he insisted, like so many others at the time. The active forgetting going on in Roosevelt's letter is noteworthy: "We practically have 'Dixie' as a national tune everywhere. There isn't the slightest reason why we should not have Julia Ward Howe's hymn as our national anthem. It is mere waste of time to get people of set purpose to write such an anthem."[46] TR meant his questions to be rhetorical, never supposing that some Americans, even outside the South, might have compelling reasons to reject the "Battle Hymn" as a national anthem.

Letters to the *New York Times* showed how controversial this proposal was. The *Times* heard from its readers soon after it complied with the appeal for help by Harris's *Home Magazine*. These writers opposed the suggestion for different reasons, but all contested that the "Battle Hymn" was entitled to be the nation's anthem. A Shakespeare scholar weighed in about the poem as literature. Whatever the merits of the "Battle Hymn" in the public's mind, the song would never be adopted, because "its words mean nothing, convey no impression, and, as a matter of fact, never have been used except as a tour de force when somebody ordered or procured them to be sung. There is no idea of battle conveyed. Imagine an army bawling 'In the beauty of the Lilies Christ was born across the sea'! And what would a soldier assume was meant by 'Let the Hero born of Woman crush the serpent with his heel,' or 'As you deal with my contemners so with you my Grace will deal'?" If President Roosevelt had asked the public or even Howe herself to explain the meaning of these words, they could not have done it. "Mrs. Howe's words are prohibitive—they mean nothing, convey no impression, express no purpose or aspiration. What soldier going into battle would remark, 'Prepare my soul to meet him—Be jubilant, my feet'?"[47]

The *Times* published one reply to this complaint, but it seemed only to reinforce its point. The critic charged that for the writer to condemn the "Battle Hymn" he "must either be atrophied in some parts of his psychological being, or his literary education must have been neglected in certain directions." Perhaps too many Americans lacked the knowledge, taste, and discernment necessary to embrace the "Battle Hymn" as their national anthem, the writer suggested. "There echoes in every word and line of the poem the poetic thought and religious ecstacy [*sic*] of the old

Hebrew prophet and poet who could sing of 'the mountains that skipped like rams, and the hills like lambs of the flock' and mean no more than any poet since who has felt at moments the dancing joyousness of nature and talked nonsense and music in the same breath in trying to express his ecstacy [*sic*]."[48]

Defending the ideal of a secular republic, a Jewish reader responded to Roosevelt that "the poem possesses very few qualifications to entitle it to reception by the American people as a national hymn, either for war or peace. Apart from some confusion in metaphor, besides obscurity in not a few lines which renders them to a great extent meaningless, there is a great deal of literary excellence in the hymn, which is fervid, musical, and polished, albeit lacking in that simplicity which is so essential and necessary in a national anthem." He thought it "more suitable for a church or Salvation Army ode than for the purpose for which it was intended." "However," he added, "all these are minor disqualifications compared with its sectarian and non-secular element." As proof, he cited the poem's references to Christ, his death, and God's justice and grace. "The American Nation and Army are not all Christians," he reminded the readers of the *Times*. "In both bodies there are many who prefer a different religion to what Christ taught; and there are many who have no religion at all." The "Battle Hymn" pushed the limits of toleration unnecessarily: "The only religious element that can be properly introduced into any battle hymn or national ode is: God and the Right. Any other religious sentiment in a vast cosmopolitanism is superfluous and undesirable." Above all, and this as a matter of conscience, no unbelieving soldier should be asked by the government to profess an alien faith in the face of battle. At the moment of ultimate cost, "he certainly does not desire his last breath to be a lie to his conscience and to the sacred heritage of his convictions."[49]

Similar concerns surfaced five years later when several students at the Jewish-majority Public School No. 7 in Brooklyn refused to sing the "Battle Hymn" because of its references to Christ. The principal had tried unsuccessfully for several days to get them to cooperate. According to one press report, the superintendent of schools backed the pupils and thought it reasonable that they "not be forced to sing any selection against their religious principles." The principal relented.[50] The accommodation not granted to Kate McGean in 1863 in the heat of war was now possible by 1913.

One further letter to the *Times* in 1908, this time written from a soldier's perspective, opposed adoption of the "Battle Hymn" as ill suited to the realities of combat. This veteran of the Spanish-American War thought the suggestion ludicrous. "The soldiers of our armies will not, as companies or regiments or brigades, sing the words of the 'Battle Hymn.'" Some individual might dare to "sing these sentimentally religious lines to his comrades, but just as surely as he does he will be hooted down." A regiment would ridicule any brother-in-arms who would "sing the words: 'In the beauty of the lilies Christ was born across the sea.' And yet, if that same man had started up with the words, to the same tune: 'Hang Jeff Davis on a sour apple tree' a thousand voices would have joined with his—provided, of course, that his regiment be made up of Northern men." And if soldiers would not sing it, it would never become the national anthem: "Few men go into battle with prayer on their lips; those who do generally run away at the first gun shot. If they sing it will be something harsh and stern." Recalling his own experience in battle in 1898, he assured the *Times* he could not "think of that regiment of strong men singing the words of Julia Ward Howe's 'Battle Hymn,' marching up that hill—they were under too great stress and strain."[51]

Just as the *Times* published these letters, Archie Butt wrote to Howe directly about the president's plan for the "Battle Hymn." In reply, she confessed that she had not heard much about the proposal until a Boston reporter called her for her opinion. She took the opportunity of Butt's letter to send him an account of how she wrote the "Battle Hymn," and told him "it would gratify a dear wish of my heart if the south would adopt my verses." "Like our beloved President," she added with family pride, "I have in my veins a strain of Southern blood."[52]

Perhaps no American statesman better represented the combination of imperialism, nationalism, and progressivism than Teddy Roosevelt, and Howe's "Battle Hymn" helped him tie these ambitions together. So closely associated in the popular mind did Roosevelt become with the "Battle Hymn" that the satirical *Life* magazine in 1907 depicted him in a cartoon with raised fists in the midst of an impassioned speech. The caption read, "Battle Him of the Republic."[53] The *Baltimore Sun* joined in the punning by calling TR "the real Battle Him of the Republic!"[54] The "Battle Hymn" became ubiquitous in Roosevelt's 1912 bid for the presidency

Figure 16. Nelson Harding, "The Battle Him of the Republic," *Brooklyn Daily Eagle*, October 12, 1912.

under the banner of the Progressive Party. The *Brooklyn Daily Eagle* returned to the "Battle Him" pun in a cartoon showing Roosevelt dressed as a Rough Rider, swinging a club as he reaches the summit called "Armageddon."[55] The socialist poet Bernice Evans mocked the former president in 1917 with the same play on words: "There's a Horrible Grin, / Up on Oyster Bay, / Sometimes known as / The Battle Him of the Republic.[56]

Howe's daughters lined up loyally behind this "Battle Him." Maud Howe Elliott, getting word of Taft's renomination for president in June 1912, described herself as "much cast down about the result of the Republican National Convention in Chicago." "Roosevelt will try and form a third party," she hoped. She attended a large banquet for Bull Moose supporters on August 7 at the Point of Pines resort outside Boston. Roosevelt, fresh from delivering his "confession of faith" in Chicago, "likened the forming of the Progressives to the founding of the Republican party by the abolitionists and the liberals of that time. The Golden Rule and the Decalogue must animate all our legislation." Maud called "the enthusiasm" for Roosevelt "heartfelt and magnificent." Enlisting in the cause, she founded the Newport County Women's Progressive League and headed up the wider Rhode Island women's campaign. When she attended a Progressive Party meeting in Providence in September 1912, she "was greeted with the 'Battle Hymn', the audience rising and singing the Glory Halleluiah with a will. It was very moving and I felt it deeply. It is all for Mother."[57]

At the 1912 Progressive Party convention in Chicago, the "Battle Hymn" stood out for the way in which the insurgent movement appropriated the Civil War anthem to capture the energy and idealism of the Progressives' domestic war for righteousness. The Progressive Party met in the Windy City just six weeks after the Republicans had gathered there and renominated the incumbent William Howard Taft. Roosevelt staked out a position to the ideological left of the Democratic candidate Woodrow Wilson. Herbert Croly, among the Progressive movement's leading public intellectuals, author of the landmark book *The Promise of American Life* (1909), and soon a founding editor at the *New Republic*, gave form and content to much of Roosevelt's "New Nationalism." Roosevelt combined the populism of the recall, initiative, and referendum with a vigorous nationalism, a strong centralized state, a modern army and navy, and a degree of government regulation of the economy not yet seen in American life. This was Roosevelt's "strenuous life" enacted on a national scale.

His widely reported speech at the Progressive convention repeated much of what he had told Republicans on the same stage weeks earlier. On August 6, he declared in what he called, as Maud noted, his "confession of faith," that the National Progressive Party was "a movement of truth, sincerity, and wisdom, a movement which proposes to put at the service of all our people the collective power of the people, through their Governmental agencies, alike in the Nation and in the several States." This campaign battled for America's future. It had all the marks of a crusade and a religious revival. "Our cause is based on the eternal principles of righteousness," he promised the crowd. He praised his faithful followers as those who had pledged themselves "to spend and be spent in the endless crusade against wrong." Repeating his closing words from the Republican convention, he declared once more, "We stand at Armageddon, and we battle for the Lord."[58]

Delegates sported red bandannas to capitalize on TR's cowboy image. Symbols of the purported reconciliation of North and South also abounded at the convention, such as the brass band of the GAR playing "Dixie." The tent-revival atmosphere handed the daily press and popular weeklies the dominant theme for their reporting. "It was not a convention," the *New York Times* cautioned its readers. "It was an assemblage of religious enthusiasts. It was a Methodist camp meeting done over into political terms."[59] The crowd of 15,000 struck reporters as aglow with piety. While the press might have been amused, this was a convention without a trace of irony. Edward Lowry, in *Harper's Weekly*, thought that "while there was absolutely no conscious humor in the meeting, the singing was the best ever heard at any national convention." The crowd released its "surcharged emotions" with "Onward, Christian Soldiers" and the "Battle Hymn of the Republic," mixed with patriotic standards.[60]

The novelist, playwright, and war correspondent Richard Harding Davis found the singing the "most surprising part" of the convention. True, the hymns "might have been sung better by a church choir," but the voices "carried a harmony that could not have been imparted by any music master." "It reminded [him]," he added significantly, "of the psalm singing of the Boers before the battle of Sand River." These saints in Chicago stood at "Armageddon" and mustered for battle: "They were young men with the look of the Pilgrim Fathers and Cromwell's army; their faces showed that they still possessed illusions, still held to high ideals."[61] Davis may have missed the women seated in the auditorium, but he caught the crowd's unbounded idealism.

All agreed the convention's highlight had been the keynote address by former Indiana senator Albert J. Beveridge. Beveridge is best known today for his pro-imperial speeches during and immediately after the Spanish-American War, speeches that mixed the Bible and US expansionism into a heady theo-political cocktail. At the 1900 Republican convention in the Auditorium Building in Chicago, Beveridge had summoned America to embrace world empire with a clear conscience. His "Star of Empire" had been a tour de force filled with promises of regeneration, progress, and bright prospects for God's chosen people armed with a national mission. His vision ranged as far as Constantinople, and he imagined the day when a powerful United States would preside over a "Congress of the Nations" as the "most righteous of judges" to remap the world. Beveridge had capped off his prophecy in 1900 with an allusion to the "Battle Hymn": America's call to be a world force for righteousness "is the high and holy destiny of the American people, and from that destiny the American bugle will never sound retreat."[62]

Back in Chicago twelve years later, Beveridge delivered what everyone at the Progressive Party convention hailed as the greatest achievement of this celebrated orator's career in public service. "Pass Prosperity Around"—the Progressives' motto—defined the senator's call for reform. He went after the "invisible government" that pulled the wires behind both major parties. The Progressives stood for rule by the people in place of this sham of democracy. He took on big business, called for a modernized Sherman antitrust law, tariff reform, an end to child labor, the vote for women, and a Constitution understood and interpreted as a "living thing" in the service of a "perfect union" and the "general welfare." This was an agenda for a righteous nation that God himself would favor. Beveridge rallied the delegates and the American people to enlist in this holy cause. "Never doubt that we are indeed a Nation whose God is the Lord," he said, quoting Psalm 144. And he ended with an appeal that grabbed headlines, the same justification for empire he had used in 1900: "The call that comes to us is the call that came to our fathers. As they responded so shall we. 'He hath sounded forth a trumpet that shall never call retreat.'"[63]

At that instant, the *New York Times* reported, "the whole convention burst out spontaneously in song. They sang every verse of Mrs. Howe's majestic hymn except one, and nobody had to tell them the words."[64] Soon, the "Battle Hymn" was handily available for the campaign ahead as hymn no. 33 in *Progressive Battle Hymns*, the official songbook of the third-party movement that aimed to break the grip of the Republican and Democratic establishment.[65]

Howe did not live to hear her apocalyptic anthem mobilized for Roosevelt's Armageddon. She had died in October 1910 at the age of 91, having lived from the presidency of James Monroe to that of Taft. Boston held a memorial service at Symphony Hall in early January 1911.[66] Dignitaries, family members, and friends gathered to say farewell. Four thousand in all came to honor Howe's legacy and to express their gratitude. Representatives of the Greek, Armenian, and Italian communities joined the mourners. None of the speakers was old enough to remember the Civil War. The service closed with everyone singing the "Battle Hymn of the Republic." Of the older generation of reformers, only Franklin Sanborn and Thomas Wentworth Higginson survived, and only Higginson was well enough to attend.

Howe's eulogists included Boston's mayor, the president of Mount Holyoke College, and an assistant US district attorney. Mayor Fitzgerald's tribute stressed how far beyond America's shores the "Battle Hymn" had reached. John F. Fitzgerald, the first Irish Catholic mayor of Boston, whose daughter Rose would marry Joseph P. Kennedy in 1914, summed up Samuel and Julia Howe's achievement with the single word "emancipation." "The life motto of these two companion souls," he said, "[was] inarticulate or semiconscious, perhaps, until Lincoln crystallized it in an immortal word, . . . Emancipation." Thanks to that guiding vision that crossed all national boundaries, "the whole world . . . knew her as a friend. The Greek, for whom her husband fought; the blind and the imbecile, whose infirmities he strove to soften; the negro, whose shackles she helped to rive asunder; the Italian patriot, the oppressed Armenian, the ever-suffering Israelite; the myriads of her own sex, whose rights she championed, mourned an ardent sympathizer when she passed away." Mayor Fitzgerald then came to the "Battle Hymn," a song "chanted around a thousand camp fires during the Civil War" and one that, "through its

Hebraic imagery and prophetic fervor, will live as long as the memories of that momentous conflict endure."[67] The poet Robert Grant likewise announced, "To every votary in the world / Oppressed though struggling to be free / Her heart leapt like a flag unfurled, / Knew barriers none of race or sea."[68]

William Lewis represented not only the city's younger generation of leaders but more importantly and symbolically the fruits of emancipation after fifty years. The Virginia-born Lewis was the son of former slaves. From these bleak prospects, he rose to attend Amherst College, win recognition as a debater and football player there, attend Harvard Law School, and then, on the Harvard team, become the first African American All-American. He coached football at Harvard for about a decade before going on to practice law in Boston. Having met Lewis through their mutual friend Booker T. Washington, President Roosevelt appointed Lewis to the position of assistant US attorney for Massachusetts, and then in 1911 Taft appointed Lewis to serve as assistant US district attorney, the first African American to fill that position. Lewis specialized in civil rights cases.[69] In his eulogy he reminded the audience of Howe's debt to transcendentalism and Unitarianism, linking her to Emerson, Fuller, Parker, and Clarke, and to the reformation in American thought and culture they had launched.[70]

In the audience sat Howe's daughter, Florence Howe Hall. In a later book, she praised all the speeches, but thought "none, however, equaled in heartfelt eloquence the speech of Lewis, the distinguished negro lawyer, as he poured out the gratitude of his race to the woman who had written the 'Battle Hymn of the Republic.'" "I suddenly realized," she continued, "what the words meant to the colored people. The appeal, 'Let us die to make men free,' was for all men and for all time, yet in a special sense it was meant for the despised slave for whose freedom the soldiers of the Union laid down their lives in those dark days of the 'sixties.'"[71] Had Florence grown up in a home where the "Battle Hymn" had always been a song about humanity in general rather than the slave in particular? Florence's obtuseness about black freedom could indicate that her mother had always intended her "Battle Hymn" to be primarily about something more than the liberty of chattel slaves. On the other hand, Florence's flash of insight could simply point to one of the many ironies that would dog her mother's poem as generation after generation used and reused it in ways that obscured the freed race's title to the song.

The final encomium to Howe at Symphony Hall came from former Massachusetts governor Curtis Guild. He too looked abroad to find the poet's greatest contribution and to grasp the ultimate significance of the "Battle Hymn": "Greece knew and received her bounty. Hungary's champion found in her a helper. Italy was almost as beloved by her as her own land. The oppressed of far-off Armenia found in her alike the tenderness of a woman and the sturdy championship of a man. As an exponent of the abstruse doctrines of philosophy she stood as a teacher on the lecture platform; as an apostle of the religious creed that was hers she even occupied the pulpit."[72] In nearly the last words of Howe's memorial service, Guild promised that "Julia Ward Howe stands with Rouget de Lisle [author of the "Marseillaise"] and Theodore Korner and those other happy mortals to whom it has been given to awake a nation's very soul."[73] Crowning the moment, the choir and audience sang the "Battle Hymn" supported by Symphony Hall's great organ.

Howe's memorial service paid tribute to the poet and her poem, the maker and the making. The event gathered prominent Americans to eulogize one of the nation's and the world's leading reformers. It gathered sentiments appropriate to the occasion and took one last opportunity to assess the significance of the "Battle Hymn" in American life. But William Lewis's mood would grow somber later as he reflected on the Progressive Party and pondered the irony of its use of the "Battle Hymn." He attended the convention in Chicago in 1912. He heard Beveridge demand full recognition of the rights of man: "For an hour and a half the great orator developed his theme. I listened to the strains of music of 'John Brown's Body' and the 'Battle Hymn of the Republic.' My heart sank within me when I thought that there were men outside clamoring for admission who were denied on account of their race and color. Since all men did not include Southern Negroes, I could not feel that John Brown's soul was marching there. When that vast audience sang the 'Battle Hymn of the Republic,' 'as Christ died to make men holy let us die to make men free,' I felt that human cant and hypocrisy could go no further; it had reached its fitting climax."[74]

5

THE ANGLO-AMERICAN "BATTLE HYMN"

Rudyard Kipling made an ambitious trek across the United States in 1889. He was only twenty-four. His story "How I Found Peace at Musquash on the Monongahela" lampooned the imaginary town of Beaver, Pennsylvania, and his encounter there with the earnest Methodists of Beaver College.[1] Kipling's parents had both been Methodists, and he understood the targets of his gentle satire. Americans, he observed, nurtured a provincial faith in their own superiority and confidence in the power of the "Democratic Idea" to overcome every obstacle Necessity might throw in their way. They were naive, yes, "but the men and women [of America] set Us an example in patriotism. They believe in their land and its future, and its honour, and its glory, and they are not ashamed to say so. From the largest to the least runs this same proud, passionate conviction to which I take off my hat and for which I love them." By contrast, "an average English householder seems to regard his country as an abstraction to supply him with policemen and fire-brigades." True, the American might be a sharp dealer who ignores laws he does not like, but "he understands what manner of thing his Republic is."

Kipling found the American citizen's zeal for singing "My Country 'Tis of Thee" to be disarming. "I have heard a few thousand of them engaged in that employment," he marveled; and for such gusto "I respect him." "There is too much Romeo and too little balcony about our [British] National Anthem. With the American article it is all balcony. There must be born a poet who shall give the English *the* song of their own, own country—which is to say, of about half the world. Remains then only to compose the greatest song of all—The Saga of the Anglo-Saxon all round the earth—a paean that shall combine the terrible slow swing of the *Battle Hymn of the Republic* (which, if you know it not, get chanted to you) with *Britannia needs no Bulwarks*, the skirl of the *British Grenadiers* with that perfect quickstep, *Marching through Georgia*, and at the end the wail of the *Dead March*. For We, even We who share the earth between us as no gods have ever shared it, we also are mortal in the matter of our single selves. Will any one take the contract?"[2] When Kipling quoted an American song in his first novel two years later, he chose not "My Country 'Tis of Thee" but the "Battle Hymn of the Republic" with its "terrible slow swing."

Lippincott's Monthly Magazine published *The Light That Failed* in January 1891, Kipling's first successful attempt at long-form fiction.[3] Unfortunately for Kipling's reputation, modern critics and biographers remember that magazine's version of his novel only for its painfully sentimental "happy ending"—soon replaced by a much longer and sadder version. The 1891 original lets the hero, aspiring artist Dick Heldar, reconcile himself to the blindness that ends his career and reunites him with his childhood sweetheart, Masie. This ending, while regrettable on literary grounds, gives early evidence for the strange ways Howe's poem became tangled up in British culture and the empire's wars. The "Battle Hymn of the Republic" was well on its way to becoming an Anglo-American anthem extolling a wider political religion that was more than nationalist but less than internationalist.

Kipling set his novel in 1880s London and on the far-flung battlefields of the Sudan. In the closing paragraphs, he reunites Dick Heldar with his close circle of fellow war correspondents and artists. The final scene gathers several characters: the battle-hardened correspondent known only as

Torpenhow, adept at writing for the masses reached by a large newspaper syndicate; the equipment-laden Cassavetti, who wrote for a European syndicate; a bulky journalist nicknamed the "Nilghai" for his resemblance to the Asian antelope of that name; and another nicknamed the "Keneu" after the "Great War Eagle." About to be abandoned by these comrades as they head off to cover the Sudan campaign, Dick is sorry not to be one of them. As they drink together, Dick starts to hum a tune. "By the instinct of association," the narrator says, "he began to hum the terrible Battle Hymn of the Republic. Man after man caught it up—it was a tune they knew well, till the windows shook to the clang, the Nilghai's deep voice leading:

'Mine eyes have seen the glory of the coming of the Lord;
He is trampling out the vintage where the grapes of wrath are stored;
He hath loosed the fateful lightning of his terrible swift sword.
His truth is marching on.'

'How does the next verse go?' said the Keneu. And they swept off again, beating time on the table.

'He has sounded forth the trumpet that shall never call retreat;
He is sifting out the hearts of men before his judgment-seat:
Oh, be swift, my soul, to meet him! Be jubilant, my feet!
Our God is marching on.'

Then Cassavetti, very proud of his knowledge—'In the beauty of the lilies—'
    'Hold on,' said Torpenhow. 'We've nothing to do with that. It belongs to another man.'
    'No,' said Dick to himself under his breath, 'the other man belongs.'"

With this sentence, the "happy ending" version of *The Light That Failed* came to an abrupt and ambiguous end.

By calling Howe's poem the "*terrible* Battle Hymn of the Republic," Kipling may not have meant anything other than what Howe herself had meant by God's "*terrible* swift sword"—namely, a terror- or fear-inducing judgment. If Kipling had chosen to give Torpenhow the last word, then the novel's closing scene could have served as a sobering warning to anyone tempted to confuse the British Empire's Africa campaign with Christ's

atoning death. That kind of suffering belonged to "another man," not to
the British. And yet, up to this point, Torpenhow had not objected to linking
Britain with God's truth marching on in all the other stanzas. The novel's
last line instead goes to Dick, in words he muttered "under his breath."
He added, almost silently, that the "other man," that is, Christ, indeed
belongs. But "belongs" where, exactly? Belongs to whom? In what sense
does the "other man" belong in the mouths of cynical, inebriated British
journalists on their way to cover a colonial war? Kipling never explained.

Florence found nothing ambiguous about Kipling's purpose. The quotation flattered her mother and America and its humanitarian mission.
Florence's Spanish-American War essays for *The Independent* made that
clear. "Rudyard Kipling," she wrote, "himself a man of genius, has fitly
described Mrs. Howe's most famous war lyric as 'the terrible Battle-Hymn
of the Republic.'" Had the mark of his genius been that he had recognized
the Battle Hymn's excellence? If so, he saw more. "He saw that only a
republic, a mighty nation of freemen, patient and slow to wrath, but terrible when once aroused, could have inspired such a song. Yet when, in
'The Light that Failed' he makes a group of Englishmen and men of other
nationalities sing this hymn as a fitting prelude to their departure for the
scene of war, he recognized also, its *universal* quality—a hymn for men
of every clime who love liberty and are willing to lay down their lives for
its sake."[4]

Florence's interpretation seems naive at best. But as her reaction to
Lewis's 1911 eulogy for her mother also indicated, she had a knack for
missing the point. Kipling drew no obvious connection between, on the
one hand, the "Battle Hymn" and a warrior republic and, on the other,
the "Battle Hymn" and an international crusade for liberty. But if Kipling
did not intend these connections, they certainly captured the public imagination. Indeed, Roosevelt assured Howe in 1902 that "Kipling alone had
understood the meaning of [her] 'Battle Hymn,' and that he admired him
therefor."[5] In 1908, the president told Archie Butt, in words Butt reported
to his mother, that "when he had talked with Kipling once about his Recessional Hymn the poet had said to him that the Battle Hymn was the
greatest hymn ever written, that it would never be touched."[6]

Since Kipling had heard small-town patriots sing the "Battle Hymn"
on his travels across the United States, this may have been another way
for him to urge his British readers to get their own national song of equal

power. Perhaps he put the "Battle Hymn" into the mouths of British war correspondents because such men really did know the song and sang it around the empire. Perhaps he simply used the "Battle Hymn" in the "happy ending" version of his novel to flatter his American audience and by doing so left his British readers baffled. In 1899, Howe did not mention Kipling or his novel in her *Reminiscences*. Perhaps she knew only the novel's final version. Surely, though, she would have read Florence's articles. Regardless, Kipling's ambiguous use of three stanzas of her "Battle Hymn" points to the unexpected but welcomed ways in which the poem was put to use as a global anthem—at least a global anthem on American or Anglo-American terms.

England's reading public had known the "Battle Hymn" since its original publication, and it turned up in all sorts of settings. London booksellers carried the *Atlantic Monthly* in their stalls and advertised the February 1862 issue.[7] At times America's cousins found it difficult to remember the difference between the John Brown song and the "Battle Hymn." Recalling events from 1863, Hallam Tennyson wrote of his father's "indignation against Russia for her treatment of Poland," calling it "boundless." Lord Tennyson had been "filled with horror too at the gigantic civil war in America, although he had always looked forward to the total abolition of slavery: but he had hoped that it might have been accomplished gradually and peacefully." In a footnote to this passage, Hallam added, "[Lord Tennyson] would sing with enthusiasm the great chorus of the 'Battle-hymn of the Republic': 'Singing "Glory, Glory, Hallelujah!" / His soul goes marching on.' "[8] These were not the words of the "Battle Hymn," of course, but of "John Brown's Body."

A much more colorful British encounter with the "Battle Hymn" happened in 1864 to George Augustus Sala. Sala was an artist, travel writer, journalist, associate of Charles Dickens, frequent contributor to the *London Daily Telegraph*, and author of Victorian erotica. In 1865, he published *My Diary in America*, a memoir of the year he spent traveling the United States during the Civil War. He knew Julia's oldest brother, Samuel Ward, and wrote to him in November 1864 with a special request. The letter captures Sala's wit. He wanted his friend to know how much he admired his sister's "magnificent war-lyric." American reviewers might call him a "malignant penny a liner" or a "bloated miscreant" but that did not dim his affection for the "Battle Hymn." He marveled at "the impression made by those really Thor-Hammer lines on my rhinoceros-hided soul." "I think the doctrine it strives to inculcate, exceedingly mischievous; and I *do* believe that could Christ come across the sea to the Shenandoah Valley, He would weep tears of blood at the aspect of a conflict which seems to be carried on more by the Devils of the Pit than by human beings." But as a poem, "its sonorous ring and sounding march, its wonderful English, its almost inimitable construction have made me very enthusiastic and very envious."[9]

In *My Diary in America*, Sala featured Howe and her "Battle Hymn" in the context of explaining the North's justification for war. Many Northerners insisted to him that they aimed not primarily at subjugation of the South and reunification but at emancipation, "a crusade in favour of human freedom." And nothing captured that animating spirit better than Howe's poem. He called it "the Confession of Faith of the North," and found its power undeniable. "I have heard it sung to the familiar antislavery air of 'John Brown,' by a Massachusetts regiment twelve hundred strong, and the effect under those circumstances was almost inconceivably fine. You must excuse the seemingly blasphemous 'vigour' of some of the expressions. Those expressions are accounted utterances of genuine and heartfelt piety in New England, where there yet dwell descendants of Captain Hew-Agag-in-pieces-before-the-Lord, and Lieutenant Bind-their-Kings-in-chains-and-their-Nobles-with-links-of-iron, and where children are still christened with long-winded scriptural appellations, recalling 'If Christ-had-not-been-born-thou-would'st-have-been-damned-Barebones.'"[10] Sala had no doubt the spirit of Cromwell and the Puritan revolution marched on in the army of the North.

Sala returned to the "Battle Hymn" thirty years later in his two-volume memoir, *Things I Have Seen and People I Have Known*. This time he wrote with less levity and more reverence. Many Union soldiers had fought "for conscience' sake," he granted, "and would have regarded the cause of emancipation of the negro as a kind of Holy War. These, the worthy descendants of the old Puritans, were practically the leaven that gave life and vigour to the whole Federal army." In the spirit of the ancestors, "it was reserved for a New England lady—Mrs. Julia Ward Howe—to adapt to the hackneyed tune of 'John Brown' words of burning and commanding eloquence. Of this thrilling *grida di guerra* [battle cry] I remember just two stanzas." Here followed Sala's mostly accurate quotations of the first and last verses. "These lines may strike the fastidious or the cynical as stilted, if not slightly irreverent," he conceded; "but by those who have heard, as I have, Mrs. Julia Ward Howe's verses sung in unison, with a thunderous refrain of 'Glory, Glory, Hallelujah!' by a Massachusetts regiment on the march, two thousand strong, the effect on the imagination, both of the soldiers and the spectators, by this sonorous chant may be readily imagined."[11]

Whatever Kipling, Tennyson, and Sala made of the "Battle Hymn" and its meaning, Howe's poem took an unexpected leftward turn in the 1880s when British socialists adopted the "Battle Hymn" as one of their movement's anthems, either in whole or in part, or as the rhythm of other words meant to echo the original. The radical English periodical *To-Day* printed the "Battle Hymn" in 1885 along with a footnote about Howe's 1871 Detroit lecture in which she had explained the poem's birth.[12] In the magazine's first issue in January 1884, the editors promised that their new magazine would "point to organisation as the only beacon light that steadily shines before us." Only "a scientific system of collective and constructive Socialism," they explained, "can by any possibility save us" from the impending anarchy of unrestrained competition.[13] The editors absorbed the "Battle Hymn" into this campaign for economic transformation.

William Morris, the visionary utopian socialist who admired the guild system of medieval England, modeled his poem "The March of the Workers" (1885) on Howe's original. The opening lines ask, "What is this the sound and rumour? What is this that all men hear?" And the chorus answers, "'Tis the people marching on!"[14] The poem appeared in *The Commonweal* in February 1885 and then in *Chants for Socialists*, a penny pamphlet published by the Socialist League the same year. In 1903, an editor included stanzas from Morris's hymn in her *Essex House Song Book*, a beautiful volume, rendered in a black and red calligraphic font, that gave voice to the movement's ideals. She combined four of Morris's verses with two of Howe's from the "Battle Hymn of the Republic," thinking that Howe's lines had actually been written by a socialist poet from Bristol and claiming that that was how "our boys in East London used to sing" it.[15]

Matching the socialists' zeal, British churches adopted the "Battle Hymn" for public worship. Over a twenty-five-year period, Howe's anthem gradually made its way from theologically more radical to more mainstream publications, ending up in the very proper Anglican hymnal during World War I. In 1891 three verses appeared at the end of *Christian Hymns*, edited by Stopford A. Brooke, pastor of Bedford Chapel, Blooms-bury.[16] Reverend Brooke included the "Battle Hymn" among his selection of Unitarian liturgies and hymns. In a note at the back, he explained his reasoning: "These three verses are a part of 'The Battle Hymn of the Republic' made during the great struggle in America. The other two verses are not, as the three given are, capable of being spiritualized into a hymn of the universal war waged between Good and Evil. But that the whole of this fine poem may be known, and because the war was itself part of the world's war against evil, I place here the second and third verses."[17] He added the two stanzas to his editorial note, making the poem complete. As much as any visionary American, Brooke treated the "Battle Hymn" as an anthem for "the universal war" and the triumph of good and handled the Civil War as but one phase in the "world's war against evil." Brooke's enthusiasm for the "Battle Hymn" serves as a reminder that American religious nationalism was not only being manufactured by Americans themselves but often by true believers abroad who proved eager to extol the American mission, at times in even more extravagant terms than Americans themselves. That tendency continued unabated into the 1890s.

Howe's death in 1910 brought the poet and her poem before the British public once more. The London *Times* carried an obituary accompanied by a longer story about her life and association with the Civil War.[18] "Her fame," the *Times* reflected, "rests chiefly on 'The Battle Hymn of the Republic,' written for the Northern armies in 1864 [*sic*] during the crisis of the American Civil War. It is emphatically a hymn, full of the fervour of religious enthusiasm. On its appearance it immediately became the national anthem of the North. We quote the following stanzas of this historic poem:—" and then followed verses one, two, five, and the paper's attempt at deciphering the unpublished sixth verse:

> He is coming like the glory of the morning on the wave;
> He is wisdom to the mighty, He is succor to the brave;
> So the world shall be His footstool, and the soul of Time His slave:
> Our God is marching on.

The *Times'* publication, presumably copied from Howe's *Reminiscences*, may have been the first time the rejected verse appeared in print outside of that book. The *Times* reported the "Battle Hymn" "never lost its hold on the American people, and when the Spanish-American War broke out it was heard once again on all sides." The paper also had the bad manners to point out (correctly) that Howe had been an "expansionist" who "warmly advocated the annexation of San Domingo to the United States as long ago as the early 'seventies.'" It then cited remarks by a friend of Howe's that "we were all expansionists in those early days. . . . What long, frightful years of suffering and bloodshed would have been saved to unhappy Cuba if we had succeeded." That friend had been Henry Brown Blackwell, coeditor with Howe of the *Woman's Journal*, who had joined Julia and Samuel in the Samana Bay Company's civilizing efforts in Santo Domingo in the early 1870s.[19]

Britain's declaration of war on August 4, 1914, revealed how easily exportable the "Battle Hymn of the Republic" had become in the age of empire. The British added Howe's poem to their own religious nationalism and did so in ways beyond anything Kipling had gestured toward two decades earlier. British composers, arrangers, and choristers picked up the "Battle Hymn" immediately and have yet to put it down. Starting in 1915, several versions of the "Battle Hymn" appeared, sold in numerous arrangements, set to various tunes, and available as sheet music or in songbooks. Among the most notable were the choral arranger Martin Shaw's popular version of the words set to his own tune and another offered by the organist and composer Henry Walford Davies.[20]

Davies edited a wartime hymnbook for the Church of England's Society for Promoting Christian Knowledge (SPCK). The society published *In Hoc Signo: Hymns of War and Peace* in 1915.[21] Davies served as organist at the Temple Church, London, and later in the war effort as music director for the Royal Air Force. His SPCK collection included American Civil War texts by John Greenleaf Whittier, Oliver Wendell Holmes, James Russell Lowell, and Howe. The Latin title of this hymnbook means "in this sign," the "sign" being the cross on the front cover, the sign in which Britain would be victorious. This phrase originated in accounts of the emperor Constantine's vision of the cross of Christ before the Battle of Milvian Bridge in the fourth century. The words, therefore, connected wartime Britain to one of the most powerful evocations of Christendom and holy war in the history of the West. The choice was not accidental. Near the end appeared the five verses of the "Battle Hymn," though without the "Glory, hallelujah" chorus. With the exception of a few quirks in the text—"fatal lighting" for "fateful lightning"—and changes in punctuation, this is Howe's published version from 1862. The tune was left anonymous, but it was Davies's own "Vision." Within the Great War's first year, the Church of England had mobilized Howe's poem to help conquer the Kaiser under the sign of the cross.

The "Battle Hymn" flourished in England early in the war thanks in large part to the English choral composer and arranger Martin Shaw. Shaw wrote a new melody and arrangement for the "Battle Hymn" set for soloist or unison chorus. It was published in December 1915 in the music magazine *The Treasury*. On the first page, under the poem, the sheet music carried a note about Julia Ward Howe's visit to Washington, DC, in 1861. The publisher promoted these verses as "so marvelously suitable to the present war, that one would like to think of our own brave lads marching with these noble words on their lips, and they might well be sung at home[,] in church and elsewhere." Shaw's new version, the publisher promised, "will be acknowledged as a fine attempt to grip the military ardour and the fervent piety of the words."[22] Shaw's decision to include the sixth stanza, available to the public only since Howe published her *Reminiscences*, helped popularize a verse that some in England would soon honor as their favorite and prove reluctant to let go of.

Londoners who happened to be near Trafalgar on the right days in the spring and summer of 1916 would have heard Shaw's arrangement sung in the city's streets. Shaw taught his new setting to a volunteer choir he trained for a series of wartime processions in central London. The Church League for Women's Suffrage organized three "Processions of Prayer and Intercession Services" held in 1916. Their militant piety followed the same script each month. An afternoon "procession of prayer" moved from the sanctuary of St. Martin-in-the-Fields into Trafalgar and then to Hyde Park. After a service of dedication led by the vicar, clergy in their vestments led the procession of laity and choir with the cross at their head and a hand-lettered banner in their midst that said, "To Witness for God in Time of War." Pausing in Trafalgar, they recited the Lord's Prayer. As they marched they sang hymns, among them Shaw's version of the "Battle Hymn." They called on the nation to repent. "We were not a righteous nation and the one hope for us was to come back to God," they confessed.[23] After women won the vote in 1918, the Church League for Women's Suffrage reorganized itself as the League of the Church Militant.

Shaw's setting of the "Battle Hymn" reached a much wider audience when patriots in the arts community publicized the anthem as part of an effort to sustain Britain's wartime religious nationalism after the armistice. Shaw's "Battle Hymn," again with six verses, appeared in volume 1 of *The Motherland Song Book*, produced by a new organization calling itself the League of Arts for National and Civic Ceremony. Members included Geoffrey and Martin Shaw, the composers Charles Villiers Stanford and Edward Elgar, and the Christian apologist G. K. Chesterton.[24] The league sought to propel the fusion of war, nation, and religion into the postwar era of reform. The second volume, also published in 1919, was coedited by Martin Shaw, the composer Ralph Vaughn Williams, and Geoffrey Shaw, Martin's brother, who had organized the music for the church processions in 1916. Each song in the *Motherland* collection was also available separately as sheet music.[25]

The League of Arts launched its nationwide movement on the day Germany signed the armistice in November 1918. The organization did not waste a moment. Its statement of objectives explained its broad vision: "To give adequate expression to our national joys, sorrows, and aspirations; to bring art and public life into contact; to preserve national and civic tradition; to bring every individual, as far as possible, into the creative life of the community; to assert that spiritual glory is the chief test of a nation's greatness; to forge bonds of unity through a common purpose and endeavours; and to symbolize that unity in public celebrations; to develop a religious sense of nationality and citizenship." The group's intention to cultivate "a religious sense of nationality and citizenship" matched the Civil War–era aspirations of Henry Bellows and other political preachers to make their nation sacred. To the league, war provided an impetus to the formation of religious nationalism, an opportunity not to be wasted. According to one contemporary report, "The league provides musical and dramatic performances, concerts, exhibitions of pictures, and of arts and crafts, and can provide lecturers on music, painting, architecture, and the history and meaning of art, at reasonable fees. It is in a position to give advice and help to those seeking to spread good art in their own neighbourhood."[26] The League of Arts also published "a book on the management of public processions" with advice for local communities about suitable flags, decorations, costumes, music, and dancing.[27]

Evidently, every hamlet in England was meant to benefit from the league's help in the promotion and management of this vaguely "religious" nationalism. That might mean popularizing folk songs and sea shanties, or other real and pseudo-"heritage" for the sake of national unity and fortitude, but it also meant deploying the "Battle Hymn." An article entitled "Art and Patriotism" in the London *Times* reported on the league's upcoming inaugural Sunday concert.[28] Available for such events were 25,000 copies of the first edition of volume 1 of *The Motherland Song Book*. In 1919 the League of Arts also published a fifth volume in their series, *The League of Nations Song Book*, and it, too, included the "Battle Hymn," bringing aspirations for an internationalist anthem for a global civil religion that much closer to reality.[29]

Prior to and independent of any military alliance between Britain and the United States, the "Battle Hymn" enjoyed a remarkable second career in the United Kingdom. In this role, it inspired troops and reassured the public about their war's righteousness. Less surprisingly, Britain used the hymn to acknowledge and honor its American partner once the United States entered the war in April 1917, while Americans in London used it to seal the two allies' relationship in public displays of fraternal bonds of affection. On April 20, St. Paul's Cathedral in London held the largest of the services honoring the nascent transatlantic alliance. Its organizer was none other than Walter Hines Page, Howe's former editor at Houghton Mifflin and now Woodrow Wilson's ambassador to the Court of St. James. Thousands lined London's streets on what was promoted as "America Day" and waved Old Glory and the Union Jack to greet the king and queen in royal procession, a parade that included twenty elderly veterans of the American Civil War.[30]

Known as the "American Dedicatory Service," the ceremony at St. Paul's gathered a capacity congregation of 3,500, including the king and queen, other members of the royal family, former Liberal prime minister H. H. Asquith, the archbishop of Canterbury, and the diplomatic corps. Two weeks after the service, an excited Ambassador Page wrote from the American Embassy in London to Frank N. Doubleday, his friend and publishing partner since 1900. He boasted how he had scrambled after Congress's declaration of war on Good Friday to coordinate and contain the enthusiasm of some "twenty American organizations" in London eager to celebrate the alliance. "I got representatives of 'em all together," he boasted, "and proposed that we hold our tongues till we'd won the war—then we can take London." In place of patriotism run amok, he arranged a single program, the dedicatory service at St. Paul's. There in the cathedral, "the Stars and Stripes hung before the altar," he noted, and "a double brass band played the Star Spangled Banner and the Battle Hymn of the Republic." "If you had published a shilling edition of the words of the Star-Spangled Banner and the Battle Hymn," he claimed, "you could have sent a cargo of 'em here and sold them."[31]

As planned, the St. Paul congregation and choir sang "O God, Our Help in Ages Past" and the "Battle Hymn." The *Musical Times* called the singing "very impressive."[32] The "Battle Hymn," accompanied by the band of the Royal Horse Guards, immediately preceded the sermon by Charles Henry Brent, the Canadian-born American Episcopal bishop of the Philippines since 1902. In that post, he had worked closely with the preparedness leader Leonard Wood and with John J. Pershing. Brent's conception of the religious calling of the nation suited him well for this supreme moment of righteous nationalism. In 1904 he had confided to his diary, "If one could only make that clear—the sacred character of the nation *as* a nation, not because the Church says so, not because the church is in the nation, but because *the nation is a divine creation*."[33] The bishop's scripture reading for the St. Paul service came from Isaiah 61:1–9, but once he ascended the pulpit flanked by the Union Jack and the Stars and Stripes he preached from the account of Judas Maccabeus in the Apocrypha and the words "victory is God's." Ambassador Page called Brent's performance "a red-hot American sermon."[34]

Brent had confirmed General Pershing in the Episcopal Church and at Pershing's invitation became chaplain to the American Expeditionary Force's headquarters in France. An advocate of ecumenism and the unity of Christendom, the bishop later became one of the founders of the World Council of Churches and made the cover of *Time* magazine in 1927. After the benediction, the service at St. Paul's closed with "The Star-Spangled Banner" and "God Save the King." In September 1917, in a devotional book for Lenten observance, Bishop Brent wrote that the first line of the "Battle Hymn" "is the watchword for our times."[35] The Lord's glory was still coming fifty years after Appomattox.

A number of locals managed to make it to St. Paul's for the service. The best-selling English novelist and playwright Hall Caine, whom Howe had known in Rome on her last winter there in 1898, actively promoted

US intervention in the European war and now rejoiced in the "national marriage" between Great Britain and the United States. In a dispatch for the American press on this occasion, he depicted the war in purely Wilsonian terms. In sentiments that could have been lifted straight out of the president's war message on April 2, Caine portrayed the United States as the exceptional nation that had entered the war without material motives, selfish ambition, or base pride. America intervened with "high humanity, splendid self-sacrifice and complete disinterestedness . . . with nothing to gain and everything to lose." "It was not for nothing that the flags of Great Britain and America hung side by side under the chancel arch on Friday morning. At one moment, the sun shot through the windows of the great dome and lit them up with a heavenly radiance. Was it only the exaltation of the moment that made us think the invisible powers were giving us a sign that in the union of nations which those emblems stood for lay surest the hope of the day when men will beat their swords into ploughshares and know war no more?"[36] Constantine had been given his sign of conquest; America and the Allies now had theirs under the dome of St. Paul's.

Just as many Americans in 1898 had found singing the "Battle Hymn" to be evidence of national unification through war, some now saw the "Battle Hymn" as proof of *international* unification. The United States had been reunified for the sake of the nation's calling in history, and now America and Britain joined hands in an expanding mission. The editor of the *London Daily News*, who was also present at St. Paul's, later said, "It seemed to those of us who were privileged to hear the Battle Hymn of the Republic sung within the walls of St. Paul's Cathedral that the ancient feud could never again be revived, and that the two people, so tragically estranged in the past by despotic folly, were at last free to take up the performance of that task to which their common ancestry and common ideals so obviously predestined them."[37]

The American press noticed all the flattering attention Britain lavished on the "Battle Hymn." In an article for the *Deseret News* (Salt Lake City) Edward Marshall noted that the "Battle Hymn," "embodying as it does, the moral purpose which, from the first, has inspired the Allied peoples in this world conflict, has been quoted again and again in England since the beginning of the struggle." The former muckraker had worked for Hearst's *New York Journal*, had known Stephen Crane in the Spanish-American War, and had lost a leg serving with Teddy Roosevelt's Rough Riders. He promoted American interests abroad by writing a weekly column for the London *Sunday Times*. He praised Walford Davies's new setting of Howe's anthem. Thanks to this organist, he wrote, "the 'Battle Hymn' is now more frequently sung than any other at the famous old church which is so closely associated with the Knights Templar who fought in the Crusades, and where the bones of so many of them lie. Among the many occasions upon which it has been rendered was at the impressive memorial service which was held at the Temple Church by the City of London Schoolboys in honor of their comrades who have fallen in the war." An American major said of the new tune and Temple Church: "It is the more appropriate because all of us on the Allied side regard this war as a crusade, because we are inspired by the same idea that those old fellows [the crusaders] had. The words of the Battle Hymn express it: 'As he died to make men holy, / let us die to make me free, / While God is marching on!' "[38]

To this day, St. Paul uses the "Battle Hymn" in public worship. Every year, the cathedral features it in its Thanksgiving Day service for Americans living in London. Not to be outdone in the quest for Anglo-American solidarity in the Great War, however, Westminster Abbey also added the "Battle Hymn" to its own liturgy of a transnational religion. On July 4, 1918, the Dean of Westminster held a special service to celebrate America's Independence Day. The order of worship featured the playing of "The Star-Spangled Banner" and the singing of the "Battle Hymn."[39] The next year, the abbey held another memorial service, this time for the American war dead, and once more the "Battle Hymn" was sung.[40] A Boston publisher who was present recalled his exhilaration upon hearing the congregation sing the "Battle Hymn": "The circumstances naturally called forth every spark of patriotic fervor, and no American could have listened to the singing of those marvelous words in such an environment without experiencing a thrill that rarely repeats itself in a lifetime." Only in that moment, he said, did he come to know "the flaming passion of patriotism" pulsing in Howe's words.[41]

While hobnobbing with royalty, Downing Street, and the diplomatic corps at St. Paul's and Westminster, the "Battle Hymn" also appeared in the humble wrappers of mass-marketed popular fiction in the United Kingdom and America. In 1917, the best-selling novelist Boyd Cable published his latest war story, *Grapes of Wrath*, in London and New York.[42] Boyd Cable was the pen name of Ernest Andrew Ewart, a man with a keen sense of the Anglo-American market for sensational and sentimental war stories. Ewart had been born in India in 1878, fought in the Boer War, and then moved to Australia. He became celebrated for his ability to depict war from the soldier's point of view. By 1917 he had already published the popular war novels *Between the Lines* and *Action Front*. The title *Grapes of Wrath* was immortalized years later when John Steinbeck used the same words from the "Battle Hymn of the Republic" as a book title, but unlike Steinbeck's classic, Ewart's story of the Battle of the Somme became a forgotten relic of pulp fiction. Nevertheless, the story of four friends during the "big push" in France in 1916 shows another way in which the "Battle Hymn" became useful to Britain and the United States as they forged their wartime alliance. The publisher gave a nod to Kipling when it called the new novel "as uplifting as the terrible, slow swing of the *Battle Hymn of the Republic*."[43] The "Battle Hymn" provided Ewart not only with the novel's title but also with the lens through which his American hero interprets the whole war. For good measure, he included all the verses of the "Battle Hymn," even the discarded sixth.

Laura Richards objected to the publication of the sixth verse. She wrote to the *New York Times* to express her dismay over the kind of publicity the stanza was getting. True, her mother had authorized Houghton Mifflin to publish a facsimile, and she and Maud had indeed agreed to feature it again in their 1916 biography of their mother. But these steps had been taken for historical purposes, she insisted, and the family never meant for the abandoned verse to be reattached to the "Battle Hymn" and sung and admired. Ewart/Cable's decision to include the verse "is much to be regretted," she wrote. "The stanza is a fine one, but the poem is complete without it, and in any case, I conceive, no one has a moral right to publish as the work of an author anything which that author has deliberately discarded." "My mother's judgment was final," she warned. "I feel secure that public opinion will respect it."[44]

Ewart made no effort to hide his propaganda purpose. He addressed himself to true believers in righteous war, giving them more reasons to believe what they already believed. The novel's hero strikes modern readers as improbable at best, but he won over a number of reviewers and readers. The main character, Jefferson Lee, nicknamed "Kentucky," enlists in the British army after the sinking of the *Lusitania*. He recites the "Battle Hymn of the Republic" during the Battle of the Somme in 1916 and then as he recovers from his wounds in England. Howe's poetry so inspired the young man that he returns to No Man's Land as an ambulance driver. Ewart may have imagined "Kentucky" as the grandson of a Unionist who had fought for the North, thus accounting for his love of the "Battle Hymn." But the plausibility of Ewart's characters was beside the point. No one today will confuse the novel, with characters slipping in and out of clumsy Southern dialect, with a literary masterpiece. But as evidence for how the "Battle Hymn" was taken up to fight a new war beyond America's shores and for how that redeployment seemed self-evidently true, it is invaluable.

Ewart used line after line of the "Battle Hymn" to give "Kentucky" the ability to see the war for what it really was: a vindication of America's courage despite Woodrow Wilson's erstwhile hand-wringing that a nation might be "too proud to fight"—something idealistic young Americans had always resented, Kentucky claims. He sees the coming of the Lord just as surely as any Union soldier in 1861. The same words call men to die for freedom whether along the Potomac or the Somme. It was all there again: the lightning, the sword, the vintage of God's wrath, and the onward march of truth. The trumpet would never call retreat, not now, not ever. The fiery gospel converts this son of the South to holy war. The story's didacticism pointed to an obvious moral: clear-headed, patriotic Americans, hearing the "Battle Hymn" ringing in their ears, had wanted their nation to enter the war against Germany long before April 1917 and once in the fight sought every opportunity to crush Imperial Germany's false gospel. The United States Army was still the agent of God's vengeance. His vineyard now included the British Isles and Europe. A wide-ranging review in the *New York Times* praised Ewart's gifts as a writer and the *Grapes of Wrath* as a compelling narrative of the war told from the inside. The reviewer seemed captivated by Kentucky's determination to return to the front. In this way, "the great American hymn give[s] title and summing up to this picture of the army of one of our allies, a picture etched with steel in lines of fire and blood and heroism unsurpassed. 'Grapes of Wrath' is indeed a memorable book."[45]

The novel turned out to be anything but memorable. Nevertheless, it showed that the "Battle Hymn of the Republic"—imported by British socialists, sung by congregations, and mobilized for the British war effort after 1914—had now been reexported to America via popular fiction, affirming the nation's righteousness. This cycle of international exchange raises the question of whether the version of the "Battle Hymn" that returned to the United States in 1917 was the same "Battle Hymn" that England had admired since the 1860s. The words were the same, of course, aside from the addition of the sixth verse, but were the sentiments indeed the same once they were sung by different people, in a different place, under different circumstances, and for a different purpose? Could Americans ever sing the same "Battle Hymn" once it had been sung in St. Paul's and Westminster Abbey, once it had reportedly inspired British troops along the Somme? The "Battle Hymn" of 1917 came back draped in layers of experience it had never worn before.

Clearly, the "Battle Hymn" had been made "international" in the narrow sense that Howe's words were being applied more literally and directly than ever before to another nation and its war aims. But in a wider sense, once American military victory played so critical a role in Allied victory, the "international" "Battle Hymn" returned to the United States in a condition more likely to be *nationalized* than ever before. The First World War gave Americans a second "Battle Hymn." While it was still a song of apocalyptic vengeance and victory, it was now given momentum as a song of national pride, feeding Americans' picture of themselves as a warrior people indispensable to campaigns waged on the right side of history.

Not every American was smitten with Howe and the "Battle Hymn," of course. In the first spring of the Great War, a young American poet and philosophy student at Oxford described a few of the eccentric people he had met there. The St. Louis native and Harvard graduate stayed busy at Merton College with his dissertation but not too busy for dinner parties. "Besides Belgians," he wrote to his cousin, "there is a very pretty Miss Cobb . . . whose mother was a Bostonian (I don't know what her name was); the mother is an odd fluttering person who is evidently looking out for her daughter, and lays compliments very thick (I know this because I have seen her laying them on to other people); she never talks to me for five minutes without bringing out Julia Ward Howe, whom she knew in Boston, and evidently considers a very illustrious person.—A very tiresome person, I should say, for all the anecdotes about her end by making her recite the 'Battle Hymn of the Republic.' "[46] Despite his Unitarian New England roots, the young T. S. Eliot found no aura of sacredness around Howe or her poem. Soon, April would be the cruelest month in a world where death had undone so many.

THE VALOR OF RIGHTEOUSNESS

God's chosen people did not need to wait for the British to show them how to deploy their own "Battle Hymn" during the Great War. Americans already in the habit of applying the "Battle Hymn" to widening spheres of service never hesitated to take up Howe's anthem for a new crusade. It proved useful to anyone eager to wage a war for righteousness. The first question it helped Americans answer after 1914 was whether their nation was ready for war and truly called to fight the German menace. Between August 1914 and US intervention in April 1917, Howe's poem featured prominently in the campaign for national preparedness. At the forefront of that movement stood former Republican president and Progressive Party candidate Theodore Roosevelt. His son, Theodore Roosevelt Jr. recalled later that his "father and mother believed in robust righteousness. In the stories and poems that they read us they always bore this in mind. *Pilgrim's Progress* and *The Battle Hymn of the Republic* we knew when we were very young."[1]

As the campaign for national preparedness heated up in 1916, Roosevelt published *Fear God and Take Your Own Part*, a popular call for

American military and moral armament. He included all five stanzas of the "Battle Hymn" at the front of the book and dedicated it "to the memory of Julia Ward Howe because in the vital matters fundamentally affecting the life of the Republic, she was as good a citizen of the Republic as Washington and Lincoln themselves." Roosevelt emphasized the demands of what he called national and international righteousness, enlisting his friend Howe in that sacred cause: "She preached righteousness and she practiced righteousness. She sought the peace that comes as the handmaiden of well doing. She preached that stern and lofty courage of soul which shrinks neither from war nor from any other form of suffering and hardship and danger if it is only thereby that justice can be served. She embodied that trait more essential than any other in the make-up of the men and women of the Republic—the valor of righteousness."[2] Westminster Abbey knew precisely which hymn to include in a memorial service for Roosevelt in February 1919.[3]

Ever-faithful Maud, Laura, and Florence helped their late mother's "Battle Hymn" attain new levels of influence during the First World War. They mobilized the "Battle Hymn" for the preparedness campaign and then dressed it in khaki for service on the western front. In 1916 Maud and Laura (with the assistance of Florence) published a two-volume biography of their mother. It won the Pulitzer Prize for biography in 1917, the first year the awards were given. The work of familial piety reads much like a nineteenth-century "life and letters," filled with extracts from family correspondence and Howe's redacted diaries, woven together with sparse narrative. When it came to the "Battle Hymn," the biography offered no surprises. It navigated safely among the various versions Howe had published. The daughters included the same facsimile of the first draft prepared by Houghton Mifflin from Charlotte Whipple's copy in 1899. Nicholas Murray Butler, president of Columbia University, who wrote on behalf of the Pulitzer committee, commended the work as the "best biography teaching patriotic and unselfish services to the people, illustrated by an eminent example."[4] While the sisters may not have intended their biography to be a direct contribution to national preparedness or to the push for intervention, Butler surely had Wilson's war of service in view. Howe had been confirmed as a national monument.

Florence also launched a solo book in 1916 dedicated to the "Battle Hymn." *The Story of the Battle Hymn of the Republic* came out from

Harper in November, the month of Wilson's reelection and five months before US intervention in the war. At the time, Florence was best known for her popular books on etiquette. In this book, she tried to account for why her mother's poem had proven so durable since the 1860s. Making a point similar to Teddy Roosevelt's in 1908, she emphasized the breadth of vision of the "Battle Hymn," which reached beyond the Civil War. "Although written in the midst of the greatest civil war that was ever fought and won," she said, "there is no word of North or South, no appeal to local pride or patriotism, no word of sectional strife or bitterness. The God to whom appeal is made is the God of freedom. The enemy to be overcome, the serpent who is to be crushed beneath the heel of the hero, is slavery."[5] National consolidation had been a precondition of victory over Spain in 1898, and that unity endured under the banner of the "Battle Hymn."

Finding the flattery still irresistible, Florence praised Rudyard Kipling again for his prescient understanding of the widest meaning of the "Battle Hymn," captured in the "happy ending" version of *The Light That Failed*: "In our war lyric we seem to hear an echo of the old cry, 'The sword of the Lord and of Gideon.' Yet we did not fully recognize its tremendous power until Kipling christened it *'The terrible Battle Hymn of the Republic.'*" Significantly, Florence claimed in the midst of another, greater war that the full meaning of the "Battle Hymn" had only gradually unfolded in the course of time and experience and that it had taken a British subject to teach America its largest truths.[6]

Florence also made sure the connection between the "Battle Hymn" and the Great War would be unmissable to her readers. She reprinted Roosevelt's heartfelt tribute to her mother from *Fear God and Take Your Own Part*. She also welcomed the YMCA's distribution of the "Battle Hymn" as a leaflet among the British soldiers and claimed that reception of the hymn in England "shows us the essential unity of the two great branches of the Anglo-Saxon race."[7] In some ways, this was a self-fulfilling prophecy. The YMCA's printing of the "Battle Hymn" was arranged early in 1916 by the suffragist Lady Julia C. Chance. "I distributed many thousands of these cards," she boasted to the editors of *Country Life*, and added as a favor that she had more copies on hand and "should be glad to let anyone have them who would undertake to get them into the hands of the troops."[8] The YMCA card carried an explanation of the hymn's origin: "This magnificent 'Battle Hymn of the Republic' was written in 1861 by a famous American lady, Mrs. Julia Ward Howe, for the Army of the Northern States of America which were then engaged in a 'Holy War' to rid the South of slavery and to preserve the Union of the States. It is said to have done more to awaken the spirit of patriotism and to have inspired more deeds of heroism than any other event of the American Civil War."[9] Evidently, Lady Chance and the YMCA hoped the "Battle Hymn" would do the same for British soldiers in 1916. Walter Hines Page's jest that he could have sold thousands of cards printed with the "Battle Hymn" in London in April 1917 may have hit close to the mark to what some were already doing free of charge.

On April 3, 1917, the day following President Woodrow Wilson's address to Congress seeking a declaration of war, the *New York Times* celebrated intervention by printing all five verses of the "Battle Hymn" on its editorial page.[10] It did so without comment. When a grateful Maud Howe Elliott saw the poem, she wrote immediately to the *Times*. She thanked the paper for publishing her mother's hymn on "this great day." "Once more," she said, the nation has been "revealed to the world as the champion of liberty." With the appearance of the "Battle Hymn" in the press, she continued, "I feel that my mother has had her part in the triumph of the cause [of US intervention] for which your paper has fought so valiantly all these long and weary months. . . . It would seem fitting that the 'Battle-Hymn' should be sung in our churches next Sunday." Her mother's confidence that God "has sounded forth the trumpet that shall never call retreat" possessed more "significance" at this historic moment than ever before. But then, her mood darkening, Maud warned, "Who hears that trumpet call and does not leap to answer it is no patriot. This world crisis is the crucial moment in our history. Democracy is on trial for its life. Liberty is at stake. Civilization itself is menaced."[11]

At the end of 1917, Laura did her part with a collection of her war poems dedicated to her son serving in France.[12] The title page identified her as a member of the Vigilantes. The civilian Vigilantes relied on the talents of over 400 writers, artists, and publicists for the American war effort. Members included the *Outlook* editor Lyman Abbott, the advertising pioneer Bruce Barton, the painter James Montgomery Flagg, the former president Theodore Roosevelt, the muckraker Ida Tarbell, and the Hoosier novelist Booth Tarkington. The organization grew out of a meeting of preparedness advocates in November 1916 who dedicated themselves to

Figure 17. Mrs. Maud Howe Elliott. *Chicago Daily News*, November 1, 1916.
Copyright: Chicago Historical Society. Courtesy of Chicago History Museum.

"rousing the spiritual forces of the country in the service of the country."
To that end, the syndicate aimed at mobilizing public opinion. Vigilantes
worked closely with government agencies such as George Creel's Committee of Public Information and with the YMCA, the Boy Scouts, the
National Security League, and the US Chamber of Commerce. Members

promoted "ideal Americanism," universal military training, and fund-raising for Liberty Loans and the Red Cross.[13]

Laura, like Maud, found the "Battle Hymn" on her mind in the heady days following Congress's declaration of war. In a dedicatory poem dated

Figure 18. Laura E. Richards, n.d.
Courtesy of Colby College Special Collections.

May 27, 1917—entitled "To My Brother and Sisters (On hearing the Battle Hymn of the Republic sung by a great company)"—she repeated her mother's images of the sounding trumpet and the glory of the Lord:

Our mother's words, the country through,
    By young and old are sung today;
Like stars, they light the war's wild night,
    Like flowers, they strew the world's dim way.

And thankful hearts her children lift,
    To hear her trumpet sounding clear;
Sweet-silver as the silver voice
    Which now our ears alone may hear.

Oh! may the land she held so dear
    Grow day by day more valiant-wise,
Tune to her note its bugle clear,
    And read God's glory through her eyes.

And, dear ones, as we follow, too,
    Along the path she leaves so bright,
Some bud of service may we strew,
    Let fall some spark of helpful light![14]

Laura urged her siblings, and through them the nation, to listen to their mother's "silver voice," to heed her summons to the path of service, to "read God's glory through her eyes." Seeing the glory of the Lord in this war became an act of faith and patriotism for Laura and her sisters. American intervention meant service to humanity, an enduring peace, and an end to tyranny. As Maud told the *Times*, this was a war for democracy, liberty, and civilization.

Howe's daughters continued to memorialize the poem well after US military intervention in 1917. For them, the Great War had become a war of fulfillment every bit as much as the Civil War and the war with Spain. Florence told the *New York Times* in July 1918 that while the crusade to abolish slavery had triumphed, the rest of humanity still awaited its own emancipation. The work of *Uncle Tom's Cabin* was done, she said, but the work of the "Battle Hymn" "still inspires men and women to do and dare."[15] In her memoirs published the same year, Florence reflected on the "Battle Hymn." She rejoiced that a hymn that long ago inspired

Union troops on the battlefields of Virginia now inspired the world: "In every hour of national crisis, whenever our country is in danger, those words flame up anew in the hearts of men." Her mother's ancestry combined the Puritan of the seventeenth century and the Revolutionary of the eighteenth. And that spirit marched on in Europe. "Nor are [the poem's words] for our country only. In this present war they have been sung with wonderful effect under the great dome of old St. Paul's in London as well as at the battle-front. For the 'Battle Hymn of the Republic,' terrible as it is, is a Christian song. No one could have written it who was not familiar with the language and imagery of the Bible, Old Testament as well as New. It was the daughter of Samuel Ward, Puritan, who wrote, 'He is trampling out the vintage where the grapes of wrath are stored.' But it was the wife of the old Revolutionist [Samuel Gridley Howe], the man whose life had been one long battle in behalf of his fellow-men, who wrote, 'He has sounded forth the trumpet that shall never call retreat.' "[16]

Launching that crusade in 1917, the United States still did not have an official national anthem to unite its people and inspire its troops. The push to make the "Battle Hymn" the national anthem gained new momentum after US intervention. One woman wrote to the *New York Times* after reading about a Russian immigrant who, reacting to news of the democratic Russian Revolution in March 1917, said, "I thought first of all of that line in your hymn 'Mine eyes have seen the glory of the coming of the Lord.' " The Lord's coming in glory accounted for democracy's supposed triumph in czarist Russia. This anecdote came from the current issue of the *Atlantic Monthly*. The award-winning short-story writer Margaret Prescott Montague published an essay she called "Good Friday, 1917," celebrating America's entry into the war as a moment akin to evangelical conversion. Congress had indeed voted for war in the early hours of Good Friday, and the redemptive connection proved too tempting for a number of authors like Montague. The nation would be "born again" by this supreme act of self-sacrifice on behalf of the peoples at war. Promises of the new birth were as prominent here as they had been in William Henry Channing's sermons at All Souls in 1861. "These are perhaps the most momentous times," Montague claimed, "the most pregnant and far-reaching, that have been vouchsafed to humanity since the coming of Christ." Montague pressed the parallel as far as imaginable: "And we who, on Good Friday, have gone to war, may well reflect deeply that the Christian ideals for which we fight, and the Resurrection of Easter, were born, not out of peace and comfort and ease, but of Gethsemane, Golgotha, and the Crucifixion." In such a holy war, the American flag itself became sacramental—"Our Stars and Stripes become 'an outward and visible sign of an inward and spiritual grace.' "[17]

Inspired by this essay and its fusion of politics and religion, of war and redemption, the writer to the *Times* thought she had an obvious solution to a national dilemma. "Why is not the 'Battle-Hymn of the Republic' our national hymn?" she asked. "It is easily sung, to a good and distinctive tune. It expresses fitly our deepest feelings; it recognizes our dependence on the divine source of life. It seems the most foolish and impossible thing to obtain a national hymn written to order. Why not use this one that we have?"[18] These words echoed the point made by Thomas Macaulay, Brander Matthews, and Theodore Roosevelt.

Would honoring the "Battle Hymn of the Republic" as the national anthem capture its real power and transcendence? Lyman Abbott, editor of the *Outlook* and like Laura a member of the Vigilantes, thought it would. The aging Social Gospeler, who habitually spoke of the Great War in redemptive terms, promoted Howe's poem as "an international battle hymn."[19] He found himself inspired by a meeting in Hampton, Virginia, in March 1917—before US intervention—that opened with "Dixie" and closed with the "Battle Hymn." Taking up a point made by Teddy Roosevelt in 1908 and Florence in 1916, he observed that Howe's poem included no language to connect it exclusively to the Civil War. That fortunate silence brought an opportunity not only for America but for the world: "This battle hymn is not merely for our Republic; it is for all republics. It would be as appropriate to-day as a national hymn for such democratic nations as Russia, France, England, Belgium, or Italy as for the United States. It is an international hymn of liberty."

Abbott convinced himself that Howe's poem transcended not only all political boundaries but all theological ones as well. It was national, international, and ecumenical: "It is pervaded by a religious spirit, but is wholly free from sectarian or theological phraseology. It is equally fitted to express the spiritual faith of Roman Catholic and Protestant, Jew and Christian, conservative and liberal, and is as beautiful in its poetic form as it is inspiring in its elevated and catholic spirit." He praised the good efforts of the American Rights League to make the "Battle Hymn" cheap, convenient, and available in bulk. He urged "clubs, camps, churches, and the managers of patriotic meetings everywhere throughout the country" to take advantage of the bargain. This was not an unbiased endorsement. Abbott was a member of the American Rights League, an organization founded in New York in 1915 to promote US intervention in the war after Germany sank the *Lusitania*. "I should be very glad if the facts here stated might come to the attention of Canadian, Australian, and English readers," Abbott concluded, "and might lead to its use by all English-speaking peoples." For good measure, Abbott ended his appeal with all five verses of the "Battle Hymn." Patriot preachers like Lyman Abbott had no doubt in 1917 that the venerable "Battle Hymn" was firmly American, Anglo-American, global, and catholic—at least on Allied terms.

The boldest claim to date for a global anthem came from the publicist Jarvis A. Wood. In 1918, Wood published a small book he called *The International Battle Hymn*. Its title was its thesis. Wood worked as an advertising executive with a Philadelphia agency with contracts with AT&T and Camel cigarettes. In his tribute, Wood aimed to inspire readers with the story of a crowd of 100,000 that had gathered in Philadelphia's Fairmount Park in October 1917 for the love of music and the love of America. Among the throng were 10,000 school children along with dozens of local choruses and glee clubs. The Community Singing Association and the Chamber of Commerce organized this "Festival of Songs and Flags." The crowd sang "America," "My Old Kentucky Home," "Old Black Joe," "Annie Laurie," "The Star-Spangled Banner," and the "Battle Hymn."[20]

Like so many before and since, Wood revered the "Battle Hymn" as a sacred text, and his book reads like a devotional tract urging readers to rededicate their lives to America. When a soloist with the Metropolitan Opera sang the "Battle Hymn" and led the crowd, "the spirit of independence, the spirit of devotion, the spirit of sacrifice, the spirit of courage took possession of all hearts. It seemed as if the Lord of Hosts might have stopped for a little at [the park's] Belmont Plateau and listened to the Glory Hallelujah as He was marching on." Emphasizing its global appeal, Wood praised Howe's poem as "the hymn adapted to all liberty-loving lands and peoples; the hymn which cheers and girds us all alike with the glorious truth that God is marching on." He then drew from the *Outlook*'s editorial, nearly paraphrasing it: "That staunch old patriot, Dr. Lyman Abbott, has recently pointed out that it contains no embalmed bitterness, no reference to 'slavery' nor 'rebellion,' no 'North,' no 'South.'" Stripped of its context, it was nonsectarian and exportable: "It acclaims no human ruler, but points to the Lord God of Hosts as He overrules in the affairs of men. It presents nothing to which Roman Catholic or Protestant, Christian or Jew cannot heartily subscribe. In fact, the Battle-Hymn cannot be confined to any one land or people." The orthodox gloss on the canonical "Battle Hymn" was a settled matter of faith by 1918.

But Woods did not leave the matter there. The expansive "Battle Hymn" was also a personal "Battle Hymn" that called for introspection. The poem was both universal and individualist, reaching to the most distant horizon and to the inner depths of the soul. Adopting one of the most durable phrases from Lincoln's Gettysburg Address, Wood hoped "the words and the meaning of the Battle-Hymn will get deep down in all hearts; in the hearts of men who fight and the women who nurse; of those who can make things to fight with and those who can produce food to fight on; of those who can give time, effort or money in order that 'government of the people by the people and for the people shall not perish from the earth.'" Getting right with America sounded a lot like getting right with Jesus, and Lincoln provided the altar call.

Lincoln's centrality to the Allied cause seemed self-evident to Wood. "I find myself quoting Lincoln, our Lincoln, humanity's Lincoln," he wrote of how he interpreted the war experience. The concentric circles radiated outward. Both Lincoln and the "Battle Hymn" belonged to all the world. Wood was sure he knew what Lincoln and the spirit of the "Battle Hymn" would do today faced with the German menace. They would march on with God. "But what about me?" he urged his readers to ask, drawing them to a moment of personal rededication. "My soul, my feet, what can *I* do to join in as God is marching on? The Battle-Hymn of the Republic is not merely patriotic—it is patriotism itself. . . . Sing it, friend, sing it. Sing it when alone; sing it when with crowds. A common need, a common hope, a common purpose, all gain in power when they are given a common voice—they are made vibrant and vital when they pour from a thousand throats in song." One can almost detect the sound of an organ quietly playing the "Battle Hymn" underneath his appeal. "So sing our great Battle-Hymn, friend, learn it and sing it, and as you sing highly resolve that the world shall be made and kept safe for democracy—safe for ourselves."

On the book's last page, Wood added a quotation from Howe to sum up his conception of the "Battle Hymn" and the duties of patriotism to which it summoned the righteous nation in this hour of need: "Our flag should go forth only on errands of justice, mercy, and so forth, and once sent forth it should not be recalled until the work where unto it has been pledged is accomplished." Wood changed the syntax and a few of the words, but these were the precise sentiments Howe had expressed to the Legion of the Medal of Honor in Brooklyn in 1900. Wood may have just read this sentence in the Howe daughters' newly released biography.[21] In this way, Wood made Lincoln, the flag, and the "Battle Hymn" sacred symbols for all of humanity. These sentiments matched Woodrow Wilson's progressive vision for America's influence in the world. Back on the Fourth of July in 1914, before the outbreak of the war in Europe, and only a week after the assassination of Archduke Franz Ferdinand in Sarajevo, President Wilson claimed to foresee the day when the Stars and Stripes would be recognized as "the flag not only of America, but of humanity."[22] Four years later, that day seemed to idealists like Woods to have arrived.

The ecumenical ideology of Americanism and the "Battle Hymn" found more literal fulfillment among prominent religious leaders in wartime. Where theology divided them, Americanism united them. Churches and preachers of all sorts mobilized the faithful for war by deploying Howe's poem between 1917 and 1919. Enthusiasts for the "Battle Hymn" ranged from the revivalist Billy Sunday to mainline Methodists to the Moody Bible Institute to the Unitarians and liberal Congregationalists to Catholics. Knowingly or not, heirs of the First and Second Great Awakenings and the Social Gospel, with a little help from Rome, made common cause when they quoted and sang Howe's anthem to explain America's role in the war and the war's role in modern history as the outworking of God's will.

Some churches needed little prompting from Maud's letter to the *New York Times* to include the "Battle Hymn" in Sunday worship. Already on Palm Sunday, April 1, the day before Wilson's war message, some preachers had appealed to the "Battle Hymn" to push for intervention. The pastor of New York's Madison Avenue Baptist Church read the full

text of the poem to his congregation as an example of women in war
and to shame the advocates of peace.[23] On April 8, Easter Day, Billy Sunday opened his tent meeting in Manhattan with a rousing sermon. Re-
cruitment stations were set up just outside his Tabernacle. Many saw the
New York campaign as the pinnacle of the revivalists' career to date.[24]
The massive purpose-built wooden Tabernacle held a capacity crowd of
20,000. The choir alone numbered 6,000. John D. Rockefeller Jr. thought
the whole spectacle of opening day "wonderful." Accompanied by two
pianists, Homer Rodeheaver led choir and audience in "The Star-Spangled
Banner" and the "Battle Hymn of the Republic." "Go to bed and sleep,
Woodrow," Sunday yelled to the Easter Day crowd. "We're coming!"[25]

Sunday and Rodeheaver had been using the "Battle Hymn" at their
mass rallies since at least 1915. At the Philadelphia evangelistic campaign
that year, 20,000 people at a Sabbath afternoon service reportedly burst
into a spontaneous rendition of the "Battle Hymn" at the end of Sunday's
sermon.[26] In Boston in 1916, the preacher did not disappoint the press
with his antics. "Demanding that Bostonians rally to the colors and do
battle with the devil," the *Springfield Republican* reported, "he picked up
a chair, climbed on his pulpit and yelled: 'Let's show the devil we don't
know how to retreat.' The choir sang 'The Battle Hymn of the Republic.' "
Eighteen thousand were on hand for the performance.[27] At the great New
York City campaign in April 1917, Sunday preached one night on the
topic "God's Grenadiers." "Our flag has never been furled," he told the
exuberant crowd, "and it is now unfurled for the liberty of the world."
"Uttering this last sentence with one foot upon his chair and one upon
the pulpit," the reporter continued, "he suddenly seized an American flag
and waved it back and forth, while his hearers cheered frantically and
finally burst out into singing: 'My County, 'tis of Thee,' followed by 'The
Battle Hymn of the Republic,' to which they kept time with a Chautauqua
salute"—a popular tradition begun at the Chautauqua meetings of wav-
ing a handkerchief in the air to add to the applause.[28]

Chaplain McCabe's Methodists continued to sing the "Battle Hymn"
in a war to make the world safe for democracy. The New York Con-
ference of the Methodist Episcopal Church, meeting at the beginning of
April 1917, as Congress debated Wilson's war declaration, "saluted the
American and French flags, gave three cheers for both, and sang 'The
Battle Hymn of the Republic.' "[29] In November 1918, when leaders and

laity in the Methodist Episcopal Church got word of Germany's defeat, they sang the stanzas of the "Battle Hymn." The Montana bishop Richard J. Cooke, a convert from Catholicism and the past president of Grant University (now the University of Tennessee, Chattanooga), exclaimed, "Glory hallelujah!" "To think that at Sedan, where Germany crushed France in 1870, the soldiers of America are crushing the oppressor of the world."[30]

Fundamentalists sang this "Glory, hallelujah" just as loudly, and not only at Billy Sunday's tent revivals. The more buttoned-up editors of the Moody Bible Institute's *Christian Workers Magazine* chose to publish all six verses of Howe's poem (a rare appearance of the sixth verse in the United States). The editors added a note at the top that matched anything Abbott, Roosevelt, Sunday, or the Howe daughters had said about the poem to date. Fundamentalists may have felt culturally alienated to a degree, but they wanted to save that culture. By the war's end, the Moody Bible Institute and the University of Chicago Divinity School traded nasty barbs about premillennialism's alleged pessimism, but the clear divides of the fundamentalist-modernist controversy of the 1920s had not yet happened. The two sides could sound a lot like each other when it came to infusing patriotism with the Christian faith and the Christian faith with patriotism. The nation's needs trumped the church's, even for leaders at Moody otherwise opposed to theological liberalism. "We reprint this great hymn of Julia Ward Howe as a patriotic duty," the editors explained in August 1917. "It is one of our national classics which many Americans think they know, but which they do not know. There is too much 'religion' in it ever to become our national hymn, but we wish it might be taught to all the boys and girls in our public schools." Simultaneously lamenting the decline of American culture and glossing over Howe's theology, the editors reassured their readers that the "Battle Hymn" could be made safe for Bible-believing Christians: "Mrs. Howe was not an evangelical Christian, her strongest sympathies being with the Unitarians, and yet as one reads the hymn, he is impressed with the fact that the Unitarianism it represents is almost more orthodox than the so-called Evangelicalism of today. A good deal must be read into it to make it a gospel song, but when that is done the singing of it stirs the soul."[31]

Unitarians, of course, as Howe's own denomination, held much clearer title to her poem. The War Work Council of the Unitarian Churches issued a series of "War Bulletins" immediately upon US intervention in 1917. Some of these were meant to be read from the pulpit, others to help raise funds for church work among the army camps, still others for food conservation and national prohibition. One of the series comprised a set of cards and leaflets "setting forth American ideals in the form of famous verse or prose." Among these were leaflets dedicated to Lincoln's second inaugural address and to the "Battle Hymn."[32] The Unitarian Association intended some of these publications for distribution at YMCA huts. The National War Work Council of the YMCA printed over a million copies of "Songs We Like to Sing," a collection of popular lyrics that included two verses of the "Battle Hymn." The YMCA also kept the "Battle Hymn" in its "Victory Songs" in 1918. These pamphlets included dozens of other patriotic, folk, and popular songs, so determining what inclusion of the "Battle Hymn of the Republic" "proves" in these instances takes some care. It at least shows that the "Battle Hymn" had become routine in the American patriotic repertoire, a standard part of how America sang about itself and its God. Its place on the war front was simply assumed, and Unitarians and evangelicals made common cause to get it into the hands of soldiers. The righteous nationalism of the "Battle Hymn" belonged to everyone in the embrace of the savior-nation.

The liberal Congregationalist Samuel McCrea Cavert, a leader in the ecumenical Federal Council of Churches, included the "Battle Hymn" in his 1917 essay, "The Missionary Enterprise as the Moral Equivalent of War." Cavert's title gave a nod to the Harvard philosopher William James's *Varieties of Religious Experience*, which the minister cited in the first paragraph. Cavert hoped for a warless world, but man's drive for competition needed to be channeled into another outlet beneficial to human welfare. The current war revealed the ordinary soldier's capacity for heroic service to others, the potential for a life lived in serious devotion to a cause higher and larger than himself. This was the self-denial of cross-bearing. The question was whether the church could sustain this consecration to service and direct it to something other than war in the new era ahead.

Cavert anticipated the worldwide triumph of God's kingdom and hoped the "missionary enterprise," broadly conceived, would provide the equivalent of war he sought. He envisioned a church totally mobilized for kingdom work at home and abroad. Achieving a warless, righteous, democratic world order was possible only through the "spirit of Jesus." Acknowledging the challenges of demobilization in the postwar world, Cavert pressed the point that the church's "missionary work is one phase of expenditure that should know no retrenchment. . . . There '. . . has sounded forth the trumpet that shall never call retreat; . . . O, be swift, my soul, to answer Him; be jubilant, my feet! Our God is marching on.' "[33] The "Battle Hymn" still had work to do in a warless world.

The coming kingdom inspired other theologians to appeal to the "Battle Hymn" as they interpreted the war in light of the Second Coming of Christ. The First World War and the Balfour Declaration in 1917 sparked a lot of speculation about the end-time and the fulfillment of prophecy. The Presbyterian theology professor James H. Snowden, in his treatise on eschatology, *The Coming of the Lord: Will It Be Premillennial?* defended a postmillennialism in which "historical acts of judgment or chastisement" pointed to the ultimate coming of Christ in judgment at the end of history. Snowden served as the Professor of Systematic Theology at the mainline Presbyterian Western Theological Seminary in Pittsburgh. Snowden's theology of history enabled him, so he thought, to identify a range of mountain peaks of divine action in the history of Western civilization and America. From the conversion of Constantine in the fourth century through the Protestant Reformation in the sixteenth, God had manifested himself in these special interventions. Such was the case in America as well. Snowden explained: "Our Civil War set forward the hour hand on the clock of Christianity. And it is no visionary fancy that sees, not a premillenarian second coming of Christ, but a real coming of God in the present great war, for we believe it marks an epochal hour and forward movement in the development of that democracy which is in spirit so closely allied to the principle of the kingdom of God and prepares the way for and fulfills its coming. Every act of judgment and justice and every new manifestation of sympathy and service is a coming of God and of Christ. It is in this faith that we sing the inspiring strains of our Battle Hymn of the Republic." He then quoted the whole first verse.[34]

American churches also brought the "Battle Hymn" directly into their worship services and national assemblies, where it joined the Stars and Stripes on display, in many cases for the first time. Even the immigrants and Catholics Howe feared started using her poem to prove their American allegiance during the war. In 1918, a Hungarian Catholic church in

Santa Barbara County, California, dedicated a service flag for the young men from the parish serving in the military. The sanctuary displayed a six-by-ten-foot American flag to the left of the altar and the service flag to the right. The choir sang "America" and the "Battle Hymn." The priest sprinkled holy water on the service flag and read the names of the twenty-eight boys in uniform. At the close, the choir sang "The Star-Spangled Banner."[35] The war had provided the occasion for Julia Ward Howe's poem to be sung not only by Hungarians whose bid for liberty she had admired but also by Roman Catholics whom she was sure were on the losing side of history.

This scene could have played out in any liberal or evangelical Protestant church in America. The General Assembly of the Presbyterian Church (USA) convened in Columbus, Ohio, in May 1917. On the first day of the annual assembly, just weeks after Congress's declaration of war, the pastors and elders could not have made the fusion of war and religion more explicit. As the press reported, "A striking incident . . . was the marching of 200 or more young men in khaki from the Columbus military barracks thru the aisles to the platform, and the 'Battle Hymn of the Republic' was seldom sung with greater fervor than on this occasion."[36]

The PCUSA at the same General Assembly voted to include the "Battle Hymn" in a wartime supplement to the denomination's hymnal. At the end of this process, the "Battle Hymn" found a home in thousands of pews as the last hymn in the book. Joint editorial responsibility for the "Supplement of 1917," as it was called, lay with Louis F. Benson and Franklin L. Sheppard. Benson was a leading hymnologist and editor of the 1895 Presbyterian *Hymnal*. Sheppard served as the editor of the songbook *Alleluia*.[37] Both had strong views. Yet in all the debate back and forth, neither one ever questioned the appropriateness of Howe's "Battle Hymn" for Christian worship. Instead, the editors focused on details about publishing a selection whose inclusion seemed too obvious to have to justify. While Sheppard considered Kipling's "Recessional" an "inappropriate piece of poetry" for worship, he did not object to Howe's Unitarianism, nationalism, or militarism. Benson, on the other hand, stressed the enthusiasm of the denomination's publications board for what he called the "British origin and imperial proclivity" of Kipling's "Recessional," regretting only that they did not have a similar French hymn for the supplement.[38] Evidently, they aimed to honor all the Allied powers.

The publications board sent a unanimous petition to the 1917 General Assembly in Columbus proposing a supplement to the hymnal that would make the "Battle Hymn," "The Star-Spangled Banner," and Kipling's "Recessional" readily available for public worship.[39] Sheppard offered the version of the "Battle Hymn" he had just completed for a separate wartime supplement intended for his own *Alleluia* songbook. "I spent a good deal of time over it," he told Benson, and liked the simplicity of the arrangement he had settled on. "The Board has put out about 100,000 copies of this, and it will hereafter be regularly bound up with the proper form in 'Alleluia.'"[40] Underneath the title of the "Battle Hymn," Sheppard added in lieu of the usual scripture text a line from fellow Presbyterian Woodrow Wilson: "'The World Must Be Made Safe For Democracy' *President Wilson's Address, April 2, 1917.*" The "Battle Hymn" had found its political proof text.

In its own report to the General Assembly in 1918, the Board of Home Missions included a section entitled "Patriotic Service." The board reminded the denomination that "the tremendous conflict in which America has taken her place with the forces that are struggling for world liberty and righteousness has demanded special service of the Board." As part of those demands, it had completed work on the "Supplement of 1917." The board also reported that a separate hymnbook, *For God and Country: Hymns for Use in War-Time*, edited by Louis Benson, was "primarily intended for the use of churches, Sabbath schools and Associations at home rather than for use in the [army] camps." It too included the "Battle Hymn of the Republic." Regarding appropriate wartime Sunday school materials, "the great conflict in Europe has been used to teach the young people about good citizenship, both in their own land and in the Kingdom of Heaven."[41] In these ways and others, the mainline Presbyterians at the denominational level brought the war into the church and the church into the war.

That two-way exchange between religion and war, with the "Battle Hymn" as a conduit, did not go unnoticed or unchallenged within the denomination. The Princeton Seminary professor J. Gresham Machen, who had served in France with the YMCA and would soon land in the center of the fundamentalist-modernist controversy and be tried and convicted as a schismatic for his conservative opposition, worried about the American churches' failure to serve as a refuge from the world's strife. "Weary with the conflicts of the world, one goes into the Church to seek refreshment for the soul," he wrote in *Christianity and Liberalism* (1923). "And what does one find? Alas, too often, one finds only the turmoil of the world." Sadly, the typical sermon looks to "human wisdom" and not to the Bible, and then the congregation sings "one of those hymns breathing out the angry passions of 1861, which are to be found in the back part of the hymnals"—exactly where the 1917 supplement had placed the "Battle Hymn of the Republic." "Thus the warfare of the world has entered even into the house of God."[42] For an old-school Presbyterian like Machen, this was the worst fate for the church and its mission.

Machen had another chance to weigh in on the "Battle Hymn" a decade later. In a review of the new Presbyterian hymnal in 1933, he was glad to see a few hymns gone from the collection, among them hymns in conflict with Reformed theology. Likewise, he was "glad that the 'Battle Hymn of the Republic' . . . is absent from the new book. Opinions may differ about the political views out of which that poem was born. Some of us may agree with them; some of us may disagree. But one thing is clear—a fiery war song like that has no place in the worship of a Christian congregation."[43] That judgment was increasingly in the minority, and one day it would be self-identified theological conservatives who would insist on singing the "Battle Hymn," as confident as the editors at Moody in 1917 that it could be redeemed from its original context and baptized for the work of Christ and his church.

Wartime Washington and the armed forces proved just as prepared as Howe's daughters and the clergy to use the "Battle Hymn" to mobilize the nation's soldiers and civilians. The government and the military appropriated the "Battle Hymn" and its potent religious nationalism for the purposes of wartime civil religion. For the American Expeditionary Force in France, the army under the command of General John J. Pershing began publishing *Stars and Stripes* in February 1918. Publication continued until the summer of 1919. A small editorial staff included a number of men who went on to distinguished careers in publishing and the arts. The eighth issue (March 29, 1918) of *Stars and Stripes* carried on its front page the "Battle Hymn" surrounded by a border of lilies. The Boston publisher, who later attended the service for America's fallen at Westminster Abbey in 1919, claimed regarding this issue of *Stars and Stripes* that the line "As he died to make men holy, let us die to make men free" had been "selected as symbolic of the spirit of the American Army in France." He had no doubt America's soldiers would have supported any movement to adopt the "Battle Hymn" as the national anthem.[44]

On the home front, members of the Wilson administration blended the "Battle Hymn" with vaguely religious and explicitly Christian language to explain the war and the sacrifices it demanded. Secretary of the Interior Franklin K. Lane spiritualized the war as much as any self-mobilized preacher. On April 3, 1918, he gave a rousing speech in which he deployed the "Battle Hymn" to full effect to justify the war and define the true meaning of Americanism. Lane himself, Canadian by birth, knew what it meant to be "Americanized," and he put the most zealous homegrown patriot to shame. In 1905 Teddy Roosevelt had appointed Lane to the Interstate Commerce Commission, and he served as Woodrow Wilson's interior secretary from 1913 to 1920.

Lane used the "Battle Hymn" to affirm American virtue and America's faith in itself—a faith that sustained a nation at war. In 1918, he published a collection of his war speeches called *The American Spirit: Addresses in War-Time*.[45] He made the theology of his religious nationalism explicit. "Take from America the youthful belief in herself as an evangel of the gospel of Freedom," he warned in the preface, "and this war means nothing to us. . . . Germany may think in terms of man power and gun power for forty years and yet we cannot fear the ultimate worst, because we sing The Battle Hymn of the Republic—'God's truth is marching on,' and we believe it; it is part of us; it is as real as our mountains and our rivers. The only real blow that we could suffer in this war, or any other, would be the destruction of this faith. It explains to us our history and those whom we call our leaders."[46]

A year and a day after Wilson's war message to Congress, as the German army made stunning advances across France in the Spring Offensive of 1918, Secretary Lane appealed to the "Battle Hymn" again in his opening address at a conference on "Americanization as a War Measure." Held at the Department of the Interior in Washington, the meeting drew leaders from politics, business, and education, including more than twenty state governors, ten representatives of the Council of National Defense, more than thirty representatives of state councils of defense, more than sixty chambers of commerce and labor leaders, about 100 industrialists, and a number of prominent educators. Rounding out the list was Wilson's publicity chief, George Creel, and the US commissioner of education. For the benefit of this impressive gathering, Lane focused not only on education's role in making Americans out of immigrants; he talked about Americanization as something that had to happen to all citizens, the conversion experience of a revival meeting transposed from the sawdust trail to war and politics.

Lane reminded the invited guests that they had convened to confer about "how there might be made a greater America, a nobler America." To this point in their history, Americans had made the mistake of thinking that the blessings of liberty came effortlessly and did not need to be taught. The war had shown them otherwise. "We know now," he said, "that there is no such thing as Americanism unless there is Americanism in our souls." Lane thought the collapse of Russia and the subsequent Treaty of Brest-Litovsk that had knocked the Bolshevik regime out of the war showed the consequences of war for a people who had not become a true nation. Once the czar was removed, the empire disintegrated, having nothing else than the monarch to fuse it into one. The Russian people had many virtues, "but they had no sense of nationality. They have never acted as a nation." They had been destroyed by ignorance and deception. But for Americans it proved otherwise. They invited Americanism into their hearts and secured unity as a people.

For the sake of that solidarity, America had to ensure that the millions coming to its shores became educated and enlightened and were formed into a true nation. "What is it to be loyal to America?" Lane asked his audience, addressing the industrial leaders primarily. "We are to preach Americanism. You are the prophets of a new day. You are the missionaries who are to go forth." But what gospel would these missionaries proclaim? "What is the story of America?" That story was not embodied in the symbol of the flag, or the story of the Pilgrim fathers, the frontier, Yorktown, Gettysburg, Santiago, or Manila. It was not found in the nation's inventors or philosophers or poets. These were indeed part of "the American spirit of adventure," but the true America lay elsewhere, in something immaterial. "America is a spirit. America is something mystical which lives in the heavens. It is the constant and continuous searching of the human heart for the thing that is better." If America was a spirit, then it was only right to worship it in spirit and in truth.

Lane carried his analogy (if it was merely that) one step further: "You are men who deal with these material things which go to make up the great prosperity of this country, but fundamentally each one of you is a religious leader. Each one of you has in his soul a mystical quality which represents your Americanism." Propelled by a "divine dissatisfaction," America worked and fought for better things. "That is the essence of Americanism. Take out of our hearts the belief that the Battle Hymn of the Republic is true, that God's truth is marching on, and you defeat America; but until you take that from us, I care not what the battles of the world may show—the spirit of America, the real America, cannot be beaten in battle." For Lane, the love he bore for his adopted homeland was a matter of genuine heartfelt religion. He preached nationalism as evangelical piety. "I want to get into your hearts, if I can at this time, a passion for Americanism, not only because Americanism is the spirit of our country, but because Americanism is the most advanced spirit that has come to man's spirit from above."[47]

While Lane soared into this heavenly realm, emotions ran high in other branches of government as well. Congressmen did not hold back from discerning the theological implications of the war, and they as much as anybody found the "Battle Hymn" useful in that task. When Senator Robert L. Owen asked where God was in the war, Howe's poem helped him answer the age-old problem of evil.[48] The Virginia-born Owen, who served as a progressive Democrat and US senator from Oklahoma from 1907 to 1925, chaired the Senate Committee on Banking and Currency. He concluded a speech in October 1918, near the war's end, with the lines of the "Battle Hymn." His book contributed to a long, ongoing discussion in the pulpit and denominational magazines, in America and Europe, about theodicy—justifying the ways of God to man in a world of evil and suffering—that troubled the thoughts of many idealists during the war. Could God's wisdom, power, and goodness be affirmed in a global catastrophe that seemed to mock progressive optimism?

Owen did not hesitate to reaffirm the moral law at work in God's universe. His thoughts turning to Germany's predatory ambition, he claimed that "William II and his war lords have been violating the Ten Commandments of Moses and exemplifying the millions of evil consequences which under the moral laws of God flow from them." The senator then went through each of the Ten Commandments, showing how

Germany had violated the moral law point by point and so, therefore, faced certain doom in God's moral economy. Bad things happen to bad people. This war was nothing less than a showdown between autocracy and democracy, and right would triumph. To tell his grand story, Owen reached back a hundred years, all the way to the founding of the Holy Alliance of Austria, Prussia, and Russia after the Napoleonic Wars. Since then, there had really been only one unified story unfolding over the course of a century. And God's moral universe of cause and effect had been at work the whole time. Now in 1918, "the Battle of Armageddon is on to determine whether or not moral and ethical laws shall stand on earth. There can be but one answer. It is the doom of William II and of the Governments which deny the doctrines of justice, of liberty, of humanity, or righteousness." In sentence piled on sentence, Owen intensified his millennial hope: "It is the end of Autocracy, the triumph of Democracy." "It means the rebirth of the world." "It means a thousand years of peace." Owen's promises reached higher and higher. For those who still asked, "Where is God?" he answered, "Everywhere! with His glorious and beautiful laws working to everlasting perfection, teaching at last by sorrow the weakest and most foolish of His children. Where is God? Let the 'Battle Hymn of the Republic' answer—." All five verses followed.[49] Teddy Roosevelt had stood at Armageddon in 1912 to wage his domestic war for righteousness; Senator Owen stood at Armageddon in 1918 to redeem the world.

Wilson propagated the same "Battle Hymn" gospel as Secretary Lane and Senator Owen. In a speech for the opening of a Red Cross fund-raising campaign in New York in 1918, the president spoke of the American people being drawn together into a single family by contributing to the work of public-service agencies such as the Red Cross. He called on the audience to "sustain the heart of the world." He wished his listeners could have the experience of hearing the anguished cry of a distressed humanity: "If you could catch some of those voices that speak the utter longing of oppressed and helpless peoples all over the world to hear something like the Battle Hymn of the Republic, to hear the feet of the great hosts of Liberty coming to set them free, set their lives free, set their children free; you would know what comes into the heart of those who are trying to contribute all the brains and power they have to this great enterprise of Liberty."[50]

When Wilson set off for the Paris Peace Conference in late 1918, he took the ideals of the "Battle Hymn" with him. Both the president and his hosts in England used the anthem as he stopped en route to the French capital. By this point, the "Battle Hymn" appeared in public almost any time the British wanted to pay tribute to their American ally. Singing the hymn had once been the most appropriate (though predictable) way to honor Mrs. Howe; now, the "Battle Hymn" served British choirs, organists, congregations, and soloists as the music that said "America" in the clearest way possible. Wilson stopped in England and headed to Carlisle near the Scottish border, where his mother had been born, to visit the Lowther Street Congregational Church, the pulpit of his grandfather, the Reverend Thomas Woodrow. As Wilson and his entourage made their way to their pews for a special service in the president's honor, the organist played the "Battle Hymn of the Republic," identified incorrectly yet significantly in the order of worship as "the American national anthem." The congregation sang the "Battle Hymn" just before the sermon. Invited to say a few words, Wilson came to the front and spoke briefly. "The knowledge that wrong has been attempted has aroused the nations," he said. "They have gone out like men for a crusade."[51]

During his return trip to Europe for the peace conference in 1919, Wilson gave a speech on Memorial Day at the American military cemetery of Suresnes outside of Paris. Among the Allied dignitaries present to honor America's war dead were Marshal Ferdinand Foch, Supreme Allied Commander, and the British and US ambassadors to France. Flowers and American and French flags decorated each grave. The platform held a table draped with French and American flags. A US Army chaplain began the ceremony with prayer. Then the crowd sang the first verse of the "Battle Hymn of the Republic," "President Wilson leading the singing," according to the London *Times*. The president spoke without notes about the new era ushered in by the great war for liberty. The world had to guarantee that this had been the final war, and must not permit selfish old ways back into the councils of nations.[52] Even after the war ended, Howe's poem remained closely identified with Wilson and his liberal internationalist vision. When the former president died in February 1924, Raymond Fosdick, wartime chairman of the Commission on Training Camp Activities, paid tribute to his hero in a radio address. "Woodrow Wilson is dead," he said, "but his truth is marching on!"[53]

One of the most remarkable testimonies to the symbolic power of the Anglo-American "Battle Hymn" came in the last weeks of the war. When US and Australian forces broke through the Hindenburg Line in 1918, Sir Arthur Conan Doyle began his dispatch to the London *Times* with none other than the words "Mine eyes have seen the glory of the coming of the Lord; / He is trampling out the vintage where the grapes of wrath are stored." If was as if an English version of Ewart's "Kentucky" had appeared in the flesh. Doyle interpreted his experience through the words of the "Battle Hymn": "The grand, sonorous, mystical lines of Julia Ward Howe rang in my head as I found myself one of the actual witnesses of this, one of the historical episodes of the greatest of wars."[54] Howe had borne witness, and now Doyle did the same with her poem. A decade earlier, Doyle had already written about the "Battle Hymn." He had cited it as an exception to his observation that Americans and Britons typically combine "the comic with their most serious work." He called the "Battle Hymn" "the most tremendous war-song I can recall. Even an outsider in time of peace can hardly read it without emotion. I mean, of course, Julia Ward Howe's 'War-Song of the Republic,' with the choral opening line: 'Mine eyes have seen the glory of the coming of the Lord.' If that were ever sung upon a battlefield the effect must have been terrific."[55] Whether or not it had ever been sung on the battlefields of the Civil War, it now came to the battlefields of France as Doyle sang it himself, a witness to American and Australian battalions assisted by British artillery batteries as they broke through the German line in the epic contest H. G. Wells had called "the war to end all wars." Wars made sense in God's moral universe when they were wars for permanent and universal peace, justice, and righteousness. The "Battle Hymn" raised earth to heaven and brought heaven to earth. The next leap forward, making sense of all the slaughter, would be the Treaty of Versailles and the League of Nations.

7

THE SACRED INHERITANCE OF MANKIND

Theodore Roosevelt's cousin, the artist Samuel Montgomery Roosevelt, finished a giant allegorical painting in 1919 inspired by reading
the "Battle Hymn of the Republic." The founding president of the National Society of Portrait Painters displayed the canvas at the Henry Reinhardt and Sons Galleries on Fifth Avenue in New York City. Roosevelt
worked on the project for a year, overcoming the obstacles of poor health
and a fractured arm. One art magazine called his "excellent" allegory
"distinct[l]y a product of the great war," and quoted the fifth verse of the
"Battle Hymn" to explain the painting.[1] In the middle, lies the sea, invoking the words "Christ was born across the sea." A dark mountain rises in
the middle, with black storm clouds and lightning on the right, dawning
day on the left, and a cluster of white crosses in the middle distance. The
largest figure is Christ. Dressed in a red robe, he stands on the left of the
sea, above three male figures, stretching his left arm out across the sea.
The spear wound from his crucifixion is visible in his side. The three men,
the magazine concluded, "show fear and despair in the divine presence,"

S. Montgomery Roosevelt
Exhibits His Allegorical War Picture From
The Battle Hymn of The Republic

"In the beauty of the lilies CHRIST was born across the sea,
With a glory in his bosom that transfigures you and me;
As he died to make men holy, let us die to make men free,
While GOD is marching on."

DECEMBER 22ND TO JANUARY 12TH
AT THE REINHARDT GALLERIES
HENRY REINHARDT & SON
565 FIFTH AVENUE

1920

Figure 19. S. Montgomery Roosevelt exhibits his allegorical war picture from the "Battle Hymn of the Republic," December 22–January 12, 1919.

while on the right, women and young girls, representing "joy, hope and welcome," look across at Christ and the male figures. Some are naked, some barely clothed, and one holds a baby out to Christ. They seem filled with anxiety but also compassion. A mysterious void separates the two groupings and the foreground from the mountain in the rear.

The year Roosevelt exhibited his allegory, the Paris Peace Conference concluded and the US Senate debated the Treaty of Versailles with its controversial provision for a League of Nations. The year 1919 also marked the centennial of Julia Ward Howe's birth and a new occasion to reflect on her "Battle Hymn" and its significance to the postwar world. The link between the war, the peace, and the poet seemed clearer than ever. Howe's old congregation, Boston's Church of the Disciples, held a centennial service on May 25, 1919. The Republican governor, Calvin Coolidge, spoke. A large number of ethnic Greeks attended to pay tribute to Howe's work on their behalf. The church was decorated with American and Greek flags, and the inscription on the Greek flag read, "To the Great Philhellene."

A letter from John J. Pershing read at the Howe ceremony testified to the general's "privilege to bear witness to the widespread effect of 'The Battle Hymn of the Republic' on the morale of the fighting men. It is unique in its religious fervor and enthusiasm, and wherever sung it can but have the same effect which it produced when it was first sung in the Civil War." Seated in the congregation to honor Mrs. Howe were her daughter Maud, Governor John Andrew's daughter, Henry W. Bellows's widow, and Mrs. Andrew Dickson White, whose husband, the founding president of Cornell, had served on the Santo Domingo Commission with Samuel Gridley Howe in 1871.[2]

In time for the May centennial, Maud published a fresh tribute to her mother. The essay for the *Ladies' Home Journal* gave her the chance to reflect on the prominence of the "Battle Hymn" in the First World War. Entitling the essay "The Hymn in the Great War," the *Journal* included one of Howe's own accounts of how she wrote the "Battle Hymn." Maud still thought in terms of sacred war. She told of how she found the "Battle Hymn" on the front page of what she misidentified as the first issue of *Stars and Stripes*. "Its presence in the American Army's journal expresses the high purpose of the soldiers for whom The Stars and Stripes was published," she wrote. "To them the Great War was a sacred war in which they were prepared to make the last sacrifice. No existing line of verse better expresses their spirit than the words: As He died to make me holy, let us die to make men free." From here, Maud recounted the many ways the "Battle Hymn" had been enlisted for the Great War. In light of its wartime service, she wrote, "It may be that a larger destiny awaits it. Will it become the International Anthem of the League of Nations?"[3] This is exactly what the Philadelphia publicist Jarvis Wood had called for. The League of Nations would not survive, peace would not prevail, but the "Battle Hymn" endured as an "international" anthem of sacred wars and self-sacrifice.

In all the turmoil of war and unstable peace, Howe's daughters tried to keep the "Battle Hymn" not just sacred but sacred in the right way. To mishandle it was sacrilege. Tampering with the original text incurred the daughters' and the public's wrath. At times the earnest effort turned humorous, though not everyone laughed. Princeton University English professor Henry van Dyke must have felt as though he had touched the ark of the covenant in 1918 when he dared update Howe's poem. Van Dyke, a liberal Presbyterian and poet of some note, served as minister to the Netherlands under Wilson and during the war held the rank of lieutenant commander as a chaplain in the United States Navy charged with overseeing singing at American naval stations. In 1901, Mark Twain had brought the "Battle Hymn" "down to date" to satirize America's imperial pretensions, but Van Dyke brought it up to date to suit the Great War. Or so he thought. Twain's parody had taken deadly aim at American greed and its "bandit gospel," while leaving the "Battle Hymn" unscathed. Van Dyke tampered directly with the holy thing itself. Reportedly, men of the army and navy were being taught to sing the new version:

> We have heard the cry of anguish
> From the victims of the Hun,
> And we know our country's peril
> If the war lord's will is done—
> We will fight for world-wide freedom
> Till the victory is won,
> For God is marching on.[4]

Van Dyke provoked indignation and ridicule for his temerity. Florence Howe Hall denounced him. Adding to the "Battle Hymn" bordered on sacrilege, she protested. She told the *New York Times*, "To add a verse to it would be like making an annex to Lincoln's Gettysburg speech or to Hamlet's famous soliloquy." As proof, she turned once more to her old standby Rudyard Kipling. "Its appeal is to lovers of freedom everywhere. The 'Battle Hymn of the Republic,' as Kipling long ago pointed out, and as all recognize in the present terrible conflict, is international; indeed it is universal." Van Dyke erred by making the hymn too particular to this war, at the expense therefore of its universality. He should write his own song: "But the 'Battle Hymn of the Republic' is a part of the sacred inheritance of mankind in general, and of America in particular, on which no hand must be laid."[5] The editors at the *Times* agreed. "[Van Dyke] would have been well advised . . . had he done no more with respect to the 'Battle Hymn of the Republic' than to join the rest of us in acclaiming its excellence—and in letting it stand exactly as it left the hands of its author."[6]

And then the dependable *Times'* readers weighed in, showing Van Dyke no mercy, at least in the letters the paper chose to print. One reader thought the blasphemy obvious: "[The 'Battle Hymn'] belongs to the eternities. As long as the English language is spoken or read so long will it stir the depths of the souls and hearts of men and inspire in them the thoughts The Eternal is thinking and make them glad, at any cost, to be 'workers together with God,' and with 'jubilant feet' to keep in step with the Infinite." Whether in northern Virginia or on the western front, it was all one battlefield. "I can see them still as I saw them in my childhood," the idealist continued. He had witnessed the Union troops marching "on their way to 'die to make men free.'" That trumpet blast still resounded in 1918:

> And tonight, in the "encircling camps" in France, where our sons and our hearts are—our sons, God bless them!—are obeying the call of "the trumpet that shall never call retreat," the trumpet call of the ever-marching-on God. And they, whose souls have been "swift to answer Him," they, the flower, the hope, the promise of America, some in little knots in the tents or in the dugouts, amid the awfulness of the "vintage of the grapes of wrath," are quietly singing the same old hymn as to how "His day is marching on."

"This inspired hymn is to thousands a holy thing," he warned. "For one to touch it is to commit sacrilege."[7]

Florence continued to stew over what Van Dyke had done to the "Battle Hymn." Three years later she told one correspondent, "We were all much troubled at Dr. Henry Van Dyke's attempt to add a verse to the Hymn, and judging from the letters we received and the comments of the press, the public agreed with us." She took delight in reporting that "some literary men and women (I do not know their names) amused themselves by treating Dr Van Dyke's poems in the same way (making additions to them). I was told that a copy was sent to Dr Van Dyke. How he liked it I do not know."[8]

Maud shared Florence's indignation. In the draft version of her 1919 essay for the *Ladies' Home Journal* she thought it appropriate "to record my mother's feeling about the literary integrity of her poem. Many times during her life people made paraphrases of the hymn, sending them to her for her approval. Several times additional verses were submitted for her sanction. From first to last she refused to consider any of these well meant additions or paraphrases. She always received the suggestions with a good deal of emotion and declared emphatically that as the Hymn was written so must it stand without change or addition. She sometimes spoke of the 'Battle Hymn' as having been 'given' to her, and I believe that she felt it to have actually been a gift from God: as such she stoutly defended it from the attacks of all would be collaborators."[9] Not one jot or tittle would pass away from America's scripture until all was fulfilled.

Howe's reputation continued to rise in the 1920s. Her place in the American pantheon, and her hymn's place in the nation's civic liturgy, were honored by many in the postwar world. But for whom did the "Battle Hymn" speak? Some sang it to turn the nation outward after the First World War; others sang it to turn the nation inward in the "return to normalcy." The twenties witnessed the bifurcation of the "Battle Hymn" into two distinct hymns of national destiny. One "Battle Hymn" supported the internationalism of the League of Nations; the other accompanied insular Americanism, the Americanization of immigrants, and opposition to the League of Nations. A similar split happened later in the twentieth century to John Winthrop's biblical metaphor of the "city on a hill." In the 1960s, as Winthrop's "Model of Christian Charity" was used for the first time by politicians, the "city on a hill" became the property of both interventionists and isolationists, a symbol for both the exemplary city and the missionary city.[10] Likewise, without changing one word of the sacred text, Howe's poem became both nationalist and internationalist, a handy invocation of both inward- and outward-directed exceptionalism.

On the nationalist side, the "Battle Hymn" was appropriated to support what the Columbia University historian Carlton J. H. Hayes, writing in 1931, called "integral nationalism" to distinguish it from older forms of nationalism. He acknowledged his label was arbitrary, but he needed a name for a cultural phenomenon emerging in Europe and America after World War I, a trend he found novel and disturbing. While the older nationalisms worked to create and sustain nations, integral nationalism worked to intensify the identity of an already united and independent nation-state. Such passionate attachment rejected internationalism, thrived on "jingoism" and mistrust, and put a premium on narrow national interests, whether economic, political, or military. Hayes did not hesitate to compare attitudes emerging in America to what was happening in Mussolini's Italy, Atatürk's Turkey, and Stalin's Soviet Union. "In the United States," he wrote near the end of the Hoover administration, "many of the post-war policies of the national government and the large electoral majorities in support of them are in keeping with widespread tendencies of integral nationalism: refusal to join the League of Nations, reluctance to cooperate with it, refusal to adhere to the World Court except on national American terms, naval rivalry with great Britain, immigration restrictions, mounting tariff barriers, steady encroachments on the independence of Caribbean peoples, growing intolerance toward minorities at home."[11] "Integral nationalism," Hayes concluded, "is essentially religious, fanatically religious."[12]

An example of the way Hayes's "integral nationalism" worked in regard to the "Battle Hymn" happened in March 1921 at a Hutchinson, Kansas, conference of evangelical churches. Speaking at the First Evangelical Church, Bishop Samuel P. Spreng, who had just been abroad, addressed his fellow pastors on the topic of "Europe after the War." He assured the group, in one reporter's summary, that the "religion of Jesus Christ is the only hope for infidel France, and philosophy-ridden Germany." The newspaper account elaborated the point, quoting Spreng's affirmation of America as an example to the world but also in needing to close its borders: "Europe is looking to America. Oh, if our immigration doors were opened America would be flooded and swamped with people

rushing here from Europe to what looks to them like heaven." Ever alert
to dangers, America needed to stay strong and independent. "I am plead-
ing that America remain true to this high position," the bishop declared.
"I am glad that America stayed out of that Godless league they made in
Paris (Applause). I am glad that we have not allowed our hands as a nation
to be tied by others." But that reassertion of national independence did
not mean America would abandon its high calling. No: "God help us to
be a beacon light, a star of hope to the people of the stricken world. Never
did Julia Ward Howe's 'Battle Hymn of the Republic' seem so splendid
and broad in application as in this day, for 'Our God is Marching On.' "[13]
Spreng's ignorance or forgetfulness stripped the "Battle Hymn" of its internationalism and its origin as a poem written by a "philosophy-ridden"
poet steeped in German thought. It could be sung as easily to denounce
foreign entanglement as to promote it.

The "Battle Hymn" was becoming all things to all men in the fractious
postwar decades. Herbert H. Gowen of Seattle, Washington, used the
"Battle Hymn of the Republic" ten years later for a purpose that was the
opposite of Spreng's as Gowen tried to advance the cause of international
cooperation. The Reverend Gowen's vision tacked closer to Maud's than
to Spreng's. An expert on Asian history and culture and rector of the Episcopal Trinity Church in Seattle, Gowen served as chair of the Department
of Oriental History, Literature, and Institutions at the University of Washington. He delivered a sermon in 1931 at a meeting of the Institute of
International Relations, headquartered at the University of Southern California. Inspired by the prophet Ezekiel's vision of wheels within wheels, he
preached on the need for "vision" more generally for the world to carry
through the inspiring plan for international cooperation. He hoped that
the long nightmare of the world war had taught nations to hate war and
to look for something more potent than the bureaucracy of the League
to rid the world of the "old diplomacy" and nationalist rivalry. Idealists
should take inspiration from the success of Jesus's apostles on the Day of
Pentecost when the Holy Spirit transformed "a few uninfluential Gali-
leans" into a movement to build "a new order" and a "new life" for a
civilization on the brink of collapse.

Gowan rejected cultural pessimism: "The new heavens and the new
earth are indeed revealing themselves before the eyes of men. . . . The
City of God is descending to earth with gates open to the four points of

the compass." Humanity's high calling at this historic moment was not to despair but "to cooperate with the designs of this Almighty and All-wise Power." Gowen then turned to the "Battle Hymn." Seventy years ago, the poet "saw in the marching feet of a great multitude of men proof that God Himself was 'marching on' for the accomplishment of His Divine Will. And today we may make the still greater Battle Hymn of a still greater Republic if we go forth in the faith of the Hebrew prophet [Ezekiel] to see behind the mystery of an eclipsing storm the call to still larger faith in the ultimate victory of God's creative, redemptive, and sanctifying purpose using as its instrument the harnessed willingness of a regenerated humanity."[14] Presumably, this coalition of the willing would be peaceful.

Expressions of religious nationalism (or nationalist religion) in the postwar era could be intense. Some took the form of worship of America and its symbols. One instance covered in the press was a worship service in New York in February 1924 at the Protestant Episcopal church of St. Mark's-in-the-Bouwerie. Columbia's Carlton Hayes found prime material in this strange ritual to prove his point about fanatical nationalism. He recounted the story in his 1926 essay, "Nationalism as a Religion," drawing from a report in the *New York Times*.[15] Notably, this zeal for religious nationalism appeared among the theological and political liberals who fused their worship of America with Wilsonian internationalism. The two had never really been incompatible, for Wilson, or for his hero Mazzini. What pious Samuel Ward would have made of the fate of the Protestant Episcopal Church in Manhattan is not hard to imagine.

The word "worship" is not too strong. St. Mark's hosted a service to honor the national flag. The liturgy came from a book published in 1918 by William Norman Guthrie, rector of St. Mark's from 1911 to 1937. Guthrie's manual for worship carried an unambiguous title, *The Religion of Old Glory*. He was born in Scotland in 1868 and was the grandson of the utopian socialist, feminist, and abolitionist Fanny Wright. Guthrie had been an Episcopal minister since 1893. In addition to liturgies for Old Glory, he wrote services for Buddha's birthday, American Indian Day, and a host of festivals not typically associated with the church calendar. Chapter 12 of Guthrie's *Religion of Old Glory* provided "An Office and Ceremony for the Worship of Old Glory."[16] The rector designed a totemic ritual for worshipping in turn the flagpole, the eagle, and each part of the flag. The liturgy culminated with the "Battle Hymn of the Republic."

As the *Times* reported, "At the conclusion the flag was allowed to drop on the flagstaff as a salute to the sanctuary, and the 'Battle Hymn of the Republic' was sung." Carlton Hayes feared that the temptation toward "syncretism of nationalism and Christianity," exaggerated by Guthrie, was finding converts among Catholics, Protestants, fundamentalists, and modernists.[17] While there is no reason to take Guthrie's display of nationalism as representative of the time, it does indicate the degree of religious nationalism the "Battle Hymn" could be made to serve.

While some used the "Battle Hymn" to promote integral nationalism and others to promote internationalism and religious nationalism, still others rejected it outright as alien to their identity as Americans. Particularism and localism still found a voice in the midst of postwar nationalism and internationalism. Nationalists and regionalists squared off over the question in the 1920s and 1930s. The Daughters of the American Revolution and the Sons of the American Revolution advocated including the "Battle Hymn" in the public-school curriculum and having children memorize it along with the "American's Creed," a prize-winning affirmation of American ideals that gained wide currency during the war and into the 1920s.[18] But at the same time the "Battle Hymn" met sustained opposition in the South from the United Daughters of the Confederacy (UDC). The UDC adopted a resolution "to prevent the use of 'The Battle Hymn of the Republic' on public occasions in the south, and particularly to see that it be not taught to southern children." The UDC emphasized the indignity of making the children of the vanquished sing the songs of the victors.[19]

Organizers campaigned against the "Battle Hymn" for decades. They wanted it out of the classroom, out of textbooks, and out of church hymnbooks. An editorial in the *Atlanta Constitution* in 1921 tried to capture the dilemma faced by patriotic Southerners as love of one country conflicted with love of another. As the American flag passed in front of onlookers in the streets of a Southern town, "and as we uncover to the tune of the 'Battle Hymn of the Republic' or to the 'Stars and Stripes Forever,' patriotism and loyalty struggle with various impulses but the spontaneous thrill which once quickened our blood does not come. The thought of Jim Crow armies, the Ku Klux [Klan], riots and insults drive down the thrills and bring up the tears of bitterness. Still this is our native land and our souls are not dead."[20]

The UDC continued its efforts into the 1930s and met resistance in the North. Black community leaders in Brooklyn denounced the UDC's neo-Confederate activism. "Charging that the United Daughters of the Confederacy 'are trying to revive the issues of the Civil War,'" a local paper reported in 1937, "members of the Crispus Attucks Community Council are starting a nationwide movement to encourage the singing of 'The Battle Hymn of the Republic.'"[21] In response, the *Nevada State Journal* stood by the women of the UDC and supported the chapter presidents of the organization who promoted the ban. In a forcefully worded editorial, the *Journal* called their stand against the Battle Hymn "a most sensible request." Why? Because the "Battle Hymn" "is one of the most ferocious war songs written during the great period of inter-American strife." In the South "it is well understood that the Lord's 'fateful lightning' and 'His terrible swift sword' were to be released against them; that the South and its institutions were the 'serpent' to be crushed under the heel of the marching Northern armies, and that the South was then to be hauled before the 'judgment seat' for proper punishment. Small wonder, therefore, that they ask that it be removed from the song books of the churches and schools of the North when it is the common wish of everyone that all of the animosities of the great Civil War shall be forgotten." True, the lyrics to "Maryland, My Maryland" were just as ferocious, but no one was singing them in church.[22]

While nationalists, internationalists, and sectionalists enlisted the "Battle Hymn" in their disparate campaigns, others brought it into the culture wars of the 1920s. The fundamentalist William Jennings Bryan took time away from teaching Sunday school in Miami Beach in 1921 to write an article entitled "The Menace of Darwinism" for his magazine. He denounced the forces of philosophical materialism. Bryan complained about a recent sermon preached by Canon E. W. Barnes of Westminster Abbey that attributed life, mind, and spiritual consciousness to processes within nature, though still "as a part of the vast scheme planned by God." Canon Barnes had already provoked controversy on both sides of the Atlantic in 1920 by his denial of a literal fall of man. He had defended an allegorical reading of Adam and of the garden of Eden at a meeting of the British Association for the Advancement of Science, and then repeated his remarks in a widely reported sermon at the Abbey. Barnes traced man's origin not to a historical Adam created by a direct act of God but back to the "fundamental stuff" of the universe.[23]

Canon Barnes had helped keep the "Battle Hymn" part of Westminster Abbey's liturgy. In 1920, at the dedication of the bronze replica of Augustus Saint-Gaudens's 1887 statue of Lincoln, which still stands in Parliament Square, the choir of Westminster Abbey sang the "Battle Hymn of the Republic" as it had many times during the war. Press photographers snapped pictures of Prime Minister David Lloyd George with his mouth wide open, singing with gusto.[24] The Abbey choir sang it again in 1921 for the service at which General Pershing laid a Medal of Honor on the slab marking the grave of the Unknown Warrior in the Abbey.[25] Adding another twist to the Anglo-American civil religion, Barnes preached a sermon in the Abbey in November 1920 on the 300th anniversary of the exile of the Mayflower Pilgrims, apologizing for the Church of England's persecution of the Separatists.[26]

For reasons known only to Bryan, Canon Barnes's theistic evolutionary beliefs led the populist to contrast Darwin's theories with the "Battle Hymn of the Republic." One can only wonder if Bryan knew how often the Abbey choir sang his beloved "Battle Hymn." "But what has God been doing since the 'stuff' began to develop?" the Great Commoner asked. "How barren of spiritual power is such doctrine when compared with the gospel of the Battle Hymn of the Republic," Bryan exclaimed, following with the fourth verse ("He has sounded forth the trumpet . . ."). "The stanza throbs with life." And then Bryan gave an altar call: "Julia Ward Howe's Jehovah is present TODAY, trumpet in hand. He is sifting hearts THIS MOMENT; an answer must be made to Him NOW."[27] By appropriating the "Battle Hymn" for his antievolutionary crusade, Bryan proved that the nationalist and internationalist "Battle Hymn" could also be populist. Other Americans would soon make it socialist.

Speaking for a more radical populism in the interwar years, the novelist John Steinbeck explored the revolutionary implications he found embedded in the "Battle Hymn." He began work in March 1938 on a book about the plight of a Depression-era Oklahoma farming family and their trek to California. The novel would win him a Pulitzer Prize. Steinbeck was already famous for *Of Mice and Men*, though he shunned publicity for the sake of staying immersed in his work. On September 3, 1938, as

European diplomats edged their way toward the Munich Agreement and the dismembering of Czechoslovakia, Steinbeck noted in his journal that his wife, Carol, had come up with the title for his novel the night before. Steinbeck was working on a draft of the chapter describing the Hooverville where the Joad family first stayed in California. He thought "Grapes of Wrath" to be "a wonderful title." He vowed he would stick with it "until I am forbidden" by his agent or publisher, Viking Press. "The looks of it—marvelous title," he wrote.[28]

A week later, Steinbeck told his agent Elizabeth Otis that "Grapes of Wrath" was "Carol's best title so far." "I like it because [the 'Battle Hymn'] is a march and this book is a kind of march—because it is in our own revolutionary tradition and because in reference to this book it has a large meaning. And I like it because people know the Battle Hymn who don't know the Star Spangled Banner." Steinbeck became so committed to the title that he included the complete words and music of the "Battle Hymn" in another letter to Otis and told her he would "like the whole thing to go in as a page at the beginning." "All the verses and the music," he insisted. "This is one of the great songs of the world, and as you read the book you will realize that the words have a special meaning in this book." Steinbeck did not want to risk any reader missing the point. "And I should like the music to be put there in case anyone, any one forgets," he insisted. "The title, Battle Hymn of the Republic, in itself has a special meaning in the light of this book."[29] Viking Press agreed to both the title and the prominent placement of the "Battle Hymn."

That "special meaning" seemed to be Steinbeck's conception of the shared place Howe's song and his novel occupied in America's "revolutionary" tradition. Because of its message of revolution, Steinbeck feared the "fascist crowd" would "try to sabotage" *The Grapes of Wrath* by calling it "communist." But he held fast to his conviction that the book was "intensely" American. The "Battle Hymn" at the front of the novel would make the connection to America's revolutionary tradition unmistakable to the public.[30]

Steinbeck happened to own a copy of Ernest Andrew Ewart's (Boyd Cable's) 1917 novel, *Grapes of Wrath*. Ewart had also put the full text of the "Battle Hymn" at the front of his book and had woven it throughout the story.[31] Perhaps Ewart gave Steinbeck the idea to do the same. But by printing both words and music inside the first edition's covers, Steinbeck and his publisher went a step beyond Ewart. Steinbeck's growing attachment to the poem seems even to have affected the novel's content after chapter 20. By the time he took Carol's suggested title, Steinbeck had already set his theme of a people's revolt stirring among the great masses of the nation's dispossessed. His characters often sense a "nervous" and "restless" "change a-comin'," culminating in chapter 25 when the narrator surveys California's abundant fruit, coffee, and vegetable harvest left to rot or systematically destroyed to prop up farm prices. Confronted with waste amid plenty, the starving people see "the failure; and in the eyes of the hungry there is a growing wrath. In the souls of the people the grapes of wrath are filling and growing heavy, growing heavy for the vintage."[32] Socialists in Britain in the 1880s had adopted the "Battle Hymn" for their cause, and now sitting on the cusp between the Great Depression and the Second World War, Steinbeck used Howe's apocalyptic vision in his own way to speak for the justice, not of Howe's God of Battles, but of a revolutionary People ready to "trample out the vintage" of their own "grapes of wrath."

Some reviewers read more religious meaning into Steinbeck's intentions than the surviving evidence shows. A writer for the *Winnipeg Tribune* wrote: "As the title indicates, the author who hears always 'the still sad music of humanity' [from Wordsworth's *Tintern Abbey*] and who hates oppression, thinks the day is coming when the Lord will 'tramp out the vintage where the grapes of wrath are stored,' and, in the language of Julia Ward Howe's Battle Hymn of the Republic, will 'loose the fateful lightning of his terrible swift sword' to avenge not only the poor tenant farmers of Oklahoma, but men everywhere who sit in the shadow of poverty because of the greed and selfishness of those in comfortable or luxurious circumstances."[33]

A sentiment similar to Steinbeck's appeared in 1946 in Saul Alinsky's *Reveille for Radicals*. The Jewish community activist, famous later for his connections to the counterculture of the 1960s and his influence still later on President Barack Obama, claimed, "The history of America is the story of America's radicals. It is a saga of revolution, battle, words on paper setting hearts on fire, ferment and turmoil; it is the story of the American Revolution, of the public schools, of the battle for free land, of emancipation, of the unceasing struggle for the ever increasing liberation of mankind." Alinsky had his own unified story of American history: "Throughout this saga [of liberation] run the strains of the song of

America's radicals. In this music there is little of tranquility or majesty but much that is stormy and wrathful. It is the martial music of anger, of faith, or hope; it is the battle hymn of the American radical, 'The Battle Hymn of the Republic.' Its words burn in the hearts of all radicals." He then quoted the first verse.[34]

Of all the admirers of the "Battle Hymn" and Steinbeck's *Grapes of Wrath*, one in particular helped catapult the novel to international success. The reviewer was the eccentric theater critic, former *Stars and Stripes* writer, *New Yorker* columnist, and radio personality Alexander Woollcott. Impressed by Steinbeck's achievement, Woollcott wrote to his friend Harold K. Guinzburg, founder and publisher of Viking Press: "I am half way through *The Grapes of Wrath* which fills me with astonishment and delight. It seems to me that in this book Steinbeck had done at last what Walt Whitman and Ernest Hemingway and Steinbeck himself and, in a way, Mark Twain tried to do. In fact, I suspect I am going to find that it is the great American book."[35]

He found what he expected. Woollcott had admired Steinbeck's work since at least Steinbeck's 1937 *Of Mice and Men*. A columnist in the *New York World Telegraph* noted at the time that "men like [American journalist and radio personality] Heywood Broun and Alexander Woollcott are making large clanking sounds in the welkin about his [Steinbeck's] work."[36] Woollcott wanted to do a broadcast about Steinbeck for his *Town Crier* radio show and contacted the reclusive novelist's agents for details about the author.[37] Steinbeck resisted having details about his life publicized. He agreed to the broadcast but asked that Woollcott "soft-pedal the personal matter." "I'm sure that of his own experience he will know that the pressures exerted by publicity are unendurable," he added.[38]

Just warming up, Woollcott broadcast a second review of *The Grapes of Wrath*, this time for a more distant audience. In the second of his series, "Letter from America," for BBC radio, airing on July 9, 1939, Woollcott compared the novel to America's classics. By putting the novel in such company, he explained, "I am not . . . forgetting such books as *Moby-Dick* and *Leaves of Grass* and *Life on the Mississippi* and *Death Comes for the Archbishop* when I say that *The Grapes of Wrath* seems to me as great a book as has yet come out of America."[39] Viking Press knew good publicity when it saw it, and used extracts from Woollcott's program in its advertisements for the novel.

Figure 20. Carl Van Vechten, *Portrait of Alexander Woollcott*, January 3, 1939.
https://www.loc.gov/item/2004663765/.

Library of Congress, Prints and Photographs Division.

Less than two months after Woollcott's BBC broadcast, Germany invaded Poland, Britain declared war, and Europe mobilized again after only two decades of unstable peace. The war would not end before engaging the United States in a global conflict that left it at the pinnacle of world power and prestige. The Allies called up the Anglo-American "Battle Hymn" once again for a tour of duty on both sides of the Atlantic. The "Battle Hymn" had taken on a personal connection for Woollcott. He had become friends with Laura Richards before the war, and they carried on an extensive correspondence in the 1930s and 1940s. He had read her children's books as a boy growing up in Germantown, Pennsylvania. A favorite had been her popular *Captain January*. He reviewed her book *Stepping Westward* in 1932 for the *New Yorker*, and that essay began more than a decade of correspondence between the two. He told his readers that as a boy of ten he had known every line of *Captain January*. "It is one of the great stories of the world, and I suspect that generations yet unborn will honor you for it," he added, addressing her directly.[40] Their friendship ended only with Laura's death on January 14, 1943. Woollcott died nine days later.

Woollcott promoted the revitalized Anglo-American "Battle Hymn" even before the United States entered the war in December 1941. On July 4, 1941, London celebrated its former colonies' Independence Day with the Stars and Stripes flying throughout the city and American patriotic music playing in the train stations. Once again, the "Battle Hymn" reverberated through St. Paul's Cathedral during a special ceremony. The occasion was the unveiling of the memorial tablet to William L. "Billy" Fiske of Eagle Squadron, the American RAF pilot who had died from his injuries two days after his plane was shot down on August 16, 1940. The tablet read, "An American citizen who died that England might live." Sir Archibald Sinclair, minister of the air force, assured those in the crypt that Fiske "has joined the company of those who from Socrates to John Brown died in the name of freedom and for the cause of freedom."[41] The American and Anglo-American religion drew very straight lines in its effort to tell the unified story of human emancipation.

Woollcott's contribution came eight months later. In March 1942, with the United States now in the war, Woollcott wrote a column on the "Battle Hymn" and Fiske's memorial tablet at St. Paul's. Conjuring up the memory of Julia Ward Howe, he wrote, "This is the story of a valiant and gracious woman to whom, in a dark hour in this nation's history and in the unmapped half-world that lies between sleeping and waking, it was given to put down on paper certain words which have since been recognized as an imponderable and inalienable part of the national wealth, words which will last at least as long as America does. Perhaps longer." Woollcott tied America to England, and the Civil War to the Second World War. "The singers [in the crypt] were the still surviving fliers from his own squadron, and certain young American volunteers who had crossed the sea to make up the Eagle Squadron. Standing together in the candle-lit dusk of the crypt, this group, symbolic of Anglo-American courage, sang Billy Fiske to his rest." Woollcott quoted most of the first verse of the "Battle Hymn." He closed with Julia Ward Howe's words on her ninetieth birthday, "I march to the brave music still." He then asked, "Do we? This year—and next—will provide the answer."[42] Woollcott, like so many others before and since, moved from "Battle Hymn" to altar call or used the "Battle Hymn" *as* altar call.

Woollcott had already been promoting Julia Ward Howe and the "Battle Hymn" in December 1940, a year before Pearl Harbor, to an American audience anxious about the war in Europe and what its role might be. Franklin Roosevelt had just won reelection in November. The "Battle Hymn" landed a corporate sponsor that year thanks to the famous New York advertising firm of Batten, Barton, Durstine, and Osborn, better known as BBDO. Famed advertising executive Bruce Barton, author of *The Man Nobody Knows*, the 1925 best seller that turned Jesus into a successful businessman, took the lead. The agency persuaded the Du-Pont chemical corporation of Wilmington, Delaware, to enhance its corporate image by sponsoring what would become the popular *Cavalcade of America*, first on CBS radio, then on NBC, and briefly on television before ending in the early 1950s.[43] Thanks to the American public's growing conviction in the 1930s that arms manufacturers had been among the special interests duping the nation into war in 1917, DuPont had to figure out how to restore the company's reputation with consumers. Its chemical products had to be marketed as a public benefit. The 1934 best seller *The Merchants of Death* had devoted a whole chapter to DuPont as America's most influential gunpowder manufacturer, with connections to both government and higher education. Public hearings held in the Senate by the Nye Committee focused even more bad publicity on the company.

Figure 21. Advertisement for DuPont's *Cavalcade of America*, *Baltimore Sun*, December 4, 1940.

With BBDO's help, DuPont reinvented itself as a corporation devoted to life, not death. Its successful advertising slogan, "Better Things For Better Living . . . Through Chemistry," linked DuPont with convenience and consumerism rather than high explosives.

A cavalcade is a public procession, and DuPont's half-hour radio program celebrated the parade of pioneers, inventors, statesmen, war heroes, and authors who had built America. Its consistent message, presented week after week through the scripts and advertisements, kept *Cavalcade of America* focused on the ingenuity, pluck, and persistence of hardworking Americans determined to build a secure, prosperous nation. From the program's inception in 1935, the staff at BBDO and the networks teamed up with historians to produce a show that brought the usable past to the nation's living rooms each week. Scholarly advisers to date had included Harvard's Arthur M. Schlesinger; James Truslow Adams, author of *The Epic of America*; and a team of Yale historians. In 1940, the show moved from CBS to NBC. That year it featured diverse programming about Abraham Lincoln, Chicago Hull-House reformer Jane Addams, and General Robert E. Lee. On December 9, after a delay of some weeks to revise the script and prepare the men's choir and orchestra to perform composer Deems Taylor's specially commissioned musical score, *Cavalcade* presented its heavily advertised program, "The Battle Hymn of the Republic." The storyteller was Alexander Woollcott, on loan from CBS for the broadcast.

Woollcott invited his audience to travel back with him to witness "the birth of a masterpiece." It is hard to listen to the broadcast or read the script without interpreting Woollcott's effort as a thinly veiled call for national preparedness for entry into the Second World War. How else to understand his crisp description of Union soldiers on the Potomac in November 1861? They were "a democracy limbering up. Good troops. Fresh troops. Young troops. But untrained. Inexperienced. Unequipped. Unled." Woollcott described Howe's visionary moment at the Willard Hotel. "Such words," he said of the "Battle Hymn," "are the stuff that dreams are made of and can vanish like the dew with the rising sun." But later Howe could read what she had scrawled in the dimness, and now "they are part of our great inheritance." Here he read the first verse. And at this point Woollcott's story evolved into a tribute to his ninety-year-old friend Laura Richards, listening from her home in Gardiner, Maine. On her ninetieth birthday, Laura quoted what her own mother had said on her ninetieth: "I march to the brave music still." These are the same words Woollcott would use again in his newspaper story on Billy Fiske in 1942. But this "march to the brave music" was underway a full year before Pearl Harbor.

Predictably, the solemn moment then arrived for soul searching and the obligatory altar call. Woollcott invited his audience to consider whether they had lived up to these ideals: "Can you and I say the same? Under every American roof from coast to coast—in every anxious American heart—those words stir a question. The answer to that question also lies just around a bend in the road of history. The next few years—perhaps the next few months—will bring that answer. Do we? *Do* we? Do we march to the brave music still?" His words led into a tympani roll and then the "Battle Hymn" performed by choir and orchestra. The announcer returned to link the lesson from history with the DuPont company by explaining the chemical firm's commitment to integrity in all its products—a virtue evident across America, a nation "advancing on all fronts with an integrity of mind and purpose and will-to-do that inspires all the world."[44]

Woollcott's production was only the first of at least three wartime *Cavalcade* broadcasts devoted to the "Battle Hymn." Six months after Pearl Harbor, DuPont programmed the "Battle Hymn" again, this time as a radio drama featuring top stars. *Cavalcade*'s "Hymn from the Night," performed on June 29, 1942, starred Helen Hayes as Julia Ward Howe. The drama opens in 1856 with the sound of gunshots in the streets of Boston as slave-hunters attempt to enforce the Fugitive Slave Law and the citizens of Boston riot. Julia and her husband are alarmed by the violence. But "Chev" consoles her with the good news about his deaf and blind patient, Laura Bridgeman, who spoke that day for the first time. Julia exclaims, "It's like the day of revelation. When the blind shall see, and the deaf shall hear and the dumb shall speak"—words from Isaiah (29:18) that Jesus applied to himself, as recorded in the Gospel of Luke (7:22).

With this messianic theme of deliverance well established, the script moved to John Brown, and as it did so it rewrote history to make Samuel Gridley Howe reluctant and skeptical about Brown's mission, warning Julia that the wild-eyed reformer is an "outlaw" and a "murderer." In the action, when Julia meets Brown, the grim abolitionist becomes the voice of prophecy to her. He pounds on the front door and announces, "It's I, John Brown, servant of the Lord God Jehovah!" As he enters, Julia praises him for his abolitionist work, but he demurs that he is "only an instrument of God's will" and warns, "Much blood will be spilt before the sins of slavery shall be washed away." He urges her to "work—work in God's vineyard." The conversation continues in this heavy-handed way as the themes of wrath, blood, and glory develop through the melodrama. Brown's great desire is that Julia would come to share his vision and see "Glory! Glory beyond this corporeal frame—mine eyes have seen it madam."

These are the words that haunt radio Julia when she makes her fateful visit to Washington, DC, and sees the Union encampments. And, of course, these are the words that she immortalizes in her "Battle Hymn." As she speaks them, the full chorus sings the "Battle Hymn" and brings the drama to a close. The announcer then shares a word from DuPont about the massive scale of nitrate production by the modern chemical industry, thereby guaranteeing that the shortages of World War I will not be repeated during the present crisis. DuPont's ability to derive "nitrogen from the air is an assurance that we'll return, some day soon, to a peaceful world in which Du Pont will once again manufacture—BETTER THINGS FOR BETTER LIVING . . . THROUGH CHEMISTRY." As the show closes, Helen Hayes returns to the microphone to remind listeners that "the days of wrath—are on the march again" and asks them to do their part for this "people's war" by bringing scrap rubber to local collection stations.[45]

Cavalcade produced "Hymn from the Night" again on September 18, 1944, three months after the D-Day invasion, this time with a revised script and the voluptuous film star Rosalind Russell in the role of Julia, and Walter Houston as the host. The broadcast begins with a DuPont "back-to-school" advertisement for interior house paints. Walter Houston emphasizes the chemical company's commitment to educating the public about the nation's heritage. That task was a critical one in time of war: "Today, our nation, foremost among free nations, is proudly discovering and recording its present and its past." And naturally this broadcast about the "Battle Hymn" was meant to make its own contribution to that "record." The program ends with the inspiring story of nylon-bristle paintbrushes produced for the US Navy and available soon to the nation's consumers. One more example of "Better Things for Better Living . . . Through Chemistry."[46]

While Du Pont and BBDO mobilized the "Battle Hymn" for another war, President Roosevelt and his staff were just as quick to recognize the song's potential to solidify America's "special relationship" with Britain and to promote the war as a sacred cause. On New Year's Day 1942, little more than three weeks after America's entry into the war, Roosevelt and Prime Minister Winston Churchill attended a special service at historic Christ Church in Alexandria, Virginia. Churchill had come down to Washington from a diplomatic mission to Canada. At Christ Church, the Allied leaders sat together in George Washington's pew, worshipping alongside surprised parishioners, gathered on short notice, and a good number of Secret Service agents.

FDR had designated January 1 as a National Day of Prayer. The president called the nation to the solemn task "of asking forgiveness for our shortcomings of the past, of consecration to the tasks of the present, of asking God's help in days to come." England, Canada, India, and other nations joined in. The Associated Press portrayed the service at Christ Church as a symbolic reconciliation of the United States and Britain and of the North and South. The point seemed to be made clear by the fact that the president and prime minister sat together and worshipped together, while a Northern-born rector, Edward Randolph Welles, preached from a pulpit in the former Confederacy.[47]

After graduating from Princeton in 1928, Welles had earned a BA and MA at Oxford where he excelled in debate and track. He had the honor of preaching at Westminster Abbey on August 27, 1939, the last Sunday before the war began. Roosevelt's call to national repentance inspired him to preach on 2 Samuel 12:13, the account of the prophet Nathan confronting King David about his sin with Bathsheba. In what could have been an awkward sermon about adultery, Welles chose instead to focus on national sins and not on the marital infidelities of his parishioners and guests. He had a more political Decalogue in mind.

America's greatest sin was "international irresponsibility," he warned. "We ought to be ashamed of our treatment of the Indians at home and of the worst features of Yankee imperialism and exploitation abroad." "But by far our greatest sin as a nation," he claimed at this critical moment, "is the sin of international irresponsibility." America ought instead to follow the example of the Good Samaritan in Jesus's parable, an example of self-sacrifice for the good of others. Jesus "endured His cross," and we the American people had to "accept our cross too. For the cross of sacrifice and danger and even death is the price of spiritual power." Welles called for national unity and for the necessary dedication to world service that came with great material and moral power. To a penitent people, God gives "pardon and power." And, like King David, the penitent "nation shall live." Welles then framed the war with Germany in the largest possible terms: "I believe that the spirit of Christ alone stands in the way of successful Nazi world domination, for it alone can inspire a successful will to resist and provide sufficient power to achieve victory." Reaching back to Lincoln and the Civil War, he warned that "the world cannot remain half slave and half free; half pagan and half Christian; half Nazi and half democratic." He closed by affirming FDR's "spiritual call to arms" and asked his congregation to pray for a peace attained through "the Fatherhood of God and the brotherhood of all mankind."[48] *Time* magazine called the sermon "militant."[49]

The service included written prayers from George Washington, the prayer "In Time of War" from the Anglican *Book of Common Prayer*, and an American Episcopalian prayer. Worshippers sang James Russell Lowell's "Once to Every Man and Nation," the old national hymn "America," and the "Battle Hymn of the Republic." Many years later, Churchill's granddaughter quoted Welles's claim that "Winston Churchill was so deeply moved [by singing the 'Battle Hymn'] that in the middle he wept, with great tears running unashamedly down his cheeks."[50] After the New Year's service, Roosevelt and Churchill left Christ Church and headed down through the midday rain to Mount Vernon where the prime minister laid a wreath at Washington's tomb.[51]

The British picked up where they had left off with the Anglo-American "Battle Hymn" in the 1920s. The work of creating an Anglo-American "Battle Hymn" had succeeded brilliantly from 1914 to 1919, and it seemed effortless and normal for Howe's poem to be heard again in Britain's cathedrals and at public ceremonies. When the first United Nations Day was observed in Great Britain on June 14, 1942, a large parade of workers, civic organizations, and Allied soldiers passed in review in front of Buckingham Palace. The Ministry of Information produced an eight-minute color film about the event. The footage shows a choir of British men, women, and children singing the "Battle Hymn of the Republic" to honor American troops. The film ends with "our God is marching on."[52]

As the war in Europe neared its end, Roosevelt seemed to occupy the role of national pastor. The "Battle Hymn" provided the backdrop for national consecration. The task of making (or keeping) America sacred continued for a new generation fighting a new war. On June 5, 1944, the president took to the airwaves to announce that Allied forces had entered Rome. On June 6, he addressed the nation again via radio to announce that the D-Day invasion of Normandy was underway.[53] The president led the nation in a prayer he had written for the occasion. The

White House had already released the full text of the prayer to the press. Newspapers across the country carried it on June 6 in advance of the broadcast. Churches held special prayer services that evening, promising to let out in time for the president's broadcast. *Newsweek* noted the day's solemnity: "With uncanny oneness of gesture, America turned to prayer." The popular newsweekly estimated FDR's listening audience at 100 million.[54] At 10:00 p.m. CBS and NBC brought the president's prayer to the nation's living rooms.

Roosevelt offered a nonsectarian petition addressed simply to "Almighty God." He asked for divine blessing on the nation's "mighty endeavor, a struggle to preserve our Republic, our religion, and our civilization, and to set free a suffering humanity." FDR knew that soldiers, sailors, and airmen would die in the invasion, and for these he interceded: "Embrace these, Father, and receive them, Thy heroic servants, into Thy kingdom." NBC followed with a sung benediction performed by Fred Waring's Pennsylvanians. The choir modulated into a rendition of "Onward, Christian Soldiers" accompanied by full orchestra. Waring then introduced the "Battle Hymn of the Republic," and the choir performed a stirring rendition. On June 8, the *Los Angeles Times* published a political cartoon showing a muscular arm wielding a sword and lightning bolts striking Nazi forces in the heart of Europe. The caption read, ". . . The Fateful Lightning of His Terrible Swift Sword."[55]

That summer, Waring and his choir staged a popular show at Twentieth Century Fox's Roxy Theater in New York. *Billboard* expected Waring "to make plenty of moola." His radio shows for Chesterfield and Owens-Illinois Glass had made him a household name. Audiences expected a rousing performance, and they got it, complete with the "Roxyettes." Twentieth Century Fox hired Waring's choir, orchestra, and soloists for screenings of its new biopic, *Wilson*. The finale, *Billboard* reported in its clipped style, "is a flag-waver, Battle Hymn of the Republic, with payees asked to join in final chorus. This, more than anything else, is Waring's forte. His money-making ability comes from the fact that while seemingly slick on the surface, he, in reality, is right down in the corn where customers can grasp everything he does."[56] Vaudeville knew how to turn the "Battle Hymn" simultaneously into cash and patriotism.

President Roosevelt's death the following spring meant the "Battle Hymn" was heard once more in St. Paul's Cathedral, London. On

'... Hath loosed the fateful lightning of His terrible swift sword'

Figure 22. Bruce Russell, ". . . The Fateful Lightning of His Terrible Swift Sword," *Los Angeles Times*, June 6, 1944, drawing.

April 17, 1945, the cathedral choir sang the "Battle Hymn" for the president's memorial service. The king and queen and the prime minster came to honor the Allied leader. Churchill wept.[57]

The "larger destiny" Maud anticipated for the "Battle Hymn" did not happen quite the way she had hoped in 1919 when expectations for the League of Nations ran high among Progressives. The larger destiny that awaited the "Battle Hymn" carried it across the seas to Europe, Africa,

Asia, and the Pacific. It was used to tell the American story, encourage moral and material rearmament, unite a nation behind war mobilization, send "the fateful lightning" to defeat Germany, Italy, and Japan, and consecrate the sacred nation to seeing it all through to decisive victory. A durable, adaptable anthem of religious nationalism, the "Battle Hymn" was meant to unify a people in an emergency, inspire self-sacrifice, and strengthen the Anglo-American alliance. Immediately after the war, church and state deployed the "Battle Hymn" once more for a protracted ideological struggle, while others brought Howe's poem back much closer to its origins during the civil rights movement. For some, the "larger destiny" meant renewing the "Battle Hymn" as a song of judgment against an unrighteous nation.

8

EXOTIC MEDLEY

The United States hardly missed a beat following the Second World War in the effort to keep America sacred. The Cold War turned to a tried-and-true strategy and kicked it up a notch. As part of that effort, the nation's founding and refounding documents became holy relics to a degree not yet seen in politics and culture. That elevated status had begun after the First World War. By 1930, planning was underway for the architect John Russell Pope's new home for the National Archives in Washington, DC. President Hoover called the monumental Roman structure the "temple of our history" and "an expression of the American soul." In 1952, the Declaration of Independence, the Constitution, and what purported to be the Bill of Rights were enshrined in the "Rotunda of the Charters of Freedom" of the temple, as Pope had intended.[1] Hoover had called them "the most sacred documents of our history." Stored for safekeeping in Fort Knox during World War II, the artifacts took a 30,000-mile tour of the United States in 1947 among a large collection of essential documents of democracy. The "Freedom Train" exhibited these parchments along with Washington's Farewell Address and Lincoln's Emancipation Proclamation and Gettysburg Address. Truman's attorney general promoted the tour as an answer to "shocking evidence of disloyalty to our government" and threats to national unity. Three hundred communities across the country had the chance to see these treasures and reaffirm their faith in democracy. In response, local governments, schools, and civic organizations hosted weeklong events of "rededication to American freedom" to prepare for the train's arrival, while churches kept the Sabbath by observing "religious freedom day."[2]

The "Battle Hymn" would have been an obvious choice for the 1947 Freedom Train. In hindsight, its absence seems to require an explanation. In 1942, the Library of Congress had included Howe's verses in a wartime exhibit called "Poems of Faith and Freedom," curated by the Librarian of Congress, Archibald MacLeish. Howe's poem joined Rupert Brooke's "The Soldier," John McCrae's "In Flanders Fields," and John Magee's "High Flight,"[3] the star attraction. But the library's manuscript of the "Battle Hymn" was a later copy, not the original, though some, including Woollcott, thought it was. Though community choirs hailed the Freedom Train with renditions of the "Battle Hymn of the Republic" in 1947, Howe's manuscript would have to wait until a revival of the Freedom Train in 1976. Only then would Howe's poem physically join the company of America's other sacred texts. Still in private hands, the "Battle Hymn" manuscript remained out of sight, but its message helped the United States lead what was now called the "free world" against the threat of Communism.

Just because the "Battle Hymn" manuscript remained unavailable did not mean it was denied a starring role in the Cold War as in every war since 1861. In February 1947, the US State Department began broadcasting deep into the Soviet Union. The radio program soon to be known as the "Voice of America" opened its first Russian-language broadcast with the "Battle Hymn of the Republic." Programming originated in studios in New York City and was beamed into Soviet territory from an 85,000-watt station in Munich. The announcer told his Russian audience that the purpose of the broadcast was to present "a picture of life in America, to explain our various problems and to point out how we are trying to solve them." The lineup offered news, an explanation of American federalism, folk music, and stories of scientific advancement. Listeners were treated to renditions of "Turkey in the Straw," a selection from Aaron Copland's *Rodeo*, and Cole Porter's "Night and Day." The broadcast ended, according to press reports, close to how it began, with the "last bars of the 'Battle Hymn of the Republic.' "[4]

Cold warriors' appropriation of the "Battle Hymn" came at a time of explosive growth in religious nationalism. Militant Americanism and political Christianity confronted Communism and atheism in the struggle with the Soviets and Maoist China. If, during the First World War, Randolph Bourne had been right that war was "the health of the state," war had also proven to be the health of religious nationalism. The Cold War followed this pattern. Indeed, the global ideological conflict may have engineered and reengineered more religious nationalism than any "hot war" in American history. The Truman and Eisenhower administrations with the help of Congress led the way. The 1950s alone saw the addition of the phrase "under God" to the Pledge of Allegiance, adoption of "In God We Trust" as the nation's motto, and the appearance of the same phrase on currency and postage stamps. The National Prayer Breakfast also became a fixture of political life in the capital. Hollywood got into the act with biblical epics such as the 1956 film *The Ten Commandments* that blurred the line between ancient Israel and the United States as God's chosen people.[5] The following year brought a Rock Hudson star-vehicle called *Battle Hymn*, in which Hudson played a veteran World War II pilot and minister who volunteers for service in Korea in search of a way to atone for a bombing raid that had destroyed a German orphanage.

Tensions between Russia and the United States were nothing new in 1947. Howe herself had fit Russia into her sweeping epic of history as redemption. She knew that one day the Russian Empire, like the Austrian and Ottoman Empires, would be overcome by the onward march of democratic revolution. She had been part of the popular anti-czarist movement in America in the 1890s, putting her name to public appeals for Russian liberty and self-government.[6] She opposed an extradition treaty with the czarist regime as "repugnant" to American sentiment and "an offense to the moral sense of mankind."[7] Perhaps it was more fitting than anyone realized that the State Department now targeted Soviet despotism with her "Battle Hymn." The Cold War, like any war, hinged on strategic, economic, and less tangible psychological and ideological factors. In that contest, the "Battle Hymn" was supposed to serve as musical shorthand for the American way of life, but its use by both church and state also projected righteous nationalism into the complex geopolitics of the US-Soviet test of wills and sustained religious nationalism at home. Whether the apocalypticism of the "Battle Hymn" would also be injected into the worldwide struggle was another matter.

The experience of every US military engagement since the Civil War made promotion of the "Battle Hymn" during the Cold War easy. Both nation and church sang the "Battle Hymn" to reaffirm righteous nationalism in a time of global testing. Religious groups prone to mix religion and patriotism used the "Battle Hymn" during the Cold War, and in the hot wars of the 1950s and 1960s, to reaffirm America's mission and their own entitlement to be counted an authentic part of the nation's identity. Evangelicals, Catholics, and Mormons seemed to intuit that the "Battle Hymn of the Republic" had been turned into one of the most effective emblems of the savior-nation. To be part of America meant to sing the "Battle Hymn." The "Battle Hymn" was called on once more to build a national community, to make one out of many to an extent Julia Ward Howe never intended.

As memories dulled, as the rough edges wore off the Civil War, and as Howe became a generic figure of Americanism suitable for postage stamps, the "Battle Hymn" became easier and easier to sing, moving freely across denominational, theological, and sectional boundaries. And this was true even in the midst of commemorations of the centennial of the Civil War. How many Americans in the post–World War II era knew much of anything about who Howe was and what she believed about God, Christ, and the church? How many, for that matter, had bothered to learn about the authors of any of the hymns they sang each Sunday, let alone the "Battle Hymn"? Howe's anthem had appeared in their churches' hymnbooks immediately in 1862. Its popularity had grown exponentially. Howe's "Battle Hymn" had been reinvented into a "gospel hymn."[8] There seemed to be no denominational or theological impediments to its use in Sunday schools, worship services, reform movements, missionary societies, and revival meetings. There had never been enough explicitly Unitarian theology in its verse to distract Trinitarians from singing about their faith in America—not Chaplain McCabe, not the Moody Bible Institute, not Billy Sunday, not William Jennings Bryan. Everyone could be part of the unified story of America and sing about national greatness as often as the spirit moved them.

That spirit moved evangelicals in large numbers in the 1950s. Howe may have thought she left revivalism far behind as an adult, but revivalism turned out to be the biggest supporter of her "Battle Hymn," to the point of becoming so closely identified with conservative evangelicals that Howe's anthem started to sound to some like bigotry and intolerance. Two Wheaton College graduates helped renewed evangelicals' affinity for the "Battle Hymn": Jim Elliot and Billy Graham. Elliot, one of the most admired figures in American Christianity in the 1950s, adopted the "Battle Hymn" as his theme song. The Plymouth Brethren missionary worked among the tribes of Ecuador and was killed there in 1956. Early in his career, he launched an evangelistic radio program in Illinois. He called it *The March of Truth*. In a letter to his parents in January 1951, he explained his vision: "Never have I sensed such a great responsibility to do and say the right thing for God. We have entitled the program 'the March of Truth,' taking our theme from the Battle Hymn of the Republic, 'His truth is marching on.' Pray daily for this, as we are children here, needing more each day to know His grace to demonstrate that promise of Jesus' own lips."⁹ Elliot may have meant Jesus's promise that his "words shall not pass away" (Matthew 24:35).

The evangelist Billy Graham left a much bigger mark than Elliot on the history of the "Battle Hymn." He made it his signature song on radio and television, and in film and countless revival meetings. Graham was born in Charlotte, North Carolina, in 1918, days before the armistice ending World War I. He attended fundamentalist Bob Jones University in Cleveland, Tennessee, for a semester, transferred to Trinity College in Florida, and then took his degree in 1943 from evangelical Wheaton. That same year, he married, began a brief pastorate in the Chicago suburbs, and launched his first radio program, *Songs of the Night*. For a time, he worked with the new "Youth for Christ" organization and spoke at its conferences in Britain and Europe before founding the Billy Graham Evangelistic Association. Graham came to national attention with his "Christ for Greater Los Angeles" rallies held at the Rose Bowl in Pasadena in the fall of 1949. The aging newspaper publisher William Randolph Hearst publicized Graham's Southern California revival with an editorial predicting great success for the young preacher. Suddenly Graham was headline news. With an apocalyptic edge that would later soften, his sermons warned that God's judgment would fall on the United States within two years without a national revival.[10] Carl F. H. Henry, a leading intellectual in what was called the New Evangelicalism, praised Graham's LA sermons for "[drawing] the line clearly between Christianity and Communism, in the midnight hour of western culture." Up to then, "multitudes had been aware that Communism was on the march in the Orient, but the Rose Bowl left no doubt that God was on the march in America, too."[11] From LA, Graham and his team went from success to success in a series of evangelistic campaigns in 1950 in Portland (OR), Minneapolis, and Atlanta. Graham's swing through the South continued in 1951 with crusades in Fort Worth, Shreveport, and Memphis. By 1951, publicity for the Graham phenomenon was able to boast of the crusader's "impact on millions of Americans."[12]

From the start, Graham and his team exploited a range of media, from radio to television to feature films. Music became central to the Graham message. Plans for a radio program began to take shape during the Minneapolis crusade in 1950. Graham's team settled on their choice for the show's producer (the Christian film producer Dick Ross), on the show's title *Hour of Decision*, and on a "militant" theme song, the "Battle Hymn of the Republic," to be sung by the crusade choir. The "Battle Hymn" debuted on Graham's program on November 5 with a broadcast from the crusade in Atlanta. Carried on the ABC radio network, the program soon set Nielsen records for audiences for religious broadcasting.[13] There in the heart of the South—in the city General Sherman's troops had burned to the ground eighty-six years before, marching through Georgia accompanied by army bands playing "John Brown's Body"—Howe's poem came to Dixie dressed in a business suit and mobilized to promote an up-to-date American evangelicalism.[14]

The "Battle Hymn" continued to accompany Graham through his short-lived *Hour of Decision* television show, through his more successful film-production company, at the White House during several Democratic and Republican administrations, and on his overseas crusades, especially in the former Soviet Union. In 1951, Dick Ross joined with Billy Graham Pictures to found a new production company called World Wide Pictures.

In 1962, as a production of the "Billy Graham Team Musicals," the company released *One Nation under God*. *The Sure Defense* followed two years later. These films were often shown together by church groups and advertised widely to their communities through local papers. Publicity for *One Nation under God* described the patriotic film as "a musical sing-along with Beverly Shea, Cliff Barrows, U.S. Army Chorus and Jubilaires Choir." Movie audiences were invited to join in by following the subtitles to "America" and "My Country 'Tis of Thee." The production of *The Sure Defense* in 1964 offered "a colorful tour of Washington, D.C." and footage of the Reverend Graham holding "a special meeting in The Pentagon." George Beverly Shea sang "Lift Up Your Heads, O Ye Gates," and the Army Chorus sang "The Lord Is in His Holy Temple" and, naturally, the "Battle Hymn."[15]

During his long public career, Graham became acquainted with every American president since Harry Truman, and his association with the White House made him into something close to the nation's pastor, with an honored place set for him at party conventions, inaugurations, state funerals, and memorial services. The appearance of the "Battle Hymn" at these events may have had little to do with Graham's own enthusiasm for Howe's poem per se and much more to do with a particular president's own fondness for it, or with its long-established place in the national religion, but by the 1970s Graham and the hymn had become entwined symbols on display at the nation's most solemn civic rituals. In 1973, Graham gave the graveside eulogy at Lyndon Johnson's burial in Texas. The former Oklahoma beauty queen Anita Bryant sang the "Battle Hymn." When Graham preached at Washington National Cathedral for the 9/11 memorial service in 2001 four days after the attacks, the "Battle Hymn" sounded through the nave along with "A Mighty Fortress Is Our God." Graham's words of national comfort, divine dependence, and hope for "spiritual renewal" prompted sustained applause from the audience, including an emotional President and Mrs. Bush. Graham and the "Battle Hymn" appeared prominently again at the same cathedral in June 2004 as part of former president Reagan's funeral.

Graham had always been a cold warrior. From 1949 on he emphasized what the gospel could do to rescue America in a time of cultural and international peril. The juxtaposition of Graham, the "Battle Hymn," and the Cold War found its most forceful expression right after the collapse of the Soviet Union in the early 1990s. At Graham's "Renewal '92" Moscow crusade, the "Battle Hymn" appeared twice at his mass meetings in the newly reconstituted Russian nation. The Russian Army Chorus and Band performed the "Battle Hymn" in English. Narrating the Billy Graham Evangelistic Association's online video of the event, the announcer introduces the "Battle Hymn" by saying that "perhaps nothing symbolized so graphically the changes which have swept Russia as the appearance one evening at the crusade of the Russian Army Chorus and Band." Their days of singing Communist anthems were over. When they sang the "Battle Hymn" at Graham's crusade, "they brought the audience to its feet." The band that accompanied the uniformed, all-male choir included brass, double basses, accordions, and balalaika, surely one of the most picturesque performances ever given of the "Battle Hymn." The *Washington Post* reported that Graham's own choir sang the "Battle Hymn" in Russian, rendering the chorus as "Slava, Slava, hallelujah."[16]

Second only to Billy Graham in popularizing the "Battle Hymn" among American evangelicals was the Tulsa, Oklahoma, native Anita Bryant. The eighteen-year-old Bryant, winner of the Arthur Godfrey talent show in New York and a frequent singing guest on Godfrey's television show, was crowned Miss Oklahoma in 1958. The next year she was second runner-up at the Miss America pageant in Atlantic City, New Jersey, and was awarded a $2,500 scholarship. Bryant built a successful pop singing and recording career. During the Vietnam War, she headlined frequently with comedian Bob Hope for his Christmas troupe and other tours at American bases in Southeast Asia. According to one columnist, the soldiers liked her "because she typifies the 'girl back home.' "[17] In the fall of 1966, Bryant released her newest album, *Mine Eyes Have Seen the Glory*. It included a mix of patriotic and religious hymns: "This Is My Country," "America the Beautiful," "Onward, Christian Soldiers," and the titular "Battle Hymn." Bob Hope wrote the notes for the album's back cover.[18]

Bryant used the same opening line from the "Battle Hymn" as the title of her 1970 autobiography. She was sure the dramatic role of the "Battle Hymn" in her life proved nothing less than "the awesome directness of God's force in my life."[19] It had earned her, she said, citing a story from *Variety*, "the first standing ovation in White House history." That feat was outdone only by the later occasion when she received "two standing ovations there." In 1968, Bryant and Billy Graham appeared together at the Republican convention in Miami and then at the volatile Democratic convention in Chicago, the "first Americans ever" to do so, she boasted. Delegates at both arenas heard her rendition of the "Battle Hymn" and once again honored her with standing ovations.[20]

A few years earlier, Bryant had decided to feature the "Battle Hymn" as the new closing number for her stage show, a decision she interpreted as providential. A friend had heard the Mormon Tabernacle Choir sing the "Battle Hymn" in Salt Lake City and told Bryant she should do the song in her act. God seemed to be moving in mysterious ways since she, her husband, and other staff members had all been coming independently to the same idea. Her production team worked on a new arrangement. The "Battle Hymn" spoke to her faith and to the deepening national controversy over the protracted US engagement in Vietnam. "Each of us marveled at how much this hymn expressed our feelings about God, about our American troops, and so many other things that seemed fantastically timely and right," she wrote. "The song fit into everything we stood for." One friend worried about the reception the "Battle Hymn" would get "down South." His concern surprised Bryant. "Who was thinking of the Civil War now?" she wondered. " 'You'll find the 'Battle Hymn' in all the hymn books,' I told him. 'It's a Christian hymn. With all the war in Viet Nam, that hymn sounds completely contemporary. Listen to the words!' " To impress her point on her readers, she included the first and last verses of the "Battle Hymn"—from the glory of the Lord to the beauty of the lilies.[21]

The decision to use the "Battle Hymn" drove her to her knees. "*Lord,*" she prayed, "*I feel so strongly that you want us to do this hymn for this particular audience. Something is trying to block it. If it's your will for us to perform 'Battle Hymn,' please remove whatever obstacles block our way.*"[22] Certain of God's will and defiant of any dark forces conspiring against it, she performed the song. "That night the Hymn evoked from a predominantly Southern audience a real ovation. God's message superseded any thoughts of sectionalism, and the words to a classic American hymn suddenly seemed to sing with a new authority. For me, it was a thrilling time indeed." Impressed with the success of the "Battle Hymn" that night, she kept it as her closing number. She sang it at the White House in 1968 for President Johnson and his guests, accompanied by the United States Marine Band. Before the performance, she prayed for "Christ to shine through me, that what I offer might bring a real message from God to the President and other dignitaries present that evening." And then she pleaded for God's help: "*There's a crisis in Viet Nam, Lord. These men have such weight on their shoulders. Please push Anita Bryant aside. Let your message come forth through the words I sing, to comfort and reassure them.*" As she sang, she recalled being overwhelmed by the sense of God at work in Johnson's embattled White House: "Suddenly I felt the power of the Holy Spirit within that room. As the hymn gathered force, I knew the Lord was speaking to me and to everyone else there." The president and his guests gave her a standing ovation. "What each of us felt that night, I am convinced, was the unmistakable authority of Almighty God," Bryant reported.[23] Howe herself had not been more confident that the "Battle Hymn" was the voice of God.

A decade later, Bryant enlisted the "Battle Hymn" in her campaign against gay rights. In January 1977, the Dade County Commission in southern Florida added language to the county's antidiscrimination ordinance protecting homosexuals.[24] By the mid-1970s, Bryant was best known for promoting orange juice sales in television spots for the Florida Citrus Commission. Every child knew on Bryant's authority that "a day without orange juice is a day without sunshine." Angered by the Dade County ordinance, she headed up opposition with the group Save Our Children. She reached out to churches to alert them to the threat to children in particular. At public debates with activists, she would sing the "Battle Hymn of the Republic." In one instance, she reportedly sang the hymn as her opening statement, leaving her opponent baffled. Her campaign mobilized voters and collected some 62,000 names to defeat the ordinance. Petitioners called for a referendum that summer, and the ordinance was overturned by a wide margin in June.

Brian McNaught from Detroit responded in print to Bryant with his essay "Why Bother with Gay Rights?" published in *The Humanist* magazine. Playing off Bryant's use of the "Battle Hymn" in her campaign, he warned that

> murder and defeat of civil rights under the banner of God-and-Country should be a familiar scenario to Americans who have studied the struggle for human rights in this country. The Bible and the "Battle Hymn of the Republic" have been used as a one-two punch against Jews, atheists, blacks, women, sex educators, and those who advocate separation of church

and state. This dynamic duo was even immortalized in the film *Inherit the Wind*, in which antievolutionist Matthew Brady (William Jennings Bryan) announced he was more concerned with the "Rock of Ages" than he was with the age of rocks, and his followers paraded through town with Bible, flag and familiar choruses of that old faithful "Battle Hymn," promising to hang the Darwinian schoolteacher from the old apple tree.[25]

For his last line, McNaught simply ended with "His truth is marching on . . ." After more than a century of service as an anthem of political and social emancipation, and as a call to national unity, the "Battle Hymn of the Republic" was flipped into a symbol of Bible-thumping bigotry. Even the details McNaught got wrong about *Inherit the Wind* are telling. The crowds in the streets in the 1960 film did sing about hanging the schoolteacher, but their inspiration was "John Brown's Body." The actual "Battle Hymn" did appear in the film, but at the end, when Spencer Tracy's character, "Henry Drummond"—a fictional version of defense attorney Clarence Darrow—leaves the empty courtroom accompanied by a solo female voice singing the "Battle Hymn." God's truth marches on in the movement *against* ignorant religious bigots and—the film's real point—against McCarthyites who used the Cold War as a witch hunt against suspected Communists. This cultural recycling of the "Battle Hymn" at the end of *Inherit the Wind* lay much closer to Brian McNaught's strategy in the culture wars of the 1970s than to Anita Bryant's. Could the "Battle Hymn" endure any longer as a means to national unity while being appropriated in such contradictory ways? Had it ever truly been capable of speaking the mind of a religiously and culturally diverse America?

Nineteenth-century evangelicals like Lyman Beecher had argued that Catholic immigrants could safely become part of America only to the degree that they left behind the Old World and embraced prevailing ideas about church and state, individualism, civil liberties, and the nation's largely Protestant cultural norms.[26] In the 1840s and 1850s Howe had denounced the papacy as a vestige of oppression, as part of the old order's tyranny over the mind and body of humanity. Catholics formed their own schools and fraternal organizations as they resisted cultural homogenization. Ethnic and religious enclaves also helped immigrant groups, such as confessional German Lutherans, sustain an identity in tension with

"Americanism." Catholics fought on both sides in the Civil War, but even in the victorious North they still sought a refuge among other "outs" in the old Democratic Party. In the twentieth century, prominent Catholics urged the faithful, with mixed results, to enlist in Woodrow Wilson's war for democracy and thereby prove their true Americanism. At the same time, they urged unsympathetic priests in German communities to keep quiet for the duration. Like many other religious groups, as Catholics made war alongside their fellow Americans in the twentieth century, they made their peace with religious nationalism. By the 1950s, religious pluralism and other facets of the "Americanism" once condemned by popes became part of a common heritage along with the Declaration of Independence and the "Battle Hymn of the Republic." Much of this accommodation happened well before John Courtney Murray gave philosophical and theological justification for the effort in *We Hold These Truths*, which was published just as John F. Kennedy was about to become the nation's first Catholic president.

A pioneer in the movement to reconcile Roman Catholics to Americanism was Father James Keller. He adopted the "Battle Hymn" by 1955. Keller founded the Christophers in 1945 to promote a spirit of public service among Catholics, teaching them that they each had a special mission from God. Following the war, he worked hard to mobilize Catholics in the nation's stand against Communism, arming them with a muscular version of "God and country" that embraced America's founding documents as gifts to the world, made Catholicism's peace with democracy and individualism, and upheld the United States as the only culturally and spiritually intact nation capable of resisting Communism's global menace. Recruiting Hollywood celebrities, Keller produced movies and television shows for the Christophers.

The first production, *You Can Change the World*, appeared in 1952 with the help of Jack Benny, Eddie "Rochester" Anderson, Loretta Young, Irene Dunn, William Holden, and Bob Hope. Keller wanted to use the medium of film to inspire "people of high purpose" to serve the nation in its moment "of life and death" and with the world's future hanging in the balance. Keller appears in the film. He shows a copy of a draft of the Declaration of Independence to the group to prove its affirmation of God and human dignity as the basis of just government. Lincoln's glowing tribute to the Declaration led Keller to argue that this founding document provided the key to the meaning of America and its calling in the world. Near the end, Bob Hope says that he wants to help Keller spread the word that the Constitution and the Bill of Rights have no meaning apart from the Declaration, which they fulfill.[27]

Keller named the Christophers for the third-century saint who discovered he bore the Christ child on his shoulder as he crossed a raging river. The child himself bore the world in his hands. Keller adopted the motto "It's better to light one candle than to curse the darkness." In 1955, Keller published a devotional guide, *Make Every Day Count,* providing a daily Bible verse, prayer, and inspiring story about how an ordinary person could serve the nation and humanity. Naturally it carried the papal imprimatur indicating the book was "free from doctrinal or moral error." The guide for February 25 used Howe and the "Battle Hymn" for the day's entry on the topic "The Role of Women." Howe's example reminded the prayerful Catholic what one person could do in a time of national emergency. In Keller's words, "Because Julia Ward Howe showed the imagination and initiative to bring a spiritual note into the troubled times in which she lived, she provided a splendid example of what one person can do." Father Keller assured the faithful that, as was true for Howe, "what you attempt may be known only to God, but He will bless your slightest effort." The prayer to accompany Howe's inspiring story asked, "Grant, O my Savior, that I may constantly seek an opportunity to bring Thy love and truth to all men."[28] In a remarkable convergence, Catholic piety joined with evangelical revivalism in the 1950s to call Americans to greater devotion to God and country, to the Bible and the "Battle Hymn."

It was left to a Princeton University professor to fuse the "Battle Hymn" with the Vatican itself. He did so in a best-selling book in the summer of 1979, a daunting 880-page novel.[29] Walter F. Murphy's success could be chalked up as yet another quirk in a story full of quirks were it not for the fact that he was so highly regarded as a political theorist and mentored the young Samuel Alito, future associate justice of the Supreme Court. Murphy's *The Vicar of Christ* was the story of the first American to become pope. Macmillan planned a first print run of 75,000 copies. Soon the firm sold the paperback rights for half a million dollars. It spent three months on the *New York Times* best-sellers list from May to August 1979. It debuted (on May 20) at number 14, joining a remarkable lineup of authors, including Robert Ludlum, Joseph Heller, Herman Wouk, Len Deighton,

James Michener, John Cheever, and Irving Wallace. *The Vicar of Christ* rose to number 8 on May 27 and returned to the same spot on June 17, not dropping from the top 15 until after August 12.

A Southerner and a lifelong Catholic, Murphy placed the "Battle Hymn" at the novel's climax and did so in a way that revealed just how malleable Howe's poem, and by extension the American religion as a whole, had become by the last third of the twentieth century. Born in Charleston, South Carolina, in 1929, Murphy came from Irish Catholic stock. After earning his undergraduate degree from Notre Dame, he served as a Marine Corps officer in Korea, rising to the rank of second lieutenant. He was awarded both the Purple Heart and the Distinguished Service Cross. Returning to the United States, he earned his MA at George Washington University and then a PhD in political science at the University of Chicago. He had gone to Chicago in 1955 to study with Leo Strauss. After studying with Strauss, Murphy rejected his mentor's proposal that he write his dissertation on Marcilius of Padua.[30] Instead, his interest in the Supreme Court led him to a new director for his dissertation. In 1958, Murphy took a position at Princeton where he taught for thirty-seven years. In 1968, he became McCormick Professor of Jurisprudence, the chair once held by Woodrow Wilson. He died in Charleston, South Carolina, in 2010. His ashes were buried at Arlington National Cemetery with full military honors.

Murphy's academic career seemed to prepare him to be anything but a best-selling novelist. The idea for *The Vicar of Christ* evolved from plans to write a conventional treatise on the inner workings of the Vatican. The inspiration came while he and his wife vacationed in Rome in the summer of 1965. Looking at the walls of Vatican City from a nearby café, the political scientist began to wonder how it all worked. "What I was after, essentially," he told the *New York Times*, "was to see what leadership is all about—political leadership in the best sense—to see how decisions that are good for the individual and good for society can be made into policy."[31] Murphy decided to write a novel in order to protect his Vatican sources who were few and too easy to identify. He wrote the novel from 1973 to 1974 but let the manuscript sit until he worked up the courage to send it to his agent.

Murphy set the sprawling story in Korea, Washington, and Rome. He told the story of Declan Walsh, an Irish American who becomes pope after a varied career in the US Marines, as Harry Truman's envoy to the papacy, a law professor, dean of the University of Michigan Law School, and chief justice of the Supreme Court. Murphy unfolded this complicated plot through what are supposed to be interviews with four of the pope's associates: a hardened, foul-mouthed marine; a cynical and effete associate justice of the Supreme Court; an Italian member of the Curia given to fine wine and gourmet food; and, finally, the pope's press secretary. Justice Walsh has an affair with his secretary. After his alcoholic wife's tragic death in an automobile accident, he resigns as chief justice and enters a Trappist monastery in South Carolina. Through twists in Vatican politics among the deliberating cardinals, Walsh is elected pope. He becomes a controversial reforming pope who sets out to transform the church, taking the name Francesco, or, in English, Pope Francis.

In some ways, this is the forward-looking pope for whom Howe and her friends had hoped in 1848. Murphy's Francesco launches a global "crusade" for social justice, takes Pope Gregory VI—the pope before whom Henry IV sought absolution in the snows of Canossa—as his model as he defies political corruption and thuggery, doubts the pastoral wisdom of *Humanae Vitae*'s strict stance on birth control, toys with ending clerical celibacy and admitting women to the priesthood, stuns the international community by announcing pacifism as the only stance consistent with devotion to Christ, and finally is rumored to be testing the boundaries of orthodoxy by questioning Jesus's earthly consciousness of his own divinity. Alarming his enemies, the pope's radicalism is compounded by stories spreading about the miracles he performs. The novel climaxes with the pope's assassination in St. Peter's Square and ends with his funeral.

Murphy placed the "Battle Hymn" at Francesco's funeral, though a hint of Howe's poem appears earlier in the novel in the newly elected pope's coronation homily. Accepting the triple crown, Francesco tells the crowd, "We see a world on the brink of revolution, and we are afraid. Why? Why should the people of God be afraid of change and revolution? We are the inheritors of a revolutionary tradition. Christ our Savior was a revolutionary. He preached change, peaceful change, but still a sweeping, rapid, revolutionary moral change that could not help bring social change as well." Combining Jesus's announcement that he had come not to bring peace but a sword with Julia Ward Howe's sword of justice, Francesco promises, "As Christ's Vicar I come to bring that same sword, the 'terrible swift sword' of God's love to a world that wants only to revel in material prosperity. I come to preach that same revolutionary doctrine for which Christ was crucified. I call on you, the people of God, to become seditionists, to join in a crusade, a new crusade not *against* our fellow man but *for* our fellow man. I call on you . . . to become part of a worldwide revolution of love against hatred, envy, poverty, ignorance, disease, and suffering." "People of God," the pope closes, "I have taken up the sword of Christ along with the cross of Christ. That burden is strange but it is sweet. Come, follow me."[32]

The funeral ceremony for Francesco follows the directions he had left in his will. Murphy used the pope's press secretary to describe the funeral in the last of the novel's four interviews. "As the procession organized near the altar," the secretary reports, conjuring up the scene that played out directly in front of St. Peter's, "the papal choir began chanting 'The Battle Hymn of the Republic.' It was not a display of ecumenism, but another specific order in his will that that hymn be played. As soon as the procession began to move, the [United States] marine band took up the music, shifting the soft chant of the choir into the powerful mood of the marching song of a victorious army. The words were picked up and sung by the seminarians from the North American College."[33]

The narration then switches from the press secretary to an Irish newspaper story: "The pageantry was an exotic medley of ritual Romana and martial Americana." St. Peter's Square witnessed "cardinals trying to march to the beat of the marine's drums while the voices of the choir and seminarians echoed from the façade of the great basilica and the colonnades of the piazza. The chorus was taken up by some of the prelates who knew English, then by those in the vast crowd who had any knowledge— and by thousands who had no knowledge—of the language. The words of the Civil War battle song rolled ponderously around the piazza: 'Mine eyes have seen the glory of the coming of the Lord. He is trampling out the vintage where the grapes of wrath were sown [*sic*]. . . . His truth is marching on. Glory, Glory, Hallelujah, His truth is marching on.' " "Perhaps," the fictional newspaper speculates, "some who understood English appreciated the appropriateness of the reference to the 'terrible swift sword'; or perhaps some even thought that God's truth was marching on. In Rome one cannot say. Even Romans find it difficult to tell when their playacting ends and their real emotions begin. In any case, the tears, as always, were genuine."[34]

The closest real life ever came to fulfilling Murphy's "exotic medley" of "ritual Romana" and "martial Americana" was in 2008 when Benedict XVI visited the United States for the first time since becoming pope. At the Bush White House, 13,000 people filled the South Lawn to greet the pontiff. The elaborate early-morning ceremony featured the operatic soprano Kathleen Battle singing the Lord's Prayer. The pope closed his message with the words "God bless America!" In the C-Span footage, President George W. Bush can be heard responding, "Thank you, Your Holiness. Awesome speech! We're going to sit down for one more song." That final song was the "Battle Hymn of the Republic" performed by the US Army Chorus and the Marine Band.[35] First Lady Laura Bush recalled later that none other than the papal nuncio had asked for "the song with the words 'Glory! Glory! Hallelujah.' "[36]

The conservative radio talk show host Rush Limbaugh remembered being so inspired by the White House ceremony and the choice of the "Battle Hymn" that he decided to talk with President Bush about it live on air.[37] Two years later, in 2010, Limbaugh replayed the impromptu interview, prompted to do so by having just seen footage of the dedication of the George W. Bush Presidential Library and Museum at Southern Methodist University in Dallas. While he was working at his desk, Limbaugh's attention was arrested by the sound of the US Army Chorus singing the "Battle Hymn" at the ceremony in Texas. His thoughts turned immediately to Pope Benedict's 2008 visit to the White House. Hearing the "Battle Hymn" that day "just made me stop and have total reverence for the song for what it was about, for its history, who wrote it, how it was written." Moved by Howe's words and the tune, he played the "Battle Hymn" for the next three days on his show. Now, in 2010, he rebroadcast his conversation with President Bush, cuing it up with the "Battle Hymn." The exchange was brief. They both noted the unprecedented number of guests at the event to welcome the pope. "And it was really interesting to watch people's expression during the ceremony," Bush said, "and particularly when His Holy Father got up to speak. There was this unbelievable respect, and everybody hung on his every word, and it was beautiful, and you're right, the Army Choir was just fantastic. I wish all Americans could have seen it." Greeting Pope Benedict "was a great honor for me," he continued, "and it's what you expect for the president to do, and that is to welcome a world figure, such as the Holy Father, in such grand fashion."

At this point, Limbaugh returned to his live program. He thought the Obama administration paled in comparison to the faith and dignity of the Bush years. He was struck by hearing again Bush's simple statement "It's what you expect for the president to do." "That's the kind of thing presidents are supposed to do," Limbaugh echoed. "And he's right. And it doesn't happen nearly enough. And when I heard 'The Battle Hymn of the Republic' today at his library dedication, I thought, what a coincidence, what a coincidence." "So thank you for indulging me in that," he told his audience. "I could play that song a couple more times. I obsessed over it listening to it late at night on my computer at home after everybody had gone to bed. I was just alone with my thoughts. Glory, glory, hallelujah."

The Republican Party and its agenda did not monopolize Catholic loyalties, of course, nor determine how all Catholics would choose to interpret the "Battle Hymn." Progressive Catholics thought they, too, knew what Howe's poem meant. In November 2010, Monsignor Charles Pope wrote about the "Battle Hymn" in a blog post for the website of the Archdiocese of Washington, DC. Monsignor Pope served in the city as pastor of Holy Comforter-St. Cyprian Church. In the 1990s, he led a weekly Bible study at the Capitol and later at the White House. His reading of the "Battle Hymn" tacked closer to the vision of the revolutionary Pope Francesco in *The Vicar of Christ* than to anything coming out of the Bush White House. Monsignor Pope was prompted to write by the reading for Mass on November 23. The text was Revelation 14:14–19, verses about the harvest of God's judgment and the vintage destined to be crushed in his winepress—a passage, along with Revelation 19, indispensable to Howe, Harriet Beecher Stowe, William Henry Channing, and others in the Civil War. When he heard this apocalyptic text, the monsignor thought immediately of the first verse of the "Battle Hymn," just as Howe had intended.

Monsignor Pope appreciated Howe's unflinching vision of divine justice. He retold the story of the composition of the "Battle Hymn" and the poet's "moment of inspiration." He offered his readers an exegesis of all the verses, including the abandoned sixth verse so rarely seen or heard. Line by line he showed how indebted the "Battle Hymn" was to the Old and New Testaments. Reflecting on verse 5 with its call to "die to make men free," Monsignor Pope applied the "Battle Hymn" to his readers' lives: "We are to carry our crosses as he did . . . and if necessary to die for others. As his cross made us holy, our cross can help to make others free."

"Ah, what a hymn," he sighed. "It is remarkably Christological and Bibli-cal. Some consider it controversial. But that's OK, the Bible is too, and this hymn is [a] rather remarkable stitching of Bible verses and allusions. For this reason, it is not only the Battle Hymn of the Republic, it is also the Bible Hymn of the Republic."[38] Evidently, the monsignor thought the quotations in the "Battle Hymn of the Republic" from, and allusions to, the Bible added up to Howe's poem being "biblical." Many evangelicals thought the same, as did Mormons.

If there is any group in the United States that has gone further than evan-gelicals and Catholics to baptize the "Battle Hymn of the Republic" for their own community it is the Church of Jesus Christ of Latter-day Saints. By the 1890s at the latest, the Mormons had adopted the "Battle Hymn" to ease their way into the American cultural and religious mainstream after more than half a century of opposition in the courts, the schools, and the public square, even to the point of open warfare with federal troops. Mormonism's growth in the nineteenth century had caused many to rethink the proper line between church and state. It was one thing for Protestant Christianity to influence public policy but quite another for Mormonism to do so. What the Mormons achieved with the help of the "Battle Hymn" by the end of the 1950s highlights just how malleable the poem proved to be.

Howe's hostility to Mormonism appears nowhere in books about her, and yet her attitude was well known when anti-Mormonism itself was commonplace in American public life. In 1890, Howe delivered a lec-ture on Mormonism for a Boston meeting of combined chapters of the Women's Auxiliary Conference. Howe offered what she called "A Medi-tation on the Theory and Practice of Religion Suggested by Mormonism." She was not happy. She had visited Utah two years earlier and did not like what she saw. According to a report published by the organization's secretary, Howe warned that Mormonism was having alarming success in converting the lower classes from Europe. One member of the audience called Mormonism "awful in every way" and "the next great crime to slavery."[39] Slavery had been vanquished, but Mormonism flourished. In the twentieth century, Mormonism would secure a solid reputation for promoting family values, voting Republican, and abstaining from alcohol, tobacco, and caffeine. In 1890, polite Bostonians thought the religion a national menace to be eradicated. In that year, under the threat of federal action, the Mormons' new president reversed the church's official sanction of polygamy.

Extensive notes for Howe's Boston lecture survive among her papers at Harvard.[40] She denounced Mormonism in terms far beyond anything she had said about Roman Catholicism or evangelicalism in the 1850s. "My experience in Mormonism," she said, "shows me the great lapse from rational to irrational religion upon which the church of Utah is founded." She was alarmed by the rapid headway this "irrational religion" was making in the United States and among European nations otherwise "deemed enlightened." "The mischiefs of this system are beyond words," she warned, thinking especially of polygamy's degradation of women, a system of marriage that turned a man into a "tyrant" and women into members of a "harem" to serve as the mere "instrument of his pleasure."

Howe then broadened her concern to include mass immigration from tyrannical European nations whose "unequal systems train our future citizens." "The dangers which threaten our country arising from the immorality and irreligion of other countries," she warned her Boston audience, "are too serious to be passed over with mere rhetoric, or with mere speculative consideration. The foe, despicable but dangerous, is in our midst, and has command of the highways of the ocean." Whether anarchists, Mormons, or papists, the strangers among us threatened the survival on our shores of "Christian civilization" and "republican government." As a step toward averting the danger of the wrong kind of foreign influx, Howe even proposed that American residents in Europe alert the United States to the true character of likely immigrants:

I cannot but think that American residents abroad would find many opportunities, if they sought them, of making themselves and us acquainted with the character and condition of the classes most likely to emigrate to our shores. Such an investigation might bring to light beforehand dangers which we, as a nation, are not obliged to incur. An American protective association, resident abroad, might be formed. Such an association might do much to protect us from the importation and immigration of recognized criminals, and of those whose poverty and degradation are such as are nearly akin to crime. Any action which our Government takes or tries to take in this direction could be greatly aided by private and personal research.

Howe did not choose to publish these anti-Mormon and anti-immigrant sentiments, but they nevertheless testify to the limits of her internationalism and religious tolerance and to the limits of who and what she imagined becoming part of American "nationality." If there is an inconsistency here it is not much different from the anti-immigrant editorials written around the same time by Francis Bellamy, author of the Pledge of Allegiance. Howe could think of her righteous America opening its arms just so wide, and certainly not for religions and peoples too alien for the nation's political institutions and ideals to absorb. But in little more than half a century, Mormons would be using her "Battle Hymn" as the theme song of their own irrefragable Americanism. They became patriots among patriots. With Howe's poem in hand, Mormons become the quintessential exponents of sacred nationalism. And they had it on the authority of the Book of Mormon that God, with an irrevocable covenant, had chosen America for his people, a "choice land," "free from bondage, and from captivity," and "a land of liberty."[41]

Mormons began singing their way into their starring role in religious nationalism as early as the 1890s. The Tabernacle Choir was invited to participate at the World's Columbian Exposition in Chicago in 1893, a venue at which Howe happened to lecture. The historian David W. Stowe marks this event as the moment the choir began to "establish a national audience." A deal with Columbia Records in 1910 was followed by a successful tour, an appearance at the Taft White House, and by 1919 pioneering broadcasts over the NBC radio network. So successful was the choir's rise to national prominence and respectability that Stowe dubs them "the anointed voice of America's civil religion."[42]

The choir's contracts with Columbia continued with mounting success. In 1958, the choir recorded *The Beloved Choruses* on the Columbia label, an ambitious all-classical album, performed with conductor Eugene Ormandy and the Philadelphia Orchestra. Columbia had signed the Salt Lake City choir to produce two records a year. The choir's big sound was a hit with consumers. *The Lord's Prayer*, the second collaboration with Ormandy and the Philadelphia Orchestra, followed in 1959. The "Battle Hymn of the Republic" appeared as the last song on this album and helped popularize the Peter Wilhousky arrangement, the version most often heard today. Columbia released the "Battle Hymn" as a single, and it rose to the top of the *Billboard* charts to join Bobby Darin, Paul Anka, the Coasters, and the Everly Brothers. It won that year's Grammy Award for Best Performance by a Vocal Group or Chorus. By October 1959, sales of *The Lord's Prayer* had reached 60,000, while sales of the "Battle Hymn" single reached an astonishing 300,000. The Tabernacle Choir's rendition of the "Battle Hymn" had become the definitive version for most Americans.[43]

Billboard was as surprised as anyone. " 'Battle Hymn' Sets Precedent as Pop Single," it reported. "The most unusual new pop singles hit today is 'The Battle Hymn of the Republic,' by the Mormon Tabernacle Choir and the Philadelphia Symphony [*sic*] on Columbia. It is believed to be the first time a symphony orchestra and religious choir has clicked in the rock and roll-oriented pop singles field." But how had that unprecedented achievement been possible? *Billboard* traced the takeoff of the "Battle Hymn" to station WERE in Cleveland. Local disc jockey Bill Randle "found it in an LP and started playing it steadily on his pop platter program." His engineer was the first to cut the single, and Columbia followed with its own release. "It was Randle who first spotted the pop single potential of 'Yellow Rose of Texas' when he heard it on Columbia's 'Confederacy' LP," *Billboard* continued. The music industry magazine also found a connection to the Cold War and the Soviet premier's arrival in the United States. Radio station WONE in Dayton, Ohio, was "currently programming the Mormon Choir disk daily, and plans to continue spinning it regularly thruout [*sic*] Nikita S. Khrushchev's visit to America, as what [the station producer] calls 'the sound of freedom.' "[44]

The next month, the cover of *Life* magazine featured a photo of a laughing Khrushchev holding an ear of corn, and inside explained the triumph of the "Battle Hymn" as a "pop hit." The story included pictures of Howe and of the Philadelphia Orchestra and the Tabernacle Choir rehearsing for the recording. "Moving up fast on the best-selling song lists past *Makin' Love* and *Kissin' Time*," an amused *Life* reported, "is the season's most surprising hit, the venerable *Battle Hymn of the Republic*. As socked out by the 110-man Philadelphia Orchestra and the 200-voice Mormon Tabernacle Choir led by Eugene Ormandy, the old Civil War song has more fancy fanfares, vocal polish and decibels than the loudest rock 'n' roll blasts. A single record culled from Columbia's *Lord's Prayer* has already sold more than 200,000."[45]

The choir's version of Howe's poem popularized a small change to the last verse that had circulated for years. Instead of the vow to follow

Christ's sacrifice and "die to make men free," the choir called upon the nation to "*live* to make men free." The change to the popular Wilhousky arrangement had the advantage of detaching Howe's lyrics from war and making the "Battle Hymn" applicable to any cause requiring self-sacrifice. So closely has this call to dedicated service been identified with the Tabernacle Choir that it is easy to assume the change originated with the Mormons themselves in the twentieth century.

But Howe herself was among the earliest to urge the faithful to "live to make men free." In 1891, on the platform with Susan B. Anthony and Frances Willard, she helped calm an agitated crowd at a women's rally by starting to sing the last verse of the "Battle Hymn," encouraging the audience to join her, and substituting "live" for "die." Even earlier, by the 1870s, temperance reformers had enlisted the change for the cause of national sobriety. Frances Willard often repeated the modified last verse in her campaign against demon rum, including in the pages of her autobiography. Soldiers in the US Army reportedly sang it this way in Manila at Christmas 1898 to celebrate the victory over Spanish imperialism for the sake of humanity. Fred Waring's Pennsylvanians on stage, radio, and television only popularized what had already become commonplace in American newspapers. The Mormon Tabernacle Choir seems to have solidified with its chart-topping recording a version of Howe's text that had already been inspiring reformers for generations.[46]

Thanks to its hit single and album, the choir began to appear more frequently and more prominently in the nation's civil ceremonies. President Eisenhower had already taken the initiative by inviting the choir to sing at the White House in 1958 ahead of their chart-topping success. In July 1962, the now 360-voice choir performed live from Mount Rushmore in South Dakota for the inaugural Telstar satellite broadcast to Europe. The carved heads of Washington, Jefferson, Lincoln, and Teddy Roosevelt loomed behind them in the grainy overseas transmission as they sang "A Mighty Fortress Is Our God" and the "Battle Hymn."[47] Vatican Radio hailed the broadcasts as "capable of opening the way to a growing victory of truth over error, ignorance and deceit."[48]

Democrats and Republicans embraced the choir. In February 1964, President Lyndon Johnson invited the group to sing at the White House, and it performed for him there in July. That same month, the choir sang at the Republican National Convention in California. After the Democratic victory, the press reported that the 375-voice choir had been invited to sing at LBJ's inauguration in January. The director chose the "Battle Hymn," the *Chicago Tribune* reported, because of the song's "special combination of spiritual and patriotic qualities." A few Southern congressmen questioned the choice of the Union battle anthem, but it stayed on the program. Clergy officiating at the ecumenical ceremony included the archbishop of San Antonio, a rabbi from Houston, the pastor of Washington's National City Christian Church, and the Greek Orthodox archbishop for North and South America.[49] The Mormon Tabernacle Choir returned to DC in 1969 and 1973 to perform at Richard M. Nixon's inaugurations. The choir's biggest role in any inauguration came in 1981 for Ronald Reagan. According to the choir's most recent historian, "They sang during the opening ceremony of the inaugural at the Lincoln Memorial—organized primarily by Osmond Entertainment—they rode in a seventy-foot float in the inaugural parade, stopping (per Nancy Reagan's request) at the presidential review box to sing 'The Battle Hymn of the Republic.' "[50] The Mormons' ascent in only ninety years from unassimilable national pariah to pop-culture phenomenon is an American success story. The "exotic medley" of religious nationalism added one more voice. Only dissidents dared point out the discord. But in the 1960s, the nation that strove for unity in the Cold War found itself more fractured than at any time since the Civil War.

9

A SEVERED NATION

Washington, DC's Civil War Centennial Commission hosted a gala at the National Gallery of Art on November 18, 1961, to honor Julia Ward Howe and her "Battle Hymn." The commission acknowledged a loss of confidence in the nation and around the world at the start of the decade, but that uncertainty prompted renewed affirmations of national purpose. The keynote speaker was the best-selling historian Bruce Catton, author of the 1954 Pulitzer Prize–winning *Stillness at Appomattox*. The occasion was dignified and to the point. The former pastor of the New York Avenue Presbyterian Church in DC offered the invocation.[1] In his keynote address, Catton reflected on the significance of the "Battle Hymn" after a hundred years. It had not faded: "Somehow it does not sound hollow now. . . . The hymn continues to move us." And yet he acknowledged the danger of self-doubt in a generation that might have lost sight of the path ahead. "We live today . . . in a world whose faith has grown gray and which is suspicious of the dedicated spirit." He worried that "our moments of confident affirmation—except, to be sure, when we are talking about our own strength and riches—are unfortunately few." And that is where Howe's poem could help: "The Battle Hymn . . . is the great affirmation of our belief—our belief in ourselves, in the significance of what we do and mean, in the eternal value[s] that lie beyond life. . . . It is something to be sung—and to be lived up to, by us and by all Americans, now and always."[2]

Celebrations of the "Battle Hymn of the Republic" in DC in 1961 joined the flood of national, state, and local commemorations honoring the nation's "new birth of freedom" a century earlier. School children, museums, civic organizations, and battlefield parks staged events to mark the 100th anniversaries of Gettysburg, Appomattox, and Ford's Theater. These observances began as the nation said farewell to President Eisenhower and welcomed John F. Kennedy. They continued into the years of the Bay of Pigs, the Cuban Missile Crisis, the escalation of US military involvement in Vietnam, and of one of the most active phases of the civil rights movement. The "Battle Hymn" helped the nation memorialize a heroic and tragic past. It also resumed its role—more poignantly and visibly than it had been called upon to do since Lincoln's death—as a national requiem at the funerals of Kennedy, Martin Luther King Jr., and Robert Kennedy. Singers Judy Garland and Andy Williams fused popular culture, mass media, national grief, and the "Battle Hymn" in ways not seen before; and as they did so, they attached the "Battle Hymn of the Republic" to images of profound loss, perhaps powerful enough to change the poem's symbolism, if not from destiny back into judgment, then at least from destiny into doubt.

At the same time, the 1960s brought the "Battle Hymn" under a new kind of scrutiny—from historians, sociologists, literary critics, and novelists. Just as the poem's status as a national monument seemed most secure, this attention turned it into an artifact to be studied, and for some even a problem to be solved. The "Battle Hymn" had always had its critics and dissenters. But in the Vietnam era something new was underway. Parts of American culture began to analyze a historically "situated" "Battle Hymn" and not an untouchable sacred text. A civil religious higher criticism dared to apply historical methods to American scripture. In some ways, the sacred identity of the "Battle Hymn" would intensify, and the "Battle Hymn" would take its place in the twenty-first century literally alongside holy writ in the Museum of the Bible in Washington. But if it was ever going to reach that final apotheosis it was going to have to contend with the self-consciousness, textual criticism, and historical inquiry that might rob it of its power to make America sacred. Could the "Battle Hymn" continue as an affirmation of religious nationalism in a time of deepening doubt about American virtue, cohesiveness, and prospects for success at home and abroad?

Two years after Bruce Catton memorialized Howe and her "Battle Hymn," in the days following Kennedy's assassination, tributes to the fallen president poured in from cities around the world, including Berlin, Paris, Madrid, Warsaw, Moscow, London, Cairo, and Jerusalem. The Second Vatican Council, meeting in Rome, paused in its deliberations to attend a Mass at the Basilica of St. John Lateran conducted by New York's Francis Cardinal Spellman.[3] Sunday worshippers at Westminster Abbey sang the "Battle Hymn" in Kennedy's memory. Among the 3,000 mourners were the prime minister, his cabinet, members of the opposition, and the Duke of Edinburgh.[4] The aging Winston Churchill, about to celebrate his eighty-ninth birthday, was unable to attend, but Lady Clementine Churchill and her son Randolph were there to pay their respects to the American president.[5] The congregation sang the "Battle Hymn," carrying on an unbroken tradition of honoring America in that place since World War I. On December 13, 1963, a disoriented Judy Garland closed her television show with her own tribute to Kennedy. She sang the "Battle Hymn." At times, the lyrics escaped her, but she forced her way through to the end with great emotion.

And then there was Winston Churchill's own funeral. On January 30, 1965, the BBC televised the elaborate state funeral. More than four hours of coverage followed the wartime prime minister's flag-draped coffin through the streets of London, to the nave of St. Paul's Cathedral, and then to Waterloo Station. The cathedral choristers, family, and friends sang the "Battle Hymn of the Republic." The Stars and Stripes joined the Union Jack at the front of the cathedral. Missing was a high-ranking American official, although former president Eisenhower was there. *Life* magazine was chagrined that an ailing Lyndon Johnson had not sent Vice President Hubert Humphrey to pay his respects. But the magazine thought the flag and the "Battle Hymn" appropriate tributes. Nor did anything seem odd about Queen Elizabeth, Prince Philip, and the Queen Mother singing Howe's Civil War anthem.[6] The royal family had sung it before. They would sing it again. Churchill had specially asked for the hymn to be sung at his funeral. Some said he included it to honor his American mother; others, as an expression of his hope for cordial Anglo-American relations.

The American press drew attention to Howe's poem. The Associated Press reporter Eddy Gilmore, former Moscow bureau chief and winner of the Pulitzer Prize for his journalism in 1947, began his story on Churchill's funeral with the "Battle Hymn," saying that the former prime minister had "passed into history . . . to the strains of the Battle Hymn of the Republic." He thought, mistakenly, that it might have been the first time such a gathering had sung the "Battle Hymn" together. But surely it was still notable that Eisenhower and Chief Justice Earl Warren joined Charles de Gaulle, Lady Churchill, and Queen Elizabeth to honor the former prime minister in this way. Once the casket was brought to the front, the choir began to sing the "Battle Hymn" and was then joined by the congregation for this opening hymn. For the congregation, overcome by the moment, Gilmore reported, "the emotion was more than many could bear. They wept unashamed." The BBC camera at that moment showed an American flag flying outside the cathedral.[7]

In the midst of this reverence, the English novelist Graham Greene handled the "Battle Hymn" with his characteristic dark humor and skepticism. The song seemed to capture his mixed feelings about America's role in the world. Greene wrote his novel *The Comedians* in 1965 after a dangerous excursion he had made from the Dominican Republic into François "Papa Doc" Duvalier's corrupt and violent Haiti. Greene's highly anticipated novel followed his devastating 1963 report for the London *Sunday Telegraph* aimed at toppling Duvalier's "nightmare republic." The essay appeared in November and was reprinted in the *New Republic* just days before Kennedy's assassination.[8]

The novel is set at the fictional Hotel Trianon in Port-au-Prince.[9] One of the guests, the American Mrs. Smith, is a crusading vegetarian reformer whose husband had just failed in his third-party run for the US presidency. She intervenes with surprising courage to rescue the hotel's proprietor. She expresses her disgust at the behavior of one of the Duvalier regime's ruthless henchmen. "The American accent with which the words were spoken," the proprietor narrates, "had to me all the glow and vigour of Mrs. Julia Ward Howe's *Battle Hymn of the Republic*. The grapes of wrath were trampled out in them and there was a flash of the terrible swift sword. They stopped my opponent with his fist raised to strike."[10] If Greene knew just how involved Julia and Samuel Gridley Howe had been in Santo Domingo and the Grant administration's efforts to annex the island republic in the 1870s, his use of the "Battle Hymn" showed not only brilliant insight into the moral obtuseness of the United States' eagerness to help any regime no matter how corrupt so long as it claimed to be anti-Communist but also an awareness of America's long history of humanitarian interventionism in the region.

Among American intellectuals, domestic and foreign crises in the 1960s brought an opportunity to question the role of the "Battle Hymn" in forming the American identity—even as the song continued to be sung with sincere patriotism by schools, churches, veterans groups, and countless civic organizations. Second thoughts about the "Battle Hymn" seem to have begun with the literary critic Edmund Wilson. Reverberations of Wilson's work can be detected in the later work of Robert Penn Warren and perhaps of John Updike. In 1962, Wilson published *Patriotic Gore*, his landmark study of the literature of the American Civil War. It has become a modern classic and remains in print. Wilson had been associated as editor or author with *Vanity Fair*, the *New Republic*, the *New Yorker*, and the *New York Review of Books*. As a leading literary critic and essayist, he helped cultivate a discerning readership for T. S. Eliot, Wallace Stevens, John Dos Passos, Ernest Hemingway, F. Scott Fitzgerald, and William Faulkner.

In *Patriotic Gore*, a title taken from the Confederate anthem "Maryland, My Maryland," Wilson turned to America's literary past, broadly construed, to reacquaint the public with the nation's most "articulate" war generation, as he called them. He ranged widely across the works of Harriet Beecher Stowe, Abraham Lincoln, Ulysses S. Grant, Mary Chestnut, Robert E. Lee, Alexander Stephens, Kate Chopin, and Ambrose Bierce. Coming to Howe and her "Battle Hymn," he turned his attention more generally to wars and mythmaking. "The real causes of war still remain out of range of our national thought," he wrote at the time of the centennial; "but the minds of nations at war are invariably dominated by myths, which turn the conflict into melodrama and make it possible for each side to feel that it is combatting some form of evil." If the South had its myth, a myth that long outlived the war, then the North had its myth, too: "This vision of Judgment was the myth of the North." Giving our attention only to political and economic causes, Wilson argued, can lead us to miss the mythic power of Armageddon in the Northern mind. Howe's verses gave Union troops their marching orders under the banner of this myth.[11] In Wilson's hands, the "Battle Hymn" looked like something tribal and primitive.

Wilson emerged as the most important early contributor to the cultural deconstruction of the "Battle Hymn." He influenced a generation of critics and doubters. His technique is evident in his analysis of the fifth verse. He thought Howe's evocation of Christ's death "particularly interesting on account of its treatment of Jesus, so characteristic of Calvinism." By a "Calvinist" depiction of Jesus, Wilson seems to have meant that Howe subordinated Jesus, his person and work, to the wrathful Father. The Father stands center stage, breathing fiery vengeance. If he meant that Howe was a Calvinist theologically in 1861, he missed the mark. Yes, she was proud of her Puritan ancestry, but her Calvinism was selective, and she recoiled in horror from its theology. Howe's "Christ" of the "Battle Hymn" was ill defined and mystical but fully consistent with the Christ of liberal Unitarianism she had learned from Theodore Parker and James Freeman Clarke and worked out in her poetry.

Nevertheless, Wilson seems to have had in mind a cultural Calvinism more than a theological one. "As is often the case with Calvinists," he wrote, "Mrs. Howe, though she feels she must bring Him in, gives Him a place which is merely peripheral. He is really irrelevant to her picture, for Christ died to make men holy; but this is not what God is having us do: He is a militant, a military God, and far from wanting us to love our enemies, He gives 'the Hero' orders to 'crush the serpent with his heel.' The righteous object of this is to 'make men [the Negroes] free,' and we must die to accomplish this. Note that Christ is situated 'across the sea'; he is not present on the battlefield with His Father, yet, intent on our grisly work, we somehow share in His 'glory.'" In a penetrating insight close to what John Updike would say thirty years later, Wilson thought that the odd image of the lilies worked only "to place [Christ] in a setting that is effeminate as well as remote."[12]

Wilson's interpretation of the "Battle Hymn" as myth would soon affect the work of other scholars, but in the meantime, historians helped secure the poem's centrality to American history and identity, even to the point of intensifying its symbolic power and expanding its reach. In 1966, Daniel J. Boorstin published a best-selling anthology of historical documents he called *An American Primer*. For decades, the primer was used nationwide as a supplement in college survey courses. The Harvard-trained Boorstin, who taught for many years at the University of Chicago, later won the Pulitzer Prize in history for *The Americans: The Democratic Experience* (1974) and was appointed Librarian of Congress by President Gerald R. Ford the following year.

Boorstin's two-volume collection of eighty-three documents covered over 300 years of American history, from the *Mayflower* Pilgrims to Lyndon Johnson. It ran through multiple editions into the 1990s and was translated into Spanish and French. It became a standard in classrooms, especially as a one-volume paperback. The inclusion of John Winthrop's Model of Christian Charity, just as the Puritan discourse was being integrated into American civil religion as never before thanks to the innovative use of it in 1961 by Ted Sorenson, a speechwriter for Kennedy, helped to popularize this once-obscure document and its "city on a hill" metaphor for generations of students.[13] Indeed, Boorstin used Winthrop's "city on a hill" passage as an epigram for his whole book. Tellingly, he called his anthology "a kind of American catechism—a catechism not of orthodoxy but of hopes and institutions. It introduces us to ourselves." For each catechetical document, Boorstin commissioned a prominent scholar to set the work in its historical context.[14]

For the "Battle Hymn," Boorstin chose the religious historian William G. McLoughlin, by 1966 the author of several influential books on Billy Sunday, revivalism, and Billy Graham. The Brown University professor called the "Battle Hymn" "the supreme example of the elementary urge of Americans to equate their religious and their patriotic ideals." He did not offer this assessment of the poem's significance as a warning against confusing theology, politics, and war. Rather, he thought he detected in the "Battle Hymn" America's self-understanding as a chosen nation and echoes of the Puritans' aspiration to be a city on a hill. In this way, he extended the unified story. He predicted Howe's verses would endure "as an anthem of American hope and faith, as an intonation of belief in the ultimate triumph of freedom and justice for all, and as an inspirational pledge to work for the coming of the millennium." "When it ceases to inspire Americans," he warned, "something fundamental and elemental will have departed from the national spirit."[15] The contrast between Edmund Wilson's characterization of the "Battle Hymn" as the Yankee myth of judgment and William McLoughlin's invocation of the poem's centrality to the national spirit could not have been starker. Two distinct "Battle Hymns of the Republic"—nationalist and internationalist—had emerged in the 1920s; that divide only deepened in the 1960s. This time, though, the divide came not between different camps of true believers in sacred America but between a new generation of true believers on one side divided against skeptics and outright unbelievers. Once that split happened, there seemed little reason to expect they would ever be reunited into one national church.

Though each in his own way, Wilson and McLoughlin highlight an increasing self-consciousness in the 1960s in the way scholars treated the "Battle Hymn" and religious nationalism more broadly. If we add Graham Greene to that tendency, then novelists were showing signs of the same self-consciousness about Howe's poem. That tendency was reinforced by the emergence of American civil religion itself as a distinct area of academic scholarship in the 1960s. The University of California, Berkeley, sociologist Robert Bellah launched the modern study of civil religion with an essay in 1967.[16] The study per se of the nexus of American religion, nationalism, and war was not new in the 1960s (we have only to think of Carlton Hayes's work in the 1920s or sociologist Ray H. Abrams's study of American religion and World War I in the 1930s to see otherwise). Nor was the systematic study of civil religion new, as, at least among political philosophers, it dates back to the ancients and was carried on by Machiavelli and more famously by Rousseau in his *Social Contract*. What was new in the 1960s was the degree to which discussion of civil religion became open and public and entered into the very way Americans talked about themselves and their identity. The study of civil religion became a means to national self-understanding, or at least a groping in the dark toward self-understanding. Civil religion was no longer something Americans simply "did." It was now something they talked about doing and watched themselves doing in the past and present. Civil religion was revealed as man-made and vulnerable to being unmade.

Bellah not only drew attention to the existence of a civil religion in American life but also argued that this national affirmation of faith functioned "alongside of and rather clearly differentiated from the churches [as] an elaborate and well-institutionalized civil religion in America."[17] Will Herberg (in *Protestant, Catholic, Jew*) might think the national faith was merely a generic "American Way of Life," but for Bellah civil religion was something far more substantive and in need of thoughtful study. As a sociologist, Bellah focused mostly on the way civil religion functioned as an institution, helping to bind the American community together, and operating alongside a plurality of allegiances to other religions. Just how "clearly differentiated" civil religion has been in practice from these other religions is something the history of the "Battle Hymn of the Republic" calls into question.

As his prime example of civil religion, Bellah used John F. Kennedy's inaugural address. Developing ideas he had been working on since his Fulbright lectures in Japan in 1961, Bellah argued that it would be a mistake to dismiss the Catholic Kennedy's three nonsectarian invocations of God's name in his speech as mere ritual, tradition, or empty piety, or as proof that the nation's once-robust faiths had faded into a generic aspiration of divine guidance. Kennedy's civil religion acknowledged America's God while still respecting the separation of church and state, and the private sphere from the public, Bellah insisted. The president could participate in the "beliefs, symbols, and rituals" of the American civil religion and acknowledge this "God" as the transcendent source of political legitimacy and civil liberties without violating anyone's conscience. Bellah insisted on the continuity between Kennedy's rhetoric and the American founding. It formed a unified story. Even when Kennedy claimed at the end of his speech that "here on earth God's work must truly be our own," Bellah thought the president merely connected himself to the nation's earliest "motivating spirit."

In these ways, it was not difficult for America's first Catholic president to unite himself with an unbroken tradition of vague deism stretching from Benjamin Franklin, George Washington, Thomas Jefferson, and the Declaration of Independence through Lincoln and the Gettysburg Address. Bellah refused to see the American civil religion as an impostor. Rather, "at its best [it] is a genuine apprehension of universal and transcendent religious reality as seen in or, one could almost say, as revealed through the experience of the American people." In so claiming, Bellah was unwilling to concede that civil religion, as such a potent "genuine" faith, was off limits to believers of other faiths worried about the temptation to worship other gods. Indeed, civil religion might be about to make its next big leap. Bellah envisioned the American civil religion joining a globalized civil religion promoted by a "transnational sovereignty" more potent than the United Nations.[18]

Did Bellah ever envision the "Battle Hymn of the Republic" becoming part of "a world civil religion"? If so, he may have unwittingly promoted something Howe herself anticipated more than a century before. "A world civil religion," he wrote at the end of his 1967 essay, "could be accepted as a fulfillment and not a denial of American civil religion. Indeed, such an outcome has been the eschatological hope of American civil religion from the beginning. To deny such an outcome would be to deny the meaning of America itself."[19] In 1975, Bellah paired Lincoln with Julia Ward Howe as the two Americans who best captured the meaning of America in prose and poetry. Lincoln preached his political sermons while Howe sang her beloved hymn. "In Lincoln's greatest public statements the tradition of American public oratory, infused with biblical imagery and expressed in an almost Puritan 'plain style,' attained a classic form. In Julia Ward Howe's 'The Battle Hymn of the Republic' the hymn tradition culminated in an almost perfect expression of the national spirit." Bellah highlighted the hymn's apocalypticism. Its words spoke of national testing and judgment. And in its last verse, it combined "Christian holiness and republican liberty." "It is not an accident," he insisted, "that one of the 20th century's greatest American novels of social protest, *The Grapes of Wrath*, took its title from the second line of the 'Battle Hymn' or that the old words took on apocalyptic meaning once again as a rallying cry in the great civil rights demonstrations of the late 1950s and early 1960s. A powerful fusion of imagery and feeling like that in the 'Battle Hymn' goes on working down through history."[20] But what was it about the "Battle Hymn" that led Bellah to assume that its violent stanzas would naturally work for good in history?

In 1967, Bellah's Berkeley colleague, English professor Earnest Lee Tuveson, wrote an influential account of the development of America's self-understanding as a "redeemer nation." Ranging freely over the history of American thought—too freely for some reviewers—Tuveson identified the key components of this identity: "chosen race, chosen nation; millennial-utopian destiny for mankind; [and] a continuing war between good (progress) and evil (reaction) in which the United States is to play a starring role as world redeemer."[21] All of these motifs clearly came from sources that were "religious in origin," he argued. As was true also of Bellah's foray into civil religion, the Vietnam War was never far below the surface of Tuveson's analysis, and he traced deep continuities between the earliest settlements in America and the battlefields of Southeast Asia. America's wars had been the primary means all along of intensifying this redemptive impulse in the national character. Coming to the Civil War, Tuveson engaged in a close reading of all five published verses of the "Battle Hymn." In Howe's poem, he began, the war's "apocalyptic trumpet sounded its clearest note."[22] Tuveson's analysis of the poem in these terms stands along with Edmund Wilson's as among the earliest attempts to treat the "Battle Hymn" diagnostically, as a symptom of a condition in the American mind that might turn out to be pathological. And second thoughts about the poem were never far removed from second thoughts about the poet or far removed from second thoughts about US foreign policy in the midst of Johnson's deepening war in Vietnam.

Tuveson argued that, given Howe's view of history, the poem's apocalyptic images appear not as handy poetic metaphors but rather as the key to the poet's whole attempt to locate the war in the history of redemption— in a very earthly redemption. "Taken together, [these images] are, as it were, a cipher which, decoded, conveys a message about the precise place and point of the war in the pattern of salvation." In other words, Howe wrote about the war in 1861 not *as if* it were another battle in the ongoing struggle between good and evil but as in fact the actual working out in history of the triumph of righteousness over wickedness. "Symbols thus merge, in a unique manner, with actual persons and objects." Howe's eyes were seeing the glory of the Lord coming in the Union army and its weapons of war. "The bugles Mrs. Howe had heard in the camp *were* the trumpets of God."[23] If Tuveson was right, then choirs, audiences, and congregations in modern America who downplay or ignore the ideology of the "Battle Hymn" are missing the whole point.

Tuveson also offered his own take on the seeming conflict between Howe's liberal theology and her invocation of the God of Battles. In light of Howe's Unitarianism, Tuveson suggested that at first glance she was an unlikely candidate to be the author of a poem of such "fundamentalist millennialist notions." She was, after all, a theological liberal certified by the best intellectual pedigree. She and her circle "had no faith in special revelation or mysteries in religion, and generally believed in the law of progress, and the perfectibility of human nature." Indeed, her Boston literary world "was far removed from the old grim ideas of a cosmic war of good and evil. Thus the fact that she was the poet of the American apocalyptic faith is significant; it shows how deeply such ideas must have penetrated the national mind."[24]

But rather than "far removed from the old grim ideas of a cosmic war of good and evil," Howe intensified that cosmic battle as never before, and she did so with the help of her carefully worked out war theology. Tuveson offered what could be called a "reversion thesis" as a way to account for the reappearance of "childhood teachings" in the mature Howe's most famous poem. But such a thesis is required only if we assume there was actually something that had to be accounted for in Howe's proclivity for Old and New Testament imagery of God's vengeance and blood-soaked vineyards. There is no reason to think Howe wrote her "Battle Hymn" in spite of her theology and had to find her inspiration in some primordial militant fundamentalism; she wrote her "Battle Hymn" because she interpreted the Civil War through the lens of her modern faith in history, God's justice in the here and now, and the imperative for wars for righteousness. Generations of Americans welcomed her vision into their national religious and political faith. The biblical resonance of her stanzas may have eased access for them into groups far removed from her theology, but any high-minded reformer recognized her vision of God's vineyard and answered her call to "die to make men free."

Gary Williams, professor emeritus of English at the University of Iowa, handled the question of Howe's theology more perceptively. Williams noted that in the third verse (about the "Hero, born of woman") "it seems to be Christ's courage facing torture and excruciating death, rather than the emblematic redemptive aspects of the crucifixion, that the poem likens to the sacrifice readers are asked to make. The third stanza depicts a 'Hero' born to crush the 'serpent.' This image of Christ is not necessarily Calvinistic or evangelical (and nothing at this point in Howe's life suggests a return to a mode of belief she had abandoned with relief twenty years earlier); instead, it may recall the militant, conviction-driven figure so compellingly limned in 'Whit-Sunday in the Church.' "[25] Whether churches know it or not, this is the modern Christ of Judgment that congregations still sing about as the "Battle Hymn" injects Howe's apocalypse and righteous conquest into their worship services.

Second thoughts about the "Battle Hymn" coming from literary critics, English departments, and sociologists should not obscure the fact that dissidents continued to speak up in the South where memories of the political theology of the "Battle Hymn" may have dimmed over time or become confused but had never vanished. The United Daughters of the Confederacy had campaigned against the "Battle Hymn" in the public schools and churches of the South in the 1920s and 1930s, but their opposition had been more instinctive and populist than academic. What appeared by the late 1960s was far more sophisticated. By 1968, plans were underway at St. Martin's Press in New York to bring out a new multivolume anthology of American literature. The editors for the project were Kentuckians Robert Penn Warren and Cleanth Brooks and Connecticut-born R. W. B. Lewis. Warren had been among the contributors to the Vanderbilt Agrarians' manifesto *I'll Take My Stand* in 1930 and won the Pulitzer Prize for *All the King's Men*, his fictional account of Louisiana governor Huey Long's rise and fall published in 1946. Brooks had contributed an essay to *I'll Take My Stand*'s 1936 sequel, *Who Owns America?* While an English professor at Yale, the dapper Kentuckian distinguished himself as a Faulkner scholar and a leading interpreter of Southern literature in general. Lewis, author of *The American Adam* (1955), also taught English at Yale and won the Pulitzer in 1976 for his biography of Edith Wharton, among numerous other awards.

When Warren wrote to Brooks about their ambitious project late in the summer of 1968, the "Battle Hymn" had been heard all over the nation in the preceding weeks. Anita Bryant had sung it at the political conventions that had nominated Richard Nixon and George McGovern. Andy Williams had sung it in June at St. Patrick's Cathedral in New York at Bobby Kennedy's funeral and had released it along with "Ave Maria" on the CBS label to raise funds for an RFK memorial. Warren wrote his friend on August 31 to say that he had finished a draft of his essay on Julia Ward Howe. He admitted the essay might be too long, but justified the amount of space he devoted to the poet: "The more I went into the matter the more I saw chances to get in certain things not otherwise readily available. It is the perfect—or is it?—chance to nail the apocalyptic strain in our psychology, which has been hinted at here and there." He found himself intrigued by the possibilities of Howe as a practitioner of "dream composition."[26]

Warren's final version added up to a 2,000-word introduction on Julia Ward Howe and her "Battle Hymn."[27] True to the theme announced in the anthology's subtitle, Warren attended to both the "maker" and the "making." After covering the basic facts of Howe's life and work, he plunged into an iconoclastic analysis of her (to him) questionable gifts and the "Battle Hymn." He relied in part on Wilson's *Patriotic Gore*. "The sudden, dreamlike composition of the 'Hymn' by a writer of such meager talent as Julia Ward Howe smacks of the miraculous—of automatic writing, literal inspiration, or divine guidance," he wrote. "Even she, in spite of her not inconsiderable vanity, was puzzled, even awestruck."[28] Warren, like Wilson, noted Howe's use of Isaiah 63:1–4. Her strategy, he wrote, "would focus all the echoes of the old Calvinistic sermons loaded with the ecstatic wrath of the Jew's *cherim* [or *herem*: exclusion from the community] and the fury of damnation in which the early New England (and, one is tempted to say, American) sensibility, and that of Julia Ward Howe on Bond Street [New York], had been steeped."[29]

Howe's "Battle Hymn" "precisely phrased the mood of those who felt the war as a moral crusade," Warren continued. It made her a celebrity; but more, it made her a symbol. Yes, she was "a public figure, a successful lecturer, a voluminous, if trivial, writer, the friend of the great, rich, and well-born, and, after death had removed the impediment of Dr. Howe, a doughty fighter for the rights of women. But her importance lay in the fact that she had become a national symbol." In short, "she had also become a symbol for one strain in our national psychology."[30] To reinforce his point, Warren used the report from the Philadelphia *Press* in 1899 about the dedication of a Civil War monument in Boston. A soloist sang the "Battle Hymn." Impressed, the reporter from the City of Brotherly Love believed that President McKinley would have been able to raise any number of troops to suppress insurrection in that moment as the crowd wept. "We do not know how much irony was in the reporter's nature; perhaps he did regard the Philippine operetta as a holy crusade," Warren concluded. "But we do know that the author of those lines that brought the audience to its feet ready to redeem the Philippines pasted the clipping in her journal. There was no irony in her nature."[31]

A number of years later, Warren's coeditor Cleanth Brooks remarked, "American millennialism has never been as violent as the various revolutionary movements of Europe have been—Marxism, for example—but it has remained from the seventeenth century [Puritans] onward a driving and shaping force in our history. One can find it in the essays of Emerson, in the poetry of Walt Whitman, and almost nakedly in Julia Ward Howe's 'Battle Hymn of the Republic.' It is still a powerful force right down to the present day, though it is now so familiar to most of us that we never refer to it by a term so formidable as millennialism, but speak of it rather fondly as simply the American Dream."[32]

Criticisms developed by Edmund Wilson, Robert Penn Warren, Cleanth Brooks, and others appeared later in essays of Agrarians and defenders of the Old South. M. E. Bradford, for example, placed Howe's "Battle Hymn" within what he called "the rhetoric for continuing revolution." Her poem marked the culmination of "New England self-delusion," the full throttle open on the chosen-nation imperial consciousness that had gone on to become the nation's "orthodoxy," he feared, "even in the most conservative circles."[33]

More recently, Wendell Berry, a Kentuckian who places himself in the lineage of the Vanderbilt Agrarians and yet has followed a distinctly leftward political trajectory on the environment, war, the economy, and gay marriage, spared none of his considerable rhetorical powers against the "Battle Hymn." Berry wrote about the "Battle Hymn" in the context of the Civil War's destruction of America's devotion to place, a casualty that itself belonged to a larger failure of imagination. The war's confidence in its own righteousness made the losses sustained in its prosecution invisible to most Americans. In addition to the North and the South, there had been a third side in this war: the dead. "Imagination," he wrote, "gives status in our consciousness and our hearts to a suffering that the statisticians would undoubtedly render in gallons of blood and gallons of tears." "Once dead," he continued, "the dead are conscripted again into abstraction by political leaders and governments, and this is a great moral ugliness." The more abstract the dead become, the easier it is to fight total wars to the point of annihilation. "Once the violence has started, the outcome must be victory for one side, defeat for the other—with perhaps unending psychological and historical consequences."[34]

Howe's "Battle Hymn" gave Berry the most familiar example he could call to mind to make his point about modern war and the failure of imagination that breaks down all limits. He admitted the song "has a splendid tune, but the words are perfectly insane. Suppose, if you doubt me, that an adult member of your family said to you, without the music but with the same triumphal conviction, 'Mine eyes have seen the glory of the coming of the Lord'—would you not, out of fear and compassion, try to find help? And yet this sectional hymn, by an alchemy obscure to me, seems finally to have given us all—North and South, East and West—a sort of official judgment of our history. It renders our ordeal of civil war into a truly terrifying simplemindedness, in which we can still identify Christ with military power and conflate 'the American way of life' with the will of God."[35]

Over the past century, American authors, North and South, have seemed irresistibly drawn to the "Battle Hymn" and compelled to make sense of it. Fragments of it have appeared in the poetry of Edgar Lee Masters, Ezra Pound, and e. e. cummings; in the African American playwright Alice Dunbar-Nelson's *Mine Eyes Have Seen the Glory* (1918) and David Mamet's *American Buffalo* (1975); and of course in John Steinbeck's most famous novel.[36] But perhaps no American author acknowledged himself to have been haunted more by the "Battle Hymn" than John Updike, chronicler in his Rabbit novels of post–World War II America in all its thwarted dreams, confusion, upheaval, and unexpected consolations. In his 2006 memoir, *Self-Consciousness*, Updike elaborated at some length on the degree to which Howe's words set the trajectory of his life's work, though he left a great deal unexplained in the process. In a chapter called "Getting the Words Out," the novelist recalled his painful humiliation as a child who stuttered, a malady he thought he could still sense "taunting" him as an adult as he struggled to explain himself and America.[37]

A neighbor boy named Eddie had called Updike "Ostrich" and had compounded his "fear of being misunderstood or mistaken for somebody else." Now, years later, Eddie still

> seemed to be taunting me when my first books met the criticism that I wrote all too well but had nothing to say: I, who seemed to myself full of things to say, who had all of Shillington [his hometown] to say, Shillington and

Pennsylvania and the whole mass of middling, hidden, troubled America to say, and who had seen and heard things in my two childhood homes, as my parents' giant faces revolved and spoke, achieving utterance under some terrible pressure of American disappointment, that would take a lifetime to sort out, particularize, and extol with the proper dark beauty. *In the beauty of the lilies Christ was born across the sea*—this odd and uplifting line from among the many odd lines of "The Battle Hymn of the Republic" seemed to me, as I set out [on his career as a writer], to summarize what I had to say about America, to offer itself as the title of a continental *magnum opus* of which all my books, no matter how many, would be mere installments, mere starts at the hymning of this great roughly rectangular country severed from Christ by the breadth of the sea.[38]

Tracing how Updike worked out his history of a nation "severed from Christ by the breadth of the sea" in the Rabbit novels or even in the tantalizingly titled *In the Beauty of the Lilies* is not easy. Was the "Battle Hymn" for Updike an essential way to convey the American story with its "proper dark beauty," or a great impediment to a severed nation's chance at self-knowledge? Perhaps he saw the void Samuel Montgomery Roosevelt painted in the middle of his canvas in 1919. As James A. Schiff notes, Updike consistently drew attention to America's "Protestant estrangement" from a Christ "born across the sea" and, in Updike's words, "not on this side of the ocean." "In *Lilies*," Schiff continues, "one either marches on with God and America or is left behind."[39]

Robert Penn Warren was sure (and disturbed) that "there was no irony in [Howe's] nature." But that gap left the door open to all sorts of historical ironies as the "Battle Hymn" was remade to suit any group or cause alien to Julia Ward Howe. We need only recall William Lewis's reaction to the hypocrisy of the 1912 Progressive Party convention in Chicago to see how bitter the irony could be for the children of emancipated slaves still waiting for justice in the twentieth century. In the post–World War II era, while cold warriors, evangelicals, Mormons, and Catholics sang the "Battle Hymn of the Republic," and critics dissected its stanzas, the civil rights movement enlisted Howe's poem in its own march for freedom. Blacks campaigning for civil rights, North and South, had a better claim than anyone to the original mobilization of the "Battle Hymn" against slavery, even if singing it at nonviolence rallies was a bit peculiar given its blood-bathed language. The movement's use of it in the push to become fully part of the American identity was not ironic, except for the possible shadow Howe's own racism cast over it, by then forgotten if it had ever really been acknowledged.

A typical use of the "Battle Hymn" came in February 1960 when demonstrators in Nashville sang Howe's anthem in front of the courthouse to protest the prosecution of seventy-six blacks and four whites who had violated the city's ordinance segregating lunch counters.[40] A week later, 2,000 black protestors in Montgomery, Alabama, planned to stage a rally in front of the state capitol, but as they marched toward the building they were turned back by police who threatened to disperse them with fire hoses. The crowd had assembled at the church across the street for a prayer meeting led by the Reverend Ralph Abernathy, who along with his friend Martin Luther King Jr. had founded the Montgomery Improvement Association and helped lead the bus boycott. Confronted by 10,000 white counterdemonstrators, the protestors gathered around Abernathy and sang "America the Beautiful" and the "Battle Hymn" before dispersing in small groups to head home.[41] The "Freedom Riders" would arrive in the city a year later to join in solidarity with the antisegregation movement.

The *New York Times* columnist and editor Herbert Mitgang thought he heard in the singing of the "Battle Hymn" "a clarion call in the South today." An author of popular books on Lincoln and the Civil War, Mitgang celebrated the civil rights cause as the fulfilment of the crusade begun in 1861. " 'The Battle Hymn of the Republic,' " he wrote in January 1962, at the time of its centennial, "exactly expressed the religious fervor of the abolitionists' dream 'to make men free,' and the truths of the century-old hymn—sung by Negroes besieged by a segregationist mob in Montgomery, Ala., last year—still go marching on." Howe's "Battle Hymn" had not faded into a historical artifact for this writer and for the movement he admired: "As long as Negroes, fighting for their rights in Alabama and elsewhere, sing, 'As He died to make men holy, let us die to make men free,' the lines written a century ago will be significant."[42]

Martin Luther King Jr. had been using the "Battle Hymn" in his speeches since at least 1957, and he helped turn Howe's opening lines into some of the most famous words of the civil rights movement. Preaching in April 1957 at Dexter Avenue Baptist Church, where he served as minister from 1954 to 1960, King delivered a sermon he called "The Birth of a

New Nation."⁴³ Just returned from a trip to the newly independent African nation of Ghana, he had stopped off in New York City, where he had seen the director Cecil B. DeMille's four-hour epic, *The Ten Commandments*, released in 1956. The Hebrew people had been liberated from their bondage in Egypt to become a new nation, and King was inspired by the film to think of America's own unfinished journey from the wilderness to the promised land of "cultural integration," brotherhood, and justice. Nearing the end of his Sunday morning sermon, he raised his voice as he took up the words of the "Battle Hymn":

> I say to you this morning, my friends, rise up and know that as you struggle for justice, you do not struggle alone. But God struggles with you. And He is working every day. Somehow I can look out, I can look out across the seas and across the universe, and cry out, "Mine eyes have seen the glory of the coming of the Lord. He is trampling out the vintage where the grapes of wrath are stored." Then I think about it because His truth is marching on, and I can sing another chorus: "Hallelujah, glory hallelujah! His truth is marching on."

King made it clear to his congregation that Ghana's independence marked the British Empire's setting sun. This was God's judgment on a nation and on a complacent established church that had built its power through exploitation. King's implication was obvious by the time he reached the "Battle Hymn": God would someday judge America and end America's exploitation of its subject race.

Passage of the Civil Rights Act of 1964 and the pending Voting Rights Act of 1965 provided the context for one of King's most extended uses of the "Battle Hymn." In March 1965, in a Thursday afternoon sermon preached after the march from Selma, King reviewed the history of Jim Crow segregation and focused on the push for voting rights. King called for an ongoing march until justice overcame segregated housing, segregated schools, poverty, unemployment, hunger, racism, and violence. He concluded with the "Battle Hymn." Repeating again and again the question "How long?" and hearing it echoed back from the audience, he answered, "Not long, (Not long) because

> Mine eyes have seen the glory of the coming of the Lord; (*Yes, sir*)
> He is trampling out the vintage where the grapes of wrath are stored; (*Yes*)
> He has loosed the fateful lightning of his terrible swift sword; (*Yes, sir*)

His truth is marching on. (*Yes, sir*)
He has sounded forth the trumpet that shall never call retreat; (*Speak, sir*)
He is sifting out the hearts of men before His judgment seat. (*That's right*)
O, be swift, my soul, to answer Him! Be jubilant my feet!
Our God is marching on. (*Yeah*)
Glory, hallelujah! (*Yes, sir*) Glory, hallelujah! (*All right*)
Glory, hallelujah! Glory, hallelujah!
His truth is marching on. [*Applause*]⁴⁴

But one sermon more than any other made the civil rights movement, King, and the "Battle Hymn" inseparable from each other, at least for the moment. On April 3, 1968, in Memphis, Tennessee, the night before his assassination, King preached at the Bishop Charles Mason Temple, the memorial church and resting place of the founder of the Church of God in Christ, the largest African American Pentecostal Holiness denomination. After a chilling comment about threats of violence against him, King ended with the first line of the "Battle Hymn":

Well, I don't know what will happen now; we've got some difficult days ahead. (*Amen*) But it really doesn't matter to me now, because I've been to the mountaintop. (*Yeah*) [*Applause*] And I don't mind. [*Applause continues*] Like anybody, I would like to live a long life—longevity has its place. But I'm not concerned about that now. I just want to do God's will. (*Yeah*) And He's allowed me to go up to the mountain. (*Go ahead*) And I've looked over (*Yes sir*), and I've seen the Promised Land. (*Go ahead*) I may not get there with you. (*Go ahead*) But I want you to know tonight (*Yes*), that we, as a people, will get to the Promised Land. [*Applause*] (*Go ahead, Go ahead*) And so I'm happy tonight; I'm not worried about anything; I'm not fearing any man. Mine eyes have seen the glory of the coming of the Lord. [*Applause*]⁴⁵

King tied the "Battle Hymn" to invocations of Moses and the Promised Land. The vision had ascended to the top of Mount Pisgah. If the "Battle Hymn" was in fact a poem about emancipation, equality, and racial justice, then King's use of it in the 1950s and 1960s was definitive.

Despite doubts raised in the 1960s and a generation's discovery of a severed nation, the "Battle Hymn" continued as a song of national resolve and national mourning. After the terrorist attacks of September 11, 2001, on the Twin Towers in New York, the Pentagon in Washington, and in the skies over Pennsylvania, Americans turned again as if by instinct to the "Battle Hymn." At the National Cathedral, thousands gathered three days later for a memorial service for the victims. Morning rain gave way to blue skies as the service progressed. President George W. Bush and the Reverend Billy Graham spoke. Following the president's address and his invocation of God's blessing on the nation, combined choirs, organ, and percussion led the congregation in all five verses of the "Battle Hymn of the Republic." Members of the audience wept, some overwhelmed with grief as they received the benediction.[46] That same day, London gathered at St. Paul's for its own memorial service, as it had done so many times before to honor its American friends and allies.[47]

An indication of just how completely the "Battle Hymn" had been woven into the fabric of America's national ceremonial life came during former president Reagan's funeral in 2004. The service at the National Cathedral in Washington, DC, on June 11 memorialized the Republican hero with the full rites of the American national religion. Looked at in the context of other civil ceremonies, such as presidential inaugurals that mimic worship services, complete with invocation, hymns, sermon, and benediction, the funeral blended seamlessly into the liturgy of the nation's political theology. It appropriated Jewish and Christian elements to reinforce Reagan's and, by extension, America's identity, and blended the nation's hymns and "scripture" with the funeral liturgy of the Episcopal Church's Book of Common Prayer.

The funeral paid moving tribute to the achievements of a national and international leader. The congregation stood silently as acolytes bore the cross down the center aisle as eight members of the armed services carried Reagan's flag-draped casket. Widow Nancy, children Judy, Ronnie, and Michael, along with other family members followed while the presiding Episcopal priest, the former US senator from Missouri John Danforth read scripture: "I am the resurrection and the life. . . . I know that my Redeemer liveth. . . . Blessed are the dead who die in the Lord."

Rabbi Harold Kushner, author of the 1980s best-selling *When Bad Things Happen to Good People*, read from Isaiah 40, first in Hebrew and then in English. Supreme Court Justice Sandra Day O'Connor, a Reagan appointee and the first woman to sit on the high court, then came to the pulpit, but read not from the Old Testament or the New, but from the Model of Christian Charity, the national canon's Book of Genesis that Reagan had transformed as he made it his own: "This is a reading from a sermon delivered in 1630 by the pilgrim leader John Winthrop who was aboard the ship the Arabella on his way from England to the Massachusetts Bay Colony. The 'city on the hill' passage was referenced by President Reagan in several notable speeches." One part of the short selection from Winthrop's discourse the justice proceeded to read had indeed helped define the Reagan presidency. Ironically, she began with an excerpt the president had never quoted in his speeches and may not even have known, a passage favored more by Democrats for its emphasis on social justice than by Republicans: "Now the only way to provide for our posterity is to follow the counsel of Micah, to do justly, to love mercy, to walk humbly with our God. We must delight in each other, make others' conditions our own, rejoice together, mourn together, labor and suffer together, always having before our eyes our commission and community in the work as members of the same body. The Lord will be our guide and delight to dwell among us as His own people." Justice O'Connor finished with the passage Reagan had invoked so often: "For we must consider that we shall be as a city upon a hill. The eyes of all people are upon us. So that if we shall deal falsely with our God in this work we have undertaken and so cause him to withdraw his present help from us we shall be made a story and a byword through the world."

The Roman Catholic cardinal Theodore McCarrick, at the time archbishop of Washington, DC, read Matthew 5:14–16, the verses from Jesus's Sermon on the Mount that include the famous "city on a hill" metaphor. Sacred texts from American scripture and the Bible were thus unified into the national canon in this service. John Danforth delivered his homily on Matthew 5:14, dividing it into two parts united by the theme of light. He spoke first of Winthrop's conviction about America's "special mission" and how the "Winthrop message" became the "Reagan message." Reagan's optimistic understanding of America as a city on a hill "was a vision with policy implications." "America could not hide its light under a bushel." He referred to Reinhold Niebuhr's 1944 book, *Children of Light and the Children of Darkness*—an ambiguous compliment at best, given that Niebuhr had lamented the wartime innocence of the Children of Light when dealing with the fascist Children of Darkness.[48] "If ever we have known a child of light, it was Ronald Reagan. He was aglow with it.

He had no dark side. No scary hidden agenda." In Danforth's telling, the light of America and the light of the gospel became two manifestations of one thing. The unified sacred-secular story continued.

Music for the service came from the celebrity Irish tenor Ronan Tynan, who followed Danforth's homily with "Amazing Grace" accompanied by the orchestra, and from a military choir and orchestra, performing the "Battle Hymn of the Republic." Like presidential inaugurals and many other events on the nation's liturgical calendar, the funeral service was overtly ecumenical, steeped in civil religion, and indebted to a thoroughly domesticated Christianity. For many thousands in the cathedral and watching live over cable television and the Internet, Julia Ward Howe's "Battle Hymn" could still be sung in sincerity and truth.

Among all the ways the "Battle Hymn" has been used by American preachers, politicians, activists, and advertisers—invoking divine judgment, righteous wars, national destiny, and national grief—it has also served as a Song of Innocence—innocence not in the sense of guiltlessness, and not quite in the sense of naivete, but in the sense of being untouched by experience. When the nation sings the "Battle Hymn," whether in its churches or in public squares, it does so in a way uncomplicated by the poem's long history. Americans sing it to remind themselves that they are good. Like so much else in America's national religion, it is a song of affirmation of faith in self while sounding so much like faith in God. Within the broad religious nationalism in which it holds such a hallowed place, the "Battle Hymn" enables Americans to forget their history in the midst of the act of supposedly remembering who they are. They remember abstractions. Meant to inspire but never scrutinized, the "Battle Hymn of the Republic" has been carved into monumental history. Whether or not America has been the nation "severed from Christ," as Updike thought, it has certainly become a nation, like any nation, severed from its past.

EPILOGUE

Julia's friend Charlotte Whipple played an unexpected role in preserving the original manuscript of the "Battle Hymn of the Republic." Howe gave the original to her as a memento. The publishing firm Houghton Mifflin borrowed it to make the facsimile for Howe's *Reminiscences* in 1898. With the rough draft returned to Charlotte, its whereabouts became unknown, even to the Howe daughters, and despite efforts over decades to track it down. The fact that it survives today and is on public display in Washington, DC, brings the story of the "Battle Hymn" and religious nationalism to a (temporary) conclusion.

Facing destitution late in life, Charlotte may have sold the manuscript in 1903 along with her late husband's valuable manuscript collection and library. Friends had found Charlotte in her Boston home without heat or food. The firm of C. F. Libbie handled the sale. It attracted buyers from across the country eager to get their hands on Oliver Wendell Holmes's "The Chambered Nautilus," rare first editions, and manuscripts and letters belonging to Longfellow, Hawthorne, Lowell, Whittier, and Emerson.[1]

The purchaser of the "Battle Hymn" seems to have been Mrs. Frederick M. Steele, a wealthy socialite and philanthropist who lived in Chicago and Hollywood.[2] From that point, the "Battle Hymn" evidently came into the possession of Phoebe Apperson Hearst, William Randolph Hearst's mother and a woman's rights activist, education reformer, and convert to the Baha'i faith, who knew Howe in the 1880s. Upon her death in 1918, the "Battle Hymn" would have passed to her son. The fragmentary record makes it impossible to be certain just what route the "Battle Hymn" followed from owner to owner.

Maud Howe Elliott, unaware of the fate of the "Battle Hymn," spoke at the Breakfast Club in Los Angeles in February 1932 to commemorate Lincoln's birthday. She told the story of the "Battle Hymn" and of her mother's meeting with Lincoln and said that she knew only that the original manuscript was "somewhere in California," and that Charlotte (whom she did not name publicly) had sold it to a collector. Later that day, a man in Hollywood telephoned Maud to tell her that the manuscript was indeed in the hands of a California collector and pledged his help in reuniting her with her mother's poem.[3] That did not happen.

The purported original of the "Battle Hymn" displayed in 1942 by the Library of Congress was not in fact Howe's first draft, though some, including Woollcott and the historian William McLoughlin, later thought it was.[4] The first public display of the autograph manuscript happened during the bicentennial celebrations in 1975–76. Patriotism, corporate sponsorship, and the nation's birthday converged to revive the "Freedom Train" of 1947 and finally bring the "Battle Hymn" original to the public. The idea for the train came from Ross Rowland, described in the press as "a 35-year old commodity broker with a passion for railroading."[5] He failed to get federal funding for his project and turned instead to corporate giants PepsiCo, General Motors, Prudential, Kraft, and Atlantic Richfield. His dream was to bring the bicentennial celebration right down to the level of local communities across America. Train cars featured moving walkways to ensure the exhibit could handle crowds efficiently. Specifications called for a visitor rate of 1,800 people an hour for 14 hours a day. The scale dwarfed the earlier Freedom Train. More than 500 documents and artifacts filled the dozen red-white-and-blue display cars, including George Washington's copy of the Constitution, the first Bible printed in America, Martin Luther King Jr.'s clerical robe and personal Bible, Ty

Cobb's baseball bat, a moon rock, a model of the new Dallas-Fort Worth airport, Kennedy's inaugural address, and the "Battle Hymn." Another dozen cars provided space for supplies and staff.

Inaugurated by President Gerald Ford at a ceremony in April 1975, the train toured the nation until December 1976. The journey encompassed a symbolic seventy-six cities and covered all forty-eight contiguous states. The train carried its historic cargo some 26,000 miles and hosted more than 6 million visitors. Potentially some 40 to 50 million Americans saw the train as it passed along the rails through town after town. In October 1975, Soviet cosmonauts visited the train in Salt Lake City.

Visitors discovered the "Battle Hymn of the Republic" in the "Human Resources" car—a name only a committee could have come up with. The display celebrated "individual achievements" and featured Howe's manuscript along with Tom Paine's *Common Sense*, Mark Twain's *Adventures of Huckleberry Finn*, James Monroe's dueling pistols, and various medals and awards. Not everyone was convinced the artifacts would be properly protected from damaging humidity and rough handling during their extended tour. The syndicated columnist Jack Anderson wrote a story about the Freedom Train in which he reported that he had seen correspondence from Smithsonian conservators to the train's staff complaining about temperature and humidity conditions. Sadly, the "Battle Hymn" returned to its owner with "rips in three corners."[6]

That unlucky owner was the San Francisco antiquarian book dealer David Bickersteth Magee, the Yorkshire-born son of a parish vicar, and the grandson of an archbishop of York. Magee descended from generations of obsessive book collectors. Coming to the United States on his own at age nineteen, Magee rapidly built a career in California, becoming one of America's premier collectors, dealers, and bibliographers.[7] In 1969, Brigham Young University purchased Magee's extensive collection of Victorian and Edwardian manuscripts and books that he had taken years to assemble.[8] After Magee's death in 1977, his daughter sold the "Battle Hymn" to the famed Boston book dealer Kenneth Rendell, the man later hired by *Newsweek* magazine to evaluate the authenticity of the forged Hitler diaries. Rendell still owned Howe's manuscript in 1986 when he offered to sell it to the media mogul Malcolm Forbes for $100,000. Forbes declined, and for the moment the "Battle Hymn" would not join the family's collection of Lincoln memorabilia, Victorian paintings, Fabergé eggs, and toy soldiers.[9] Rendell sold it instead to the former ambassador, secretary of the navy, and bank executive J. William Middendorf II. Through Christie's auction house, Middendorf in turn sold the "Battle Hymn" to Forbes in 1989 for $200,000, twice what the collector would have paid for it in 1986—a story Rendell loved to tell. The manuscript was still in the multimillionaire's collection at the time of his death in 1990.

The *Washington Post* reported in 2005 that the "Battle Hymn" failed to find a buyer when a large part of Forbes's collection went up for sale at Christie's. This was the third major sale of Forbes's holdings conducted by Christie's since 2002. Estimates of the value of Howe's manuscript ranged from $300,000 to $500,000.[10] Christie's finally sold it at auction in 2012 for $782,500.[11] The buyer was Steve Green, son of the founder of Hobby Lobby and the force behind the Museum of the Bible, home to his personal collection of tens of thousands of artifacts. The $800 million structure, comprising over 400,000 square feet, sits two blocks south of the National Mall. While some critics, intent on keeping the nation's capital a visible reminder of the separation of church and state, worried about the implications of having a Museum of the Bible situated so close to the Mall, no evangelical writer went on record worried about what the "Battle Hymn of the Republic" might be doing among papyrus fragments of the Greek New Testament. But then again, Elvis Presley's Bible is on display.[12]

The new home of the "Battle Hymn" in the Museum of the Bible raises important questions for any study of the relationship between religion and American life and more specifically about the connection between the Bible, politics, and war. The Museum of the Bible's president said in a press release that the "Battle Hymn" provides "a powerful example of how people throughout the ages have been influenced by the Bible."[13] That approach typifies that of historians as well as those who ask what impact the Bible has had on American history. This is a legitimate question but perhaps not the most illuminating one. If, instead of asking what the Bible did to Americans, historians were to ask what Americans did to the Bible, they would uncover a story filled with active players who have quoted, interpreted, reinterpreted, and applied the Bible. The Museum of the Bible hopes visitors will take time to reflect on how much the Bible has shaped America. But what if visitors were instead to reflect on how much Americans have shaped the Bible? The words on the page might stay the same, but appropriated for political, military, or cultural purpose unknown to the original authors, do they truly remain the same?

By reversing the question of impact, historians would open new and fruitful paths of inquiry. Merely acknowledging that Tom Paine quoted extensively from the Bible in *Common Sense* in 1776 reveals little worth knowing about American religion, politics, and war. It is hardly an aid to national self-knowledge. The simple fact that Abraham Lincoln and Woodrow Wilson quoted the Bible adds up to just as little. The same can be said of nonbiblical texts, such as the quotations from Thomas Jefferson selected for his national memorial in the 1930s. The significance of these quotations lies not in the mere words but rather in the motives and purposes of those who selected them, and then in the motives and purposes of those who quote the quotations year after year. Yes, Julia Ward Howe grew up knowing the Bible from cover to cover. In some sense the Bible influenced her. But she appropriated the Bible to achieve her own purposes, prompted by what she saw on a visit to wartime Washington—in that act of appropriation lies the real story of the "Battle Hymn of the Republic" and the building of religious nationalism.

Julia Ward Howe's "Battle Hymn" played a principal part in the creation of religious nationalism in America. It was meant to. The usable past, mobilized for the sake of nationalism, has always been selective at best and misleading if not outright fraudulent at worst. Religious nationalism has trouble holding up under exacting historical or theological scrutiny. Sacred nations need a tidy past with clear winners and losers, a clear trajectory along which the nation has become more and more truly itself, and a unified story line. A good memory subverts the purposes of nation building. Friedrich Nietzsche argued in the 1870s that modern historical consciousness was "fatal" to action, the kind of action, that is, that a civilized people needs to be able to fight for its survival. "Forgetting is essential to action of any kind," he wrote. In the modern world, "there is a degree of sleeplessness, or rumination, of the historical sense, which is harmful and ultimately fatal to the living thing, whether this living thing be a man or a people or a culture."[14] Close historical (or theological or philosophical) investigation if unchecked would melt down the civil religion that unified and sustained—and when necessary mobilized—the nation. Constant "rumination" made the "Battle Hymn" impossible to sing for anyone outside Howe's magic circle of Americanism. The "Battle

Hymn" has endured as part of the nation's "monumental" history only on the condition that the particularities of its history remained veiled by sacred vestments.

This kind of nationalist remembering requires a good deal of forgetting. But it needs more. In a celebrated lecture on nationalism in 1882, the French philosopher and historian Ernest Renan added "historical error" to amnesia as an indispensable means of nation building. "Forgetting, I would even say historical error," he wrote, "is an essential factor in the creation of a nation and it is for this reason that the progress of historical studies often poses a threat to nationality. Historical inquiry, in effect, throws light on the violent acts that have taken place at the origin of every political formation, even those that have been the most benevolent in their consequences." Indeed, "unity is always brutally established."[15]

Use and reuse of the "Battle Hymn of the Republic" quickly fell into the pattern of selective memory and strategic forgetting necessary to nation building. It was sung to honor America in ever-widening circles and on far-flung battlefields, but like any other text in the nation's religion it was stripped of its context, radically simplified, and rubbed smooth of its texture. Disembodied, it became among the most usable parts of a usable past. But it was also dogged by irony. Irony always lurked around the corner for the "Battle Hymn" and its role in national unity. As religious nationalism became ecumenical enough to draw Catholics, Mormons, and Muslims into its rites, the "Battle Hymn" became the property of anyone who chose to sing it. Howe never envisioned these alien religions—alien, that is, to her theology, nationalism, and reform idealism—as being fully incorporated into her crusade for human emancipation. They were either part of the dying past, on the wrong side of history, or so strange an aberration that they needed to be excised from America's liberal order of enlightenment and progress. They were *objects* of reform, not fellow crusaders. That certainly held true of the South. One can hardly imagine what Howe would make of a recording of the Mississippi native Elvis Presley singing her "Battle Hymn" during a laser-light show that projects patriotic images onto the giant reliefs of Robert E. Lee, Stonewall Jackson, and Jefferson Davis on Stone Mountain, Georgia. Robert Penn Warren claimed that Howe had no capacity for irony, and if that was so, then that incapacity may have doomed her "Battle Hymn" to its ironic fate from the start. Irony, along with historical consciousness, dissolves religious nationalism.

Self-consciousness presents a further threat. America's religious nationalism works like the musical creations of the avant-garde composer Charles Ives. In his music, snatches of "Bringing in the Sheaves" overlie "Columbia, the Gem of the Ocean" with borrowed bits of European masterworks tossed in. The sacred, patriotic, and traditional compete and yet combine into one dissonant piece that somehow succeeds as a work of art. Ives used the "Battle Hymn of the Republic" in several of his compositions, most prominently in *The Fourth of July*.[16] The music historian J. Peter Berkholder refers to Ives's compositional technique as "collage." This quirky celebration of Independence Day, ending in musical fireworks, combined "Columbia, the Gem of the Ocean" with "Marching through Georgia" with "The Star-Spangled Banner," with bugle calls and hornpipes, and with folk songs, sentimental favorites, and the "Battle Hymn."

Unlike the cacophony of an Ives collage, however, the tunes, words, and symbols of the American religion do not sound jumbled, unsettling, or amusing to most Americans. They sound perfectly normal and serious. To be sure, there has been conflict over the American identity. America has quarreled with itself about itself for generations. But given enough time, all the competing motifs seem to become one harmonious anthem to the ear of Americans at large. Once we dare expose national religion to historical scrutiny, though, its presumed harmony turns back into something closer to Ives's dissonance. Study of religious nationalism brings these elements to the forefront in a way similar to how a trained musician notices what Ives is up to in his scores. For Ives, that self-referential consciousness is part of the point and much of the fun.

What George Santayana wrote about Henry James's ability to liberate himself from "the genteel tradition" applies to the study of religious nationalism. In 1911, the Harvard philosopher argued that the expatriate Boston novelist had achieved this freedom "by adopting the point of view of the outer world, and by turning the genteel American tradition, as he turns everything else, into a subject matter for analysis. . . . Thus he has overcome the genteel tradition in the classic way, by understanding it."[17] By the 1960s, a number of intellectuals had turned the "Battle Hymn" into "a subject matter for analysis," furthering a self-consciousness gestured at by poets a generation or so earlier and not complete to this day. For every academic who turns the "Battle Hymn" into an object of historical or theological study, there is still a true believer who continues to sing Howe's poem as an affirmation of faith in America and its mission in the world, the very thing Bruce Catton in 1961 hoped they would do. But for others, understanding the "Battle Hymn" in Santayana's sense of what it was has enabled them to "overcome" its hold on their imagination.

Some may argue that once we remove the "Battle Hymn" or other national icon from its place in religious nationalism for purposes of historical or theological analysis, it loses all its ability to bind the national community together. Once we become too self-conscious of its origin and meaning, so the fear goes, we can no longer sing it without winks and nudges. That may be true. But cut loose from its historical meaning, something like the "Battle Hymn" does not just sit there politely and mind its manners, waiting to be used in whatever way promoters of nationalism choose. It does not remain a stable, predictable part of the civic liturgy. Stripped of its historical meaning, it becomes a blank screen onto which we can project anything we wish. Or it becomes a mirror in which we see only ourselves, whatever we happen to believe at the moment about America and its history, purpose, and future. The history of the "Battle Hymn" shows these tendencies. The choice, then, lies not between a historical meaning and a religious-nationalist meaning, but between a historical meaning and *any* meaning we dream up . . . which amounts to no meaning at all. The risk of cultural nihilism lies not in historical consciousness but in religious-nationalist manipulation of history, theology, and political philosophy.

The historian John Lukacs's advice is always worth heeding when venturing into the precarious world of the history of ideas: it is often more important to understand what people do to ideas than what ideas do to people.[18] It is *people* who have ideas, Lukacs has repeatedly cautioned students of the past. People make them and mold them, sometimes beyond recognition. Julia Ward Howe took ideas and remade them into the "Battle Hymn of the Republic." She remade her own "Battle Hymn" over the nearly half century between the time she wrote it and her death in 1910. But others remade her ideas as well, including family members, politicians, journalists, clergy, historians, and novelists, whether in America, England, or beyond. As the "Battle Hymn" has undergone new uses in new settings over the course of 150 years and counting, it has endured additions and subtractions and has been made part of national remembering and forgetting. Like any national monument expressing civic piety, the "Battle

Hymn" has had to be stripped of a great deal of context before it could be embraced by Catholics, Mormons, socialists, and others. As much as a national community might gain from such malleability, there is a price to pay for the collective amnesia required. What H. L. Mencken called the "ecstatic supernaturalism" of the "Battle Hymn" too easily masks what was really going on in its violent, apocalyptic stanzas.[19]

From the moment Julia Ward Howe drafted her "Battle Hymn" just seven months after Confederate artillery fired on Fort Sumter, she captured something larger than the Civil War, larger than America's imperiled destiny, larger even than the nation's role in the unfolding drama of redemptive history. The poem belonged to humanity. That breadth of vision owed much to Howe's development as a poet and literary critic, as a liberal Unitarian, amateur philosopher, nationalist, internationalist, and abolitionist who at the same time adhered to less-than-enlightened views on race and religious diversity. As a public intellectual, Howe kept current with the greatest movements in European and American thought and helped popularize them through her vast outpouring of poetry, lectures, sermons, journalism, and essays. Much of her poetry commented directly on events unfolding in Italy, Hungary, France, the Aegean, and the Ottoman Empire. She heard her own "Battle Hymn" sung in Istanbul in 1879.

The "Battle Hymn," and a handful of other national songs like it and with which it has had to compete for first place in the nation's affections, have served as a conduit between church and state. Theology and history flow back and forth through this poetic channel. In times of war, religion flows into politics and is made to serve its purposes. The celebration Lincoln attended in the House of Representatives in 1864 illustrates this tendency perfectly. But warfare also flows into the church as preachers and parishioners gather for Sunday worship to sing the songs of battle, honor the emblems of the nation, salute veterans, and reaffirm their faith in America. While war is not the only factory of religious nationalism, historically it has been the most productive one. War leaves behind a warehouse stocked with heroes, legends, stories of sacrifice, evocative images, popular songs, and names of once-obscure towns, farms, rivers, and islands that witnessed human agony and carnage.

The story of the maker of the "Battle Hymn," its making, and its remaking shows the complex ways in which religious nationalism finds its voice and longevity over the generations, at times even consuming itself as raw material for a new version of the old-time civil religion. The story also shows religious nationalism's remarkable capacity for adaptation and its ability to obscure the inconvenient details of theology, political theory, and history—in this case, the particularities of who Julia Ward Howe was, what she believed, and the gritty reality of the war that inspired her—as that political faith is made and molded to help make and mold a nation. The question today is whether the "Battle Hymn" serves the nation as an aid to reflection or as an impediment to genuine self-knowledge.

ACKNOWLEDGMENTS

Over the past six years of research and writing, I have accumulated many debts. It is a privilege at the close of this book to thank the people and institutions who provided help along the way. The task of recovering an unfamiliar Julia Ward Howe and an unfamiliar "Battle Hymn" has been long and difficult. But it has also been rewarding, and has provided the kinds of professional satisfaction found only among original documents discovered after long hours in an archive. I have often said that archivists are my heroes. I still marvel that archive holdings collected through other people's generosity and hard work are open to me for free. Staff at distant archives I was unable to visit provided quick and efficient answers via email to all sorts of minute questions. In particular, I am grateful to the Houghton Library at Harvard University; the Schlesinger Library at the Radcliffe Institute; the Massachusetts Historical Society; the Maine Historical Society; the Andover-Harvard Theological Library; the Princeton Theological Seminary Library; the New-York Historical Society; the

Minnesota Historical Society; the Haverford College Quaker & Special Collections; the Circulation and Interlibrary Loan Department at the University of St. Thomas; the Stuart A. Rose Manuscript, Archives, and Rare Book Library, Emory University; and my friends and colleagues at the Michael Alex Mossey Library at Hillsdale College.

Former and current students at Hillsdale College provided research assistance that proved indispensable to this project. Alex Meregaglia, now an archivist at Boise State University, has an uncanny knack for detail and never tires of tracking down resources, often in creative ways and with a technical expertise beyond my abilities. Further assistance came from Maddie Merritt in California, Adam Petersen in New York, Brett Wierenga via the Internet, and a number of undergraduates who helped me ask the right questions. Michael Lucchese helped at a critical moment with proofreading and photo credits. Hillsdale College also funded a generous summer leave grant that made an extended research trip to Cambridge and Boston possible. And my colleagues in the History Department provided, as always, an academic setting of professionalism, encouragement, and good cheer.

Critical to this book's completion have been the series editors, Darryl Hart and Laurence Moore, and the outside reader, Daniel Walker Howe. This book began when Darryl Hart walked into my office and asked if I wanted to write a book about the "Battle Hymn of the Republic" and American civil religion. Little did I realize at the time what saying yes would mean. All three scholars have given freely of their time and expertise as historians and writers. Their suggestions improved the flow and argument of this book by forcing me to think hard about what I was trying say and how I was saying it. At Cornell University Press, my editor, Michael McGandy, has been patient and has kept the project moving along without making me feel crowded or rushed, even if at times he has had to play the part of amateur therapist. Meagan Dermody helped me find my story and to tell it better with fewer words, while Sara R. Ferguson and Marian Rogers rescued me from blunders and guided me through the final stages of production with professionalism and grace.

My father did not live to see this book in print. One of the last things we talked about was the "Battle Hymn of the Republic." He said he wanted to read what I had written. For this reason, the dedication belongs to him, the humblest and kindest man I will ever know.

NOTES

Prologue

1. *National Republican* (Washington, DC), February 3, 1864.

2. *National Republican*, February 3, 1864.

3. *Second Anniversary of the U.S. Christian Commission, in the Hall of the House of Representatives, Washington, D. C., on Tuesday Evening, February 2, 1864: Order of Exercises* (Washington, DC: H. Pòlkinhorn, 1864), 1. https://www.loc.gov/resource/rbpe.20404900.

4. *United States Christian Commission for the Army and Navy: Work and Incidents; First Annual Report* (Philadelphia: United States Christian Commission, 1863), 5–7 and passim.

5. From a story in the *Sunday School Times* as reprinted in "Chaplain McCabe's Remarks and Hymn," *Buffalo Christian Advocate*, April 7, 1864.

6. Frank Milton Bristol, *The Life of Chaplain McCabe, Bishop of the Methodist Episcopal Church* (New York: Fleming H. Revell, 1908), 198–201; *Buffalo Christian Advocate*, April 7, 1864. Accounts vary as to whether McCabe or his friend Colonel William H. Powell delivered this message.

7. Bristol, *Life of Chaplain McCabe*, 203; *National Republican* (Washington, DC), February 3, 1864.

8. Ronald Beiner, *Civil Religion: A. Dialogue in the History of Political Philosophy* (Cambridge: Cambridge University Press, 2011), 1.

9. Robert N. Bellah, "Civil Religion in America," *Daedalus* 134, no. 4 (2005): 40–55; originally published in 1967.

10. Peter Kaufmann, *The Temple of Truth*, excerpted in Loyd D. Easton, *Hegel's First American Followers: The Ohio Hegelians* (Athens: Ohio University Press, 1966), 296.

11. See Charles J. Stille, *History of the United States Sanitary Commission* (Philadelphia: J. B. Lippincott, 1866), passim; appendixes A and B to Document 74, in *Documents of the U.S. Sanitary Commission*, vol. 2, no. 61–95 (New York, 1866), n.p.; see also *New-York Daily Tribune*, September 25, 1861.

12. Henry W. Bellows, *Historical Sketch of the Union League Club of New York: Its Origin, Organization, and Work, 1863–1879* (New York: Club House, 1879), 7.

13. "Speech at Great Sanitary Fair, Philadelphia, Pennsylvania," June 16, 1864, in Roy P. Basler, ed., *The Collected Works of Abraham Lincoln* (New Brunswick, NJ: Rutgers University Press, 1953), 7: 394–96.

14. George H. Stuart to Abraham Lincoln, Saturday, June 18, 1864 (U.S. Christian Commission), Abraham Lincoln Papers, Series 1: General Correspondence, 1833–1916, Library of Congress, www.loc.gov/resource/mal.3384400.

15. The North's "culture of victory" is as observable as what Wolfgang Schivelbusch calls a "culture of defeat." See Schivelbusch, *The Culture of Defeat: On National Trauma, Mourning, and Recovery*, trans. Jefferson Chase (New York: Picador, 2003).

1. The Besieged City

1. For an example of press notice of the return visit, see "Arrivals in the City," *New York Times*, November 23, 1861. The *Times* mentioned Governor and Mrs. Andrew, the governor's aide, Reverend Clarke, Samuel Gridley Howe, and Mr. and Mrs. Whipple, but not Julia.

2. For details of Julia Ward Howe's long and full life, see her own *Reminiscences, 1819–1899* (Boston: Houghton, Mifflin, 1899); Laura E. Richards, Maud Howe Elliott, and Florence Howe Hall, *Julia Ward Howe, 1819–1910*, 2 vols. (Boston: Houghton Mifflin, 1916); Deborah Pickman Clifford, *Mine Eyes Have Seen the Gory: A Biography of Julia Ward Howe* (Boston: Little, Brown, 1979); Gary Williams, *Hungry Heart: The Literary Emergence of Julia Ward Howe* (Amherst: University of Massachusetts Press), 1999; and Elaine Showalter, *The Civil Wars of Julia Ward Howe: A Biography* (New York: Simon & Schuster, 2016).

3. See Clifford, *Mine Eyes Have Seen the Glory*, 120–22. The biographer who has most emphasized the hardship of this marriage is Showalter, *Civil Wars of Julia Ward Howe*.

4. *New-York As It Is: Containing a General Description of the City of New-York . . .* (New York: T. R. Tanner, 1840), 75, 85, 104.

5. Joseph Green Cogswell, *Life of Joseph Green Cogswell as Sketched in His Letters*, ed. Anna E. Ticknor (Cambridge, MA: Riverside Press, 1874), 177–78, 206, 212–23.

6. See Harold Schwartz, *Samuel Gridley Howe, Social Reformer, 1801–1876* (Cambridge, MA: Harvard University Press, 1956); James W. Trent Jr., *The Manliest Man: Samuel G. Howe and the Contours of Nineteenth-Century American Reform* (Amherst: University of Massachusetts Press, 2012).

7. Edward Everett, "Coray's Aristotle," *North American Review*, October 1823, 420.

8. Richards, Elliott, and Hall, *Life of Julia Ward Howe*, 1:107.

9. "Julia Ward Howe," *Cosmopolitan Art Journal*, September 1858, 187.

10. See Daniel Walker Howe, *The Unitarian Conscience: Harvard Moral Philosophy, 1805–1861* (Cambridge, MA: Harvard University Press, 1970). For Unitarianism's larger context within the Whig tradition, see Howe, *The Political Culture of the American Whigs* (Chicago: University of Chicago Press, 1979).

11. Richards, Elliott, and Hall, *Life of Julia Ward Howe*, 1:106.

12. Richards, Elliott, and Hall, 143.

13. Howe, *Reminiscences*, 244.

14. Howe, 163.

15. Joel Myerson, "An Annotated List of Contributors to the Boston 'Dial,'" *Studies in Bibliography* 26 (1973): 133–66.

16. Henry Greenleaf Pearson, *The Life of John A. Andrew: Governor of Massachusetts, 1861–1865* (Boston: Houghton, Mifflin, 1904), 1:32, 33.

17. James Freeman Clarke, *A Sermon on the Principles and Methods of the Church of the Disciples . . .* (Boston: Benjamin H. Greene, 1846), 33. Clarke preached this sermon in the morning and evening on December 7, 1845.

18. Julia Ward Howe, "Review of De Lamartine's *Jocelyn*," *Literary and Theological Review* 3 (December 1836): 559–72.

19. Julia Ward Howe, review of *Select Minor Poems*, translated and edited by John S. Dwight, *New York Review*, April 1839, 393–400.

20. Nathaniel Hawthorne, *The Centenary Edition of the Works of Nathaniel Hawthorne*, vol. 16, *The Letters, 1853–1856*, ed. Thomas Woodson et al. (Columbus: Ohio State University Press, 1987), 177.

21. Samuel Gridley Howe to Julia Ward Howe, n.d., Samuel Gridley Howe-Julia Ward Howe Correspondence, Record Group 20, Yellow House Papers, Maine Historical Society. This letter was written from the Willard Hotel, Washington, DC, and says only "Friday, 24" at the top.

22. Paul E. Teed, *A Revolutionary Conscience: Theodore Parker and Antebellum America* (Lanham, MD: University Press of America, 2012), 222.

23. Julia Ward Howe, *A Trip to Cuba* (Boston: Ticknor and Fields, 1860), 12–13.

24. Howe, 212–14.

25. Edward J. Renehan Jr., *The Secret Six: The True Tale of the Men Who Conspired with John Brown* (New York: Crown Publishers, 1995).

26. "Since Then," Julia Ward Howe Papers, 1790–1951 (MS Am 2214), Houghton Library, Harvard University.

27. Julia Ward Howe, "Our Orders," *Atlantic Monthly*, July 1861, 1. This poem was reprinted in newspapers around the nation. See, for example, the *White Cloud Kansas Chief*, September 5, 1861.

28. Julia Ward Howe, "Crawford's Statues at Richmond" and "Our Country," *Atlantic Monthly*, October 1861, 416, 506; Howe, "George Sand," *Atlantic Monthly*, November 1861, 513–34.

29. "The Agricultural Fair at Barnstable," *New-York Daily Tribune*, October 18, 1861.

30. "An Unspoken Speech," *Liberator*, October 25, 1861.

31. "Unspoken Speech."

32. Basler, *Collected Works of Abraham Lincoln*, 4:331–33.

33. There is no modern biography of John Andrew. For details of his life and career, see Pearson, *Life of John A. Andrew*, esp. 1:147, 180–94.

34. Pearson, *Life of John A. Andrew*, 1:96–99.

35. Arthur S. Bolster Jr., *James Freeman Clarke: Disciple to Advancing Truth* (Boston: Beacon Press, 1954), 144, 147–48, 164.

36. James Freeman Clarke, "John Albion Andrew," in *Memorial and Biographical Sketches* (Boston: Houghton, Osgood, 1878), 58.

37. Julia Ward Howe to Samuel Gridley Howe, December 1, 1859, Samuel Gridley Howe-Julia Ward Howe Correspondence, Record Group 20, Yellow House Papers, Maine Historical Society.

38. James Freeman Clarke, "The State of the Country," May 5, 1861, James Freeman Clarke Additional Papers, 1806–1936 (MS Am 1569.8), Houghton Library, Harvard University.

39. Frank E. Howe to John Albion Andrew, October 25, October 26, October 27, November 4, and November 8, 1861, John A. Andrew Papers, Massachusetts Historical Society.

40. John Albion Andrew to James Freeman Clarke, November 7, 1861, James Freeman Clarke Additional Correspondence, 1787–1886 (MS Am 1569.7), Houghton Library, Harvard University.

41. Margaret Leech, *Reveille in Washington, 1860–1865* (New York: Harper & Brothers, 1941), 8–9.

42. Samuel Gridley Howe to Laura Howe, November 21, 1861, Julia Ward Howe Papers, 1790–1951 (MS Am 2214), Houghton Library, Harvard University.

43. James Freeman Clarke, "Washington in November," James Freeman Clarke Additional Papers, 1806–1936 (b MS Am 1569.8), Houghton Library, Harvard University; James Freeman Clarke, "Washington City in November," *Monthly Journal of the American Unitarian Association*, December 1861, 545–65.

44. James Freeman Clarke, *Autobiography, Diary, and Correspondence*, ed. Edward Everett Hale (Boston: Houghton, Mifflin, 1899).

45. Clarke, "Washington City in November," 555.

46. Clarke, 551.

47. *The Papers of Frederick Law Olmsted*, vol. 4, *Defending the Union: The Civil War and the U.S. Sanitary Commission, 1861–1863*, ed. Jane Turner Censer (Baltimore: Johns Hopkins University Press, 1986), 215; report from Olmsted, November 16, 1861, Frederick Newman Knapp Papers, Massachusetts Historical Society.

48. "Forts Runyon and Albany," *Harper's Weekly*, November 30, 1861, 767; Alfred Seelye Roe and Charles Nutt, *History of the First Regiment of Heavy Artillery, Massachusetts Volunteers, Formerly the Fourteenth Regiment of Infantry, 1861–1865* (N.p.: Published by the Regimental Association, 1917), 93, 97, 98; *Harper's Weekly*, August 31, 1861, 549, 554.

49. The best overview of Greene is found in Philip F. Gura, *American Transcendentalism: A History* (New York: Hill and Wang, 2007), 181–88. See also Gura, "Beyond Transcendentalism: The Radical Individualism of William B. Greene," in Conrad Wright and Charles Capper, eds., *The Transient and Permanent in American Transcendentalism* (Boston: Massachusetts Historical Society, 1999), 471–96.

50. Clarke, "Washington City in November," 556–57.

51. Clarke, 551, 557–58.

52. "Sermon by Rev. W. H, Channing," *Christian Inquirer*, November 23, 1861, 1.

53. Clarke, "Washington City in November," 554.

54. Julia Ward Howe, *From the Oak to the Olive: A Plain Record of a Pleasant Journey* (Boston: Lee and Shepard, 1868), 60.

55. Paul R. Baker, *The Fortunate Pilgrims: Americans in Italy, 1800–1860* (Cambridge, MA: Harvard University Press, 1964), 133.

56. J. G. Randall and David Herbert Donald, *The Civil War and Reconstruction*, 2nd ed. (Lexington, MA: D. C. Heath, 1969), 361–62,

57. Clarke, "Washington City in November," 558. See also Clarke, *Memorial and Biographical Sketches*, 48–49.

58. Howe, *Reminiscences*, 272.

59. Octavius Brooks Frothingham, *Memoir of William Henry Channing* (Boston: Houghton, Mifflin, 1886), 181.

60. William Henry Channing, "A Confession of Faith," *The Present*, September 15, 1843, 10.

61. William Henry Channing, *The Civil War in America, or, The Slaveholders' Conspiracy* (Liverpool: W. Vaughn, 1861), 1, 7–11, 32–33, 51, 90–91, 93, and passim.

62. Channing's sermon notebook for these months survives and provides a remarkable record of his thought in these crucial months, including the first sermons he preached in

wartime Washington. Channing labeled the notebook, "Sermons of 1861–62 Boston, Brooklyn, & Washington," but it also includes the notes and outlines for his last sermons in Liverpool. William Henry Channing, 1810–1884; four notebooks containing sermons, notes of sermons, and other notes; 1860–1862, Miscellaneous Collections, No. 3 (bMS 406/6 [1]), Andover-Harvard Theological Library, unnumbered pages.

63. William Henry Channing, 1860–1862, Miscellaneous Collections, No. 3 (bMS 406/6 [1]), Andover-Harvard Theological Library.

64. Octavius Brooks Frothingham, *Transcendentalism in New England: A History*, intro. Sydney E. Ahlstrom (Philadelphia: University of Pennsylvania Press, 1972), 338.

65. William Henry Channing, 1860–1862, Miscellaneous Collections, No. 3 (bMS 406/6 [1]), Andover-Harvard Theological Library.

66. Clarke, "Washington City in November," 559.

67. William Henry Channing, 1860–1862, Miscellaneous Collections, No. 3 (bMS 406/6 [1]), Andover-Harvard Theological Library.

68. Basler, *Collected Works of Abraham Lincoln*, 5:464–65.

69. Frothingham, *Memoir of William Henry Channing*, 316–17.

70. Roe and Nutt, *History of the First Regiment of Heavy Artillery Regiment*, 115.

71. Clarke, "Washington City in November," 559.

72. *Evening Star* (Washington, DC), November 19, 1861; *National Republican* (Washington, DC), November 20, 1861.

73. James Freeman Clarke, "Washington in November," 27–28, Clarke Additional Papers, Houghton Library, Harvard University.

74. Clarke, "Washington in November," 28.

75. Clarke, "Washington City in November," 562–63.

76. As reported in the *Charlotte Observer*, November 1, 1910. The Methodist *Christian Advocate* reprinted much of this interview and linked it to a story about Chaplain McCabe. "Mrs. Howe, the 'Battle Hymn' and Chaplain McCabe," *Christian Advocate*, November 3, 1910, 1527.

77. A facsimile of this draft is available in Howe, *Reminiscences* and in volume 1 of Richards, Elliott, and Hall, *Julia Ward Howe*. The handwriting on the reverse of the poem, identifying the document as the first draft, the month as November, and the location as the Willard Hotel, is not Howe's.

78. "A Model Proclamation," *Buffalo Commercial*, November 27, 1861.

2. A Rich Crimson

1. "Washington in November," *The Liberator*, November 29, 1861; also reprinted in *Christian Inquirer*, December 28, 1861.

2. James Freeman Clarke, "Washington in November," James Freeman Clarke Additional Papers, 1806–1936 (b MS Am 1569.8), Houghton Library, Harvard University, unnumbered pages.

3. "Washington in November," *Christian Inquirer*, December 28, 1861.

4. "Washington in November," *Christian Inquirer*, December 28, 1861.

5. Julia Ward Howe to James Thomas Fields, December 2, 1861, James Thomas Fields Papers, The Huntington Library, San Marino, California.

6. James C. Austin, *Fields of the "Atlantic Monthly": Letters to an Editor, 1861–1870* (San Marino, CA: The Huntington Library, 1953), 27; *Boston Daily Advertiser*, January 18, 1862; *New York Times*, January 20, 1862; *North American and United States Gazette* (Philadelphia), January 18, 1862.

7. "The Magazines," *New York Times,* January 27, 1862.

8. Austin, *Fields of the "Atlantic Monthly,"* 26–33.

9. Adam Tuchinsky, *Horace Greeley's "New-York Tribune": Civil War–Era Socialism and the Crisis of Free Labor* (Ithaca, NY: Cornell University Press, 2009).

10. Arriving at reliable circulation figures for the *Tribune* is difficult. Biographer Robert C. Williams says that in 1860 the *Tribune* had the world's largest circulation. Williams, *Horace Greeley: Champion of American Freedom* (New York: New York University Press, 2006), 1, 166. The point in establishing the *Tribune's* circulation is that, with about twice the circulation of the *Atlantic,* this one newspaper alone gave the "Battle Hymn" wider publicity than did the magazine.

11. The *Boston Daily Advertiser* carried the poem on January 15 and included Howe's name as the author. See also the evening edition of the *Daily Green Mountain Freeman* (Vermont), January 15, 1862; *The Liberator,* January 14, 1862; *Daily Cleveland Herald,* January 28, 1862; *Cass County Republican* (Cass County, Michigan), February 1, 1862; *Weekly Perrysburg Journal* (Perrysburg, Ohio), February 6, 1862; *Alleghanian* (Ebensburg, Pennsylvania), May 1, 1862; *Jeffersonian Democrat* (Chardon, Ohio), July 25, 1862; *Western Reserve Chronicle* (Warren, Ohio), February 4, 1863; *Big Blue Union* (Marysville, Kansas), December 5, 1863.

12. W. M. Fernald, "Battle Hymn," *Monthly Journal, Army Number,* October 1861, 453.

13. W. Stanford Reid, "The Battle Hymns of the Lord: Calvinist Psalmody of the Sixteenth Century," *Sixteenth Century Essays and Studies* 2 (January 1971): 36–54.

14. Henry A. Pochmann, *German Culture in America, 1600–1900: Philosophical and Literary Influences* (Madison: University of Wisconsin Press, 1957), 329, 333, 343.

15. Theodor Körner, "Battle Hymn," in David B. Tower and Cornelius Walker, eds., *A Sequel to the Gradual Reader,* 13th ed. (Boston: O. L. Sanborn, 1858), 173–74. Through textbooks such as this one, Körner's poetry was known to New England schoolchildren immediately before the Civil War.

16. Thomas Babington Macaulay, *Miscellaneous Works of Lord Macaulay,* ed. Lady Trevelyan (New York: Harper & Brothers, 1880), 4:614–16.

17. Thomas Carlyle, "Luther's Psalm," *Fraser's Magazine,* January 1831, 743–44.

18. In 1861, the Church of England published *Hymns Ancient and Modern,* but it included only one war hymn in a section entitled "In Times of Trouble," and that selection prayed for restored peace. The popular hymn "Onward, Christian Soldiers" appeared in 1864 and therefore did not influence Howe's battle hymn.

19. *Chimes of Freedom and Union: A Collection of Poems for the Times* (Boston: Benjamin B. Russell, 1861), 14–15.

20. See, for example, the *Weekly Oregon Statesman* (Salem, Oregon), July 22, 1861.

21. Julia Ward Howe, *Reminiscences, 1819–1899* (Boston: Houghton, Mifflin, 1899), 208.

22. "Whit-Sunday in the Church," in [Julia Ward Howe], *Passion-Flowers* (Boston: Ticknor, Reed, and Fields, 1854), 68–79.

23. Julia Ward Howe, *Later Lyrics* (Boston: J. E. Tilton, 1866), 21.

24. Howe, *Later Lyrics,* 40.

25. Victor Hugo to C. Caraguel, December 18, 1859, and to George Sand, January 21, 1861, in Belle Becker Sideman and Lillian Friedman, eds., *Europe Looks at the Civil War* (New York: Orion Press, 1960), 7–9.

26. Julia Ward Howe to Samuel Gridley Howe, December 2, 1859, Samuel Gridley Howe-Julia Ward Howe Correspondence, Record Group 20, Yellow House Papers, Maine Historical Society.

27. Howe, *Later Lyrics,* 12–14.

28. *Springfield Republican* (Springfield, Massachusetts), October 27, 1910, reprinted in Franklin Benjamin Sanborn, *A Transcendentalist's Opinions on American Life, Literature, Art, and People from the Mid-Nineteenth Century through the First Decade of the Twentieth*, ed. Kenneth Walter Cameron (Hartford: Transcendentalist Books, 1981), 256. A later note in the book (p. 597) gives the date as October 29, 1910.

29. Quoted in Robert N. Bellah, "Civil Religion in America," *Daedalus* 134, no. 4 (2005): 48.

30. Steven K. Green, *The Second Disestablishment: Church and State in Nineteenth-Century America* (New York: Oxford University Press, 2010), 255–61.

31. *Journal of the Board of Education of the City of New York, 1863* (New York: C. S. Westcott, 1863), 143–44; *Courier and Union* (Syracuse, NY), June 10, 1863.

32. *Journal of the Board of Education*, 172–73, 179–80, 190, 193–95. See also People ex rel. McGean v. School Board Offices (NY Supreme Court, First District; Special Term, 1863).

33. Howe Family Additional Papers, 1863–1942 (MS Am 2128), Houghton Library, Harvard University.

3. "The Glorious Freedom of His Gospel"

1. Samuel Gridley Howe to Julia Ward Howe, March 4, 1862, Samuel Gridley Howe-Julia Ward Howe Correspondence, Record Group 20, Yellow House Papers, Maine Historical Society.

2. Julia Ward Howe to Samuel Gridley Howe, March 10, 1862, Samuel Gridley Howe-Julia Ward Howe Correspondence.

3. Julia Ward Howe, Journal, May 18, 1864, Record Group 18, Yellow House Papers, Maine Historical Society.

4. Thomas Wentworth Higginson, "Julia Ward Howe," *Outlook*, January 26, 1907, 167–78; quotation at 174.

5. *Topeka State Journal*, March 9, 1881.

6. Frank Milton Bristol, *The Life of Chaplain McCabe, Bishop of the Methodist Episcopal Church* (New York: Fleming H. Revell, 1908), 182.

7. Bristol, *Life of Chaplain McCabe*, 211, 213. See also William E. Ross, "The Singing Chaplain: Bishop Charles Cardwell McCabe and the Popularization of the 'Battle Hymn of the Republic,'" *Methodist History* 28, no. 1 (October 1989): 22–32.

8. See the *National Republican* (Washington, DC), February 3, 1864; *Soldier's Journal* (Alexandria, Virginia), February 17, 1864; *Semi-Weekly Wisconsin* (Milwaukee), May 11, 1864; *Cincinnati Enquirer*, March 28, 1865. Similar meetings continued into the 1870s and 1880s.

9. Bristol, *Life of Chaplain McCabe*, 135–36 and passim.

10. Julia Ward Howe, Journal, November 8, 1898, Maine Historical Society.

11. Bristol, *Life of Chaplain McCabe*, 192, 195. See also Julia Ward Howe, Journal, September 20, 1904.

12. See Richard M. Gamble, *In Search of the City on a Hill: The Making and Unmaking of an American Myth* (London: Continuum, 2012).

13. An online copy is available at http://pds.lib.harvard.edu/pds/view/47581119.

14. *Proceedings of the Ancient and Honorable Artillery Company, of Boston, Mass., on Its CCXXVI Anniversary, June 6, 1864* (Boston: Wright & Potter, 1864), 12, 23, 32, 34, 35, 36, 42.

15. James Freeman Clarke Additional Papers, 1806–1936 (MS Am 1569.8), Houghton Library, Harvard University. This is an incomplete and undated manuscript in Clarke's hand.

16. See Gerard N. Magliocca, *American Founding Son: John Bingham and the Invention of the Fourteenth Amendment* (New York: New York University Press, 2013).

17. *Wheeling Intelligencer*, October 21, 1865. The paper described Bingham's performance as "a masterly speech" and an "eloquent vindication of noble principles."

18. John McKivigan, *Forgotten Firebrand: James Redpath and the Making of Nineteenth-Century America* (Ithaca, NY: Cornell University Press, 2008).

19. James B. Pond, *Eccentricities of Genius: Memoirs of Famous Men and Women of the Platform and Stage* (London: Chatto & Windus, 1901), xvii–xxv, 533–38. This book was first published in the United States in 1900 by G. W. Dillingham.

20. WSC to Lady Randolph, January 1, 1901, in Randolph S. Churchill, ed., *The Churchill Documents* (Hillsdale, MI: Hillsdale College Press, 2006), 2:1224–25.

21. Howe used this undated advertisement as scrap paper for a draft of some autobiographical sketches. Julia Ward Howe Papers, 1790–1951 (MS Am 2214), Houghton Library, Harvard University. In June 1872, the *College Courant* carried an advertisement for Redpath & Fall listing Howe as a speaker.

22. Pond, *Eccentricities of Genius*, 543; Pond, *New-York Daily Tribune*, October 2, 1898.

23. *Detroit Free Press*, February 5, 1871, carried a notice that Howe would speak at the Opera House that night—Sunday—on the topic "The New World." On Tuesday, the paper reported the attendance of a "large audience."

24. This version appeared in *Indianapolis News*, February 17, 1871.

25. *Boston Advertiser*, June 1886.

26. Julia Ward Howe, Journal, May 30, 1886.

27. Deborah Pickman Clifford, *Mine Eyes Have Seen the Glory: A Biography of Julia Ward Howe* (Boston: Little, Brown, 1979), 193.

28. Reprinted from the *Chicago Herald* in *The Unitarian*, July 1889, 318–19.

29. Julia Ward Howe, "The Battle-Hymn of the Republic," *Youth's Companion*, April 3, 1884, 139.

30. Richard Cutts, *Index to the Youth's Companion, 1871–1929* (Metuchen, NJ: Scarecrow Press, 1972), 492.

31. Julia Ward Howe, "Recollections of the Antislavery Struggle," *The Cosmopolitan*, July 1889, 286.

32. Howe, *Reminiscences*, esp. 269–77.

33. Walter Hines Page to Julia Ward Howe, August 1, 1898, August 29, 1898, and January 23, 1899, Houghton-Mifflin Company Records (MS Am 2030), Houghton Library, Harvard University.

34. Julia Ward Howe to Laura Richards, September 6, 1899, Howe, Julia (Ward), 1819–1910 (MS Am 2119), Houghton Library, Harvard University.

35. Higginson, "Julia Ward Howe," 167–78; quotation at 174.

36. Julian Hawthorne, "Book Reviews," *North American*, December 22, 1899.

37. Howe lectured at the Lyceum theater on May 8, at a chapel service at the university on May 9, followed by appearances at local schools and children's parties and an opportunity to meet with Union veterans. See the *Saint Paul Globe* (Saint Paul, Minnesota), May 9, 1900, May 10, 1900, and subsequent issues.

38. Julia Ward Howe Papers Concerning the *Battle Hymn of the Republic*, 1897–1906 (MS Am 2195), Houghton Library, Harvard University.

39. Julia Ward Howe Papers Concerning the *Battle Hymn of the Republic*.

40. Julia Ward Howe, Journal, January 27, 1901.

41. Julia Ward Howe, Journal, Tuesday, February 3, 1903.

42. *Ouachita Telegraph* (Louisiana), March 20, 1874; reprinted from the *Boston Transcript*.

43. Higginson, "Julia Ward Howe," *Outlook*, January 26, 1907, 174.

44. Rufus R. Dawes, *Service with the Sixth Wisconsin Volunteers* (Marietta, OH: E. R. Alderman & Sons, 1890), 28–29.

45. Julia Ward Howe, Journal, July 7, 1900.

46. Alfred Seelye Roe and Charles Nutt, *History of the First Regiment of Heavy Artillery, Massachusetts Volunteers, Formerly the Fourteenth Regiment of Infantry, 1861–1865* (N.p.: Published by the Regimental Association, 1917).

47. Julia Ward Howe, Journal, April 24, 1892. See also Louise Hall Tharp, *Three Saints and a Sinner: Julia Ward Howe, Louisa, Annie, and Sam Ward* (Boston: Little, Brown, 1956), 244.

4. Righteous War and Holy Peace

1. Laura E. Richards, Maud Howe Elliott, and Florence Howe Hall, *Julia Ward Howe, 1819–1910* (Boston: Houghton Mifflin, 1916), 2:42–43; George Washburn, *Fifty Years in Constantinople and Recollections of Robert College* (Boston: Houghton Mifflin, 1909), 88, 166; Keith M. Greenwood, *Robert College: The American Founders* (Istanbul: Boğaziçi University Press, 2003), 210.

2. Howe, "Battle-Hymn of the Republic," *Youth's Companion*, April 3, 1884, 139. See also Julia Ward Howe, "Note on the 'Battle Hymn of the Republic,'" *Century Illustrated Monthly*, August 1887, 629–30.

3. Howe Family Papers, 1787–1984. Julia Ward Howe, "Women of Eastern Europe," MC 272, Box 3, 54, Schlesinger Library, Radcliffe Institute, Harvard University.

4. Appeal reprinted in full in Richards, Elliott, and Hall, *Julia Ward Howe*, 1:302–3.

5. "A Question for Mrs. Howe," *New-York Tribune*, October 7, 1870. The letter is dated September 30, 1870.

6. *Nashville Union and American*, September 30, 1870: "A palpable hit is made on Mrs. Julia Ward Howe apropos of her intervention in the war in the name of women throughout the civilized world. It is suggested that there never was a war with which the women on each side did not heartily sympathize, and a few years ago Mrs. Howe herself wrote a stirring lyric, 'The Battle Hymn of the Republic,' the design and effect of which were to stimulate the soldiers and the people to successful fighting."

7. *Voice of Peace*, January 1875, 154.

8. "Italian Unity," *New York Times*, February 24, 1871.

9. For the text of Howe's poem, see *The Unity of Italy: The American Celebration of the Unity of Italy, At the Academy of Music, New York, Jan. 12, 1871, with the Addresses, Letters, and Comments of the Press* (New York: G. P. Putnam, 1871), 197. For the events in Rome as experienced by Americans, see William L. Vance, *America's Rome*, vol. 2, *Catholic and Contemporary Rome* (New Haven, CT: Yale University Press, 1989), 204–10.

10. James W. Trent Jr., *The Manliest Man: Samuel G. Howe and the Contours of Nineteenth-Century American Reform* (Amherst: University of Massachusetts Press, 2012), 258–66; Harold Schwartz, *Samuel Gridley Howe, Social Reformer, 1801–1876* (Cambridge, MA: Harvard University Press, 1956) 291–320; Howe, *Reminiscences*, 345–68; Richards, Elliott, and Hall, *Julia Ward Howe*, 2:320–38.

11. *American Advocate of Peace*, May 1893, 103–4.

12. Jane E. Good, "America and the Russian Revolutionary Movement, 1888–1905," *Russian Review* 41, no. 3 (July 1982): 278–79.

13. Julia Ward Howe, Journal, January 9, 1899, Record Group 18, Yellow House Papers, Maine Historical Society.

14. Maud Howe Elliott, *Three Generations* (Boston: Little, Brown, 1923), 285, 287.

15. The "Battle Hymn" also appeared without comment in the *Bangor Daily Whig & Courier*, April 20, 1898; *Butte Weekly Miner*, April 21, 1898; *Boston Daily Advertiser*, May 10, 1898; *Emporia Daily Gazette* (Emporia, Kansas), May 31, 1898 (and again on June 2).

16. *Boston Daily Advertiser*, April 19, 1898.

17. Florence Howe Hall, "The Building of a Nation's War Hymn—I," *The Independent*, September 15, 1898, 755–58; "The Building of a Nation's War Hymn—II," *The Independent*, September 22, 1898, 830–32.

18. Hall, "Building of a Nation's War Hymn—I," 755.

19. Hall, "Building of a Nation's War Hymn—II," 832.

20. *Speech of Hon. John M. Thurston, of Nebraska, in the Senate of the United States* (Washington, DC, 1898), 3, 12–13, 14–15.

21. Hall, "Building of a Nation's War Hymn—I," 755.

22. E. L. Powell, "Battle Hymn of the Republic (An Interpretation)," in *Savonarola, or, The Reformation of a City, with Other Addresses on Civic Righteousness* (Louisville: Sheltman, 1903), 99–106. This published version of the speech opens with all five verses of the "Battle Hymn."

23. Powell, "Battle Hymn," 100–103.

24. Powell, 104–5.

25. James H. Ross, "War and Peace in Hymnology," *Homiletic Review* 35, no. 6 (June 1898): 555–59.

26. *New York Times*, September 12, 1900.

27. J. B. Pond, *Eccentricities of Genius: Memories of Famous Men and Women of the Platform and Stage* (London: Chatto & Windus, 1901), 149–51.

28. Pond, 149–51.

29. *New York Times*, September 12, 1900; Pond, *Eccentricities of Genius*, 149–151. Pond's version of Howe's remarks differs in detail but not in substance from the *New York Times* account.

30. Richards, Elliott, and Hall, *Julia Ward Howe*, 2:264.

31. Trent, *Manliest Man*, 245–49.

32. Julia Ward Howe, "To the Editor of the Boston Evening Transcript," August 19, 1909, Howe Family Papers (MS Am 2119), Houghton Library, Harvard University.

33. Julia Ward Howe, Journal, May 29, 1908.

34. "Mrs. Howe's Vision," *Christian Science Sentinel*, July 18, 1908, 910; reprinted, with added commentary, from the *Boston Sunday American*, June 28, 1908.

35. "Mrs. Howe's Vision," 910.

36. Julia Ward Howe, Journal, June 26, 1908.

37. *Poughkeepsie Eagle-News*, May 31, 1899; Richards, Elliott, and Hall, *Julia Ward Howe*, 2:265.

38. Quoted in Florence Howe Hall, *The Story of the Battle Hymn* (New York: Harper & Brothers, 1916), 101–3.

39. Archibald Butt to his mother, June 15, 1908, Archibald Willingham Butt Letters, Manuscript, Archives, and Rare Book Library, Emory University; "Choose America's National Hymn," *New York Times*, August 1, 1908.

40. Archibald Butt to his mother, June 15, 1908.

41. Archibald Butt to his mother, June 15, 1908.

42. See the New York *Sun*, November 19, 1907.

43. "Choose America's National Hymn," *New York Times*, August 1, 1908.

44. "President Roosevelt Presents a Challenge to You," *Uncle Remus's Home Magazine*, August 1908, 5–6. The letter was republished in the *Army and Navy Register*, August 1, 1908, 14.

45. Brander Matthews, "The Songs of the Civil War," *Century Illustrated Monthly*, August 1887, 619–29.

46. Theodore Roosevelt to Richard Watson Gilder, November 19, 1908, in *The Letters of Theodore Roosevelt*, vol. 6, selected and edited by Elting E. Morison (Cambridge, MA: Harvard University Press, 1952), 5005; George Otto Trevelyan, *The Life and Letters of George Macaulay*, enlarged and complete ed. (London: Longmans, Green, 1908), 298.

47. *New York Times*, August 8, 1908.

48. *New York Times*, August 29, 1908.

49. *New York Times*, August 15, 1908.

50. "Pupils 'Strike' at Singing 'Battle Hymn of Republic,'" *Inter Ocean* (Chicago), November 23, 1913.

51. *New York Times*, September 19, 1908.

52. Julia Ward Howe to Archibald Butt, August 8, 1908, Archibald Willingham Butt Letters, Manuscripts, Archives, and Rare Book Library, Emory University.

53. *Life*, May 2, 1907, 622.

54. *Baltimore Sun*, May 31, 1907.

55. *Brooklyn Daily Eagle*, October 12, 1912.

56. A. Scott Berg, ed., *World War I and America: Told by the Americans Who Lived It* (New York: Library of America, 2017), 445.

57. Elliott, *Three Generations*, 353–56; see also 357 and 359.

58. *Indianapolis News*, August 6, 1912.

59. "Hail New Party in Fervent Song," *New York Times*, August 6, 1912.

60. Edward G. Lowry, "With the Bull Moose in Convention," *Harper's Weekly*, August 17, 1912, 9.

61. Richard Harding Davis, "The Men at Armageddon," *Collier's*, August 24, 1912, 10–11.

62. Albert J. Beveridge, "The Star of Empire," in *The Meaning of the Times and Other Speeches* (Indianapolis: Bobbs-Merrill, 1908), 143.

63. Albert J. Beveridge, *Pass Prosperity Around* (New York, 1912).

64. "Hail New Party in Fervent Song," *New York Times*, August 6, 1912.

65. Charles Harris Congdon and Edwin O. Grover, eds., *Progressive Battle Hymns: Songs of Peace and Prosperity; Progress and Patriotism* (N.p., 1912). Congdon was the song leader at the convention.

66. *Memorial Exercises in Honor of Julia Ward Howe* (Boston: City of Boston Printing Department, 1911), 23–33. See also *Boston Evening Transcript*, January 9, 1911.

67. *Memorial Exercises*, 5–6.

68. *Memorial Exercises*, 8–9.

69. *Dictionary of American Biography*, s.v. "Lewis, William Henry," Supplement 4 (New York: Scribner's, 1974), 492–93.

70. *Memorial Exercises*, 23–33.

71. Florence Howe Hall, *Memories Grave and Gay* (New York: Harper & Brothers, 1918), 336.

72. *Memorial Exercises*, 41, 43–44.

73. *Memorial Exercises*, 50.

74. "The Negro in Politics," *Crisis*, November 1912, 19.

5. The Anglo-American "Battle Hymn"

1. Rudyard Kipling, "How I Found Peace," in *From Sea to Sea: Letters of Travel* (New York: Doubleday & McClure, 1899), 2:154–66. On Kipling's trip, see Harry Ricketts, *Rudyard Kipling: A Life* (New York: Carroll & Graf, 2000), 141–42.

2. Kipling, "How I Found Peace," 157–58.

3. Rudyard Kipling, "The Light That Failed," *Lippincott's Monthly Magazine*, January 1891, 3–97. See J. M. S. Tompkins, *The Art of Rudyard Kipling*, 2nd ed. (Lincoln: University of Nebraska Press, 1965) 8–21. Tompkins's study is one of the few to mention the "Battle Hymn of the Republic" even in passing.

4. Florence Howe Hall, "The Building of a Nation's War Hymn—I," *The Independent*, September 15, 1898, 755–58; and Hall, "The Building of a Nation's War Hymn—II," *The Independent*, September 22, 1898, 830–32; quotation at 831.

5. Laura E. Richards, Maud Howe Elliott, and Florence Howe Hall, *Julia Ward Howe, 1819–1910* (Boston: Houghton Mifflin, 1916), 2:303–4.

6. Archibald Butt to his mother, June 15, 1908, Archibald Willingham Butt Letters, Manuscript, Archives, and Rare Book Library, Emory University.

7. *The Bookseller*, February 28, 1862, 156.

8. Hallam Tennyson, *Alfred Lord Tennyson: A Memoir* (New York: Macmillan, 1897), 1:490.

9. [George Augustus Sala] to Samuel Ward, November 15, 1864, Sala, George Augustus, 1828–1895, the Haverford College Quaker and Special Collections.

10. George Augustus Sala, *My Diary in America in the Midst of War* (London: Tinsley Brothers, 1865), 1:32–33.

11. George Augustus Sala, *Things I Have Seen and People I Have Known*. (London: Cassell, 1894), 1:246–47.

12. *To-Day: The Monthly Magazine of Scientific Socialism*, January–June 1885, 88.

13. *To-Day: The Monthly Magazine of Scientific Socialism*, January–June 1884, 1–2.

14. William Morris, *Chants for Socialists* (London: Reeves, 1885).

15. Janet E. Ashbee, letter to the editor, *Times Literary Supplement*, May 11, 1906.

16. *Christian Hymns* (London: Macmillan, 1893); originally published in 1891.

17. Note to Hymn 374, in *Christian Hymns*, 349–50.

18. "Memoir," *Times* (London), October 18, 1910.

19. Allison L. Sneider, *Suffragists in an Imperial Age: U.S. Expansion and the Woman Question, 1870–1929* (New York: Oxford University Press, 2008), 3–4.

20. Hugh S. Roberton, "Battle-Hymn of the Republic" (London: Bayley & Ferguson, 1915); Hugh Coward, "God's Truth Is Marching On" (London: Curwen, 1916); Hugh Blair, "Mine Eyes Have Seen the Glory" (London: Novello, 1916); Martin Shaw, "Battle Hymn" (London: Curwen, 1916); Walford Davies, "Mine Eyes Have Seen the Glory" (London: Curwen, 1918). In 1917, Novello published *American National Songs*, which included the "Battle Hymn."

21. *In Hoc Signo: Hymns of War and Peace* (London: Society for Promoting Christian Knowledge, 1915). In 2003 the SPCK included the "Battle Hymn" in the *Joy of Heaven*.

22. "Battle Hymn," words by Julia Ward Howe, music by Martin Shaw, *The Treasury* 26, no. 159.

23. An account signed "A. G." [Anne Gilchrist] in the *Church League for Woman Suffrage* (June 1916), reprinted in Lucy Delap, Maria DiCenzo, and Leila Ryan, eds., *Feminism and the Periodical Press*, vol. 3 (New York: Routledge, 2006); Sybil Oldfield, ed., *International Woman Suffrage: Ius Suffragii*, vol. 2, *November 1914–September 1916* (London: Routledge, 2003), 326.

24. "Studio-Talk," *International Studio*, June 1919, 103.

25. *The Motherland Song Book: For Unison and Mixed Voices*, vol. 1 (London: Stainer & Bell, 1919).

26. *Training in Music* (London: Isaac Pitman & Sons, 1922), 120–21.

27. *Musical Times*, June 1, 1919, 286.

28. "Art of Patriotism," *Times* (London), March 25, 1919.

29. *The League of Nations Song Book* (London: Stainer & Bell, 1919).

30. *Dominion* (Wellington, New Zealand), April 23, 1917.

31. Burton J. Hendrick, *The Life and Letters of Walter H. Page* (Garden City: Doubleday, Page, 1925), pt. 2, 243–44.

32. *Times* (London), April 21, 1917; "America Day: Service at St. Paul's Cathedral," *Musical Times*, May 1, 1917, 207. The editors clarified that the "Battle Hymn" was "written in 1861 by Mrs. Julia Ward Howe to the tune of 'John Brown's Body' (which, of course, is not by Martin Shaw, nor was it his arrangement that was used, as stated in the Press)."

33. Quoted in Karine V. Walther, *Sacred Interests: The United States and the Islamic World, 1821–1921* (Chapel Hill: University of North Carolina Press, 2015), 223.

34. Hendrick, *Life and Letters of Walter H. Page*, 244.

35. Charles H. Brent, *The Mount of Vision: Being a Study of Life in Terms of the Whole* (New York: Longmans, Green, 1918), xi, xix.

36. Hall Caine, "America and Great Britain Are United in Aim, Might and Glory," *Natchez Democrat*, May 4, 1917. For a profile of Caine, see J. B. Pond, *Eccentricities of Genius: Memories of Famous Men and Women of the Platform and Stage* (London: Chatto & Windus, 1901), 452–54. On Howe's contact with Caine in Rome, see Richards, Elliott, and Hall, *Julia Ward Howe*, 2:243, 248, 250.

37. A. G. Gardiner, "The Prospects of Anglo-American Friendship," *Foreign Affairs* 5, no. 1 (October 1926): 7.

38. Edward Marshall, "New Tune for American 'Battle Hymn,'" *Deseret News* (Salt Lake City, Utah), June 6, 1918. See also John Maxwell Hamilton, *Journalism's Roving Eye: A History of American Foreign Reporting*, updated ed. (Baton Rouge: Louisiana State University Press, 2009), 428.

39. *New York Times*, July 5, 1918.

40. Associated Press report in the *Fort Wayne Sentinel*, April 4, 1919.

41. William Dana Orcutt, *The Magic of the Book: More Reminiscences and Adventures of a Bookman* (Boston: Little, Brown, 1930), 192–93.

42. Boyd Cable, *Grapes of Wrath* (New York: E. P. Dutton, 1917).

43. E. P. Dutton advertisement, *New York Times*, April 7, 1917. The front page of this issue of the *Times* carried news of Congress's declaration of war.

44. *New York Times*, April 2, 1918.

45. "A Conrad Hero's Quest for the Truth," *New York Times*, April 22, 1917.

46. T. S. Eliot to Eleanor Hinckley, March 21, 1915, in Valerie Eliot and Hugh Haughton, eds., *The Letters of T. S. Eliot*, vol. 1, *1898–1822*, rev. ed. (New Haven, CT: Yale University Press, 2011), 99.

6. The Valor of Righteousness

1. Theodore Roosevelt, *Average Americans* (New York: G. P. Putnam's Sons, 1920), 3.

2. Theodore Roosevelt, *Fear God and Take Your Own Part* (New York: George H. Doran, 1916), v.

3. *New York Times*, February 10, 1919.

4. Nicholas Murray Butler to Laura E. Richards, June 4, 1917, quoted in Anne Stokes Alexander, "Laura E. Richards, 1850–1943: A Critical Biography" (PhD diss., Columbia University, 1979), 363.

5. Florence Howe Hall, *The Story of the "Battle Hymn of the Republic"* (New York: Harper, 1916), 96–97.

6. Hall, 98.

7. Hall, 99–10.

8. *Country Life* 39 (March 11, 1916): 531.

9. Hall, *Story of the "Battle Hymn,"* 99.

10. *New York Times*, April 3, 1917.

11. Maud Howe Elliott, letter to the editor, *New York Times*, April 5, 1917. The letter is dated April 3, 1917.

12. Laura E. Richards, *To Arms! Songs of the Great War* (Boston: Page, 1918).

13. See the candid promotional piece by Porter Emerson Browne, "The Vigilantes," *Outlook*, May 8, 1918, 67–69.

14. Richards, *To Arms!* This poem appears before the table of contents.

15. "Mrs. Stowe and Mrs. Howe," *New York Times*, July 21, 1918.

16. Florence Howe Hall, *Memories Grave and Gay* (New York: Harper & Brothers, 1918), 137–38.

17. Margaret Prescott Montague, "Good Friday, 1917," *Atlantic Monthly*, May 1917, 749–56; quotations at 749, 753, 754.

18. Annie W. Gould, letter to the *New York Times*, June 3, 1917.

19. Lyman Abbott, "An International Battle Hymn," *Outlook*, June 27, 1917, 321. Almost all of Abbott's editorial was reprinted in "Our 'Battle Hymn' for the Allies," *Literary Digest*, July 14, 1917, 26–27.

20. Jarvis A. Wood, *The International Battle Hymn* (Philadelphia: N.W. Ayer & Son, 1918), unnumbered pages; *Philadelphia Evening Ledger*, October 13, 1917.

21. Richards, Elliott, and Hall, *Julia Ward Howe*, 2:279.

22. Woodrow Wilson, *The Papers of Woodrow Wilson*, ed. Arthur S. Link (Princeton, NJ: Princeton University Press, 1979), 30:254.

23. *New York Times*, April 2, 1917.

24. *New-York Tribune*, April 8, 1917.

25. New York *Sun*, April 9, 1917.

26. "The 'Sunday' Meetings," *Christian Advocate*, January 14, 1915, 60.

27. "Billy Sunday and Boston," *The Pacific*, November 23, 1916, 4–5; reprinted from the *Springfield Republican*.

28. "Billy Sunday in New York City," *Sabbath Recorder*, April 30, 1917, 572–74; quotation at 574; reprinted from the *Christian Advocate*.

29. *New York Times*, April 6, 1917.

30. *Christian Advocate*, November 14, 1918, 1449.

31. "The Battle Hymn of the Republic," *Christian Workers Magazine*, August 1917, 947.

32. Reported in *Christian Register* 96, no. 20 (May 17, 1917): 460. The *Christian Register* had been published since 1821.

33. Samuel McCrea Cavert, "The Missionary Enterprise as the Moral Equivalent of War," *Biblical World*, December 1917, 348–52; quotation at 352.

34. James H. Snowden, *The Coming of the Lord: Will It Be Premillennial?* (New York: Macmillan, 1919), 128.

35. *Lompoc Journal* (Lompoc, California), August 9, 1918.

36. Reported in the *Evangelical Herald*, January 3, 1918, 6; published by the German Evangelical Synod of North America.

37. See *The Eighteenth Annual Report of the Board of Publication and Sabbath School Work* (Philadelphia: Board of Publication and Sabbath School Work, 1918), 23–24.

38. Louis F. Benson to Franklin L. Sheppard, June 7, 1917, Louis F. Benson Manuscript Collection, Special Collections, Princeton Theological Seminary Library.

39. Louis F. Benson to Franklin L. Sheppard, May 9, 1917, Princeton Theological Seminary Library.

40. Franklin L. Sheppard to Louis F. Benson, June 6, 1917, Princeton Theological Seminary Library. Sheppard included the noteworthy comment that President Wilson had directed the army and navy to drop the "braggart" third stanza from "The Star-Spangled Banner." Sheppard made the change in *Alleluia* was well. Notably, the denomination allied itself with the government first by putting the anthem in the hymnbook and then by conforming to the president's wishes by censoring words that did not suit the Anglo-American alliance.

41. *One Hundred Sixteenth Annual Report, Board of Home Missions of the Presbyterian Church in the United States of America, presented to the General Assembly, at Columbus, Ohio, May 16, 1918* (New York, 1918), 23–24.

42. J. Gresham Machen, *Christianity and Liberalism* (Grand Rapids, MI: Wm. B. Eerdmans, 2009), 151–52.

43. J. Gresham Machen, "The New Presbyterian Hymnal," *Christianity Today*, 1933, 5–6, 8–9; reprinted in D. G. Hart, ed., *J. Gresham Machen, Selected Shorter Writings* (Phillipsburg: P&R Publishing, 2004), 274–88; quotation at 277.

44. William Dana Orcutt, *The Magic of the Book: More Reminiscences and Adventures of a Bookman* (Boston: Little, Brown, 1930), 194.

45. Franklin K. Lane, *The American Spirit: Addresses in War-Time* (New York: Frederick A. Stokes, 1918).

46. Lane, *American Spirit*, v–vi.

47. *Americanization as a War Measure*, Bulletin 1918, No. 18, Department of the Interior, Bureau of Education (Washington, DC: Government Printing Office, 1918), 13–20.

48. Robert L. Owen, *Where Is God in the European War?* (New York: The Century Company, 1919).

49. Owen, 4, 49, 51–53. Owen's sweeping Whig history of the modern world covers pp. 17–53.

50. *Address of President Wilson Opening the Campaign in New York for the Second Red Cross Fund, Saturday, May 18, 1918* (Washington, DC: Government Printing Office, 1918), 6.

51. *New York Times*, December 30, 1918.

52. *Times* (London), May 31, 1919.

53. *New York Times*, February 4, 1924.

54. Arthur Conan Doyle, "The Rent in the Line," *Times* (London), October 3, 1918.

55. Arthur Conan Doyle, *Through the Magic Door* (New York: Doubleday, Page, 1909 [McClure, 1908]), 32–33.

7. The Sacred Inheritance of Mankind

1. "Roosevelt's Allegorical Painting," *International Studio*, December 1919, 78. See also "Random Impressions in Current Exhibitions," *New York Tribune*, December 28, 1919, 5.

2. Clara Bancroft Beatley, "Julia Ward Howe," *Christian Register*, June 5, 1919, 546.

3. Maud Howe Elliott, "The Hymn in the Great War," *Ladies' Home Journal*, May 1919, 43, 118.

4. "Adds to 'Battle Hymn,'" *New York Times*, March 16, 1918.

5. "'Battle Hymn' as It Is," *New York Times*, March 20, 1918.

6. "A Masterpiece Needs No Increment," *New York Times*, March 21, 1918.

7. "The 'Battle Hymn,'" *New York Times*, March 27, 1918.

8. Florence Howe Hall to William C. Edgar, August 19, 1921, William C. Edgar and Family Papers, Minnesota Historical Society.

9. Maud Howe Elliott, "Fifty-Eight Years After," Julia Ward Howe Papers Concerning the *Battle Hymn of the Republic*, 1897–1906 (MS Am 2195), Houghton Library, Harvard University.

10. See Richard M. Gamble, *In Search of the City on a Hill: The Making and Unmaking of an American Myth* (London: Continuum, 2012).

11. Carlton J. H. Hayes, *The Historical Evolution of Modern Nationalism* (New York: Richard R. Smith, 1931), 164–67.

12. Hayes, 229–30.

13. *Hutchinson News* (Hutchinson, Kansas), March 21, 1921.

14. Herbert H. Gowen, "The Spirit and the Wheels," *Proceedings of the Institute of International Relations* 7 (1931): 5–11.

15. *New York Times*, February 25, 1924,

16. William Norman Guthrie, *The Religion of Old Glory* (New York: George H. Doran, 1919), 310ff; originally published in 1918.

17. Carlton J. H. Hayes, *Essays on Nationalism* (New York: Macmillan, 1926), 121.

18. *Indianapolis News*, January 24, 1920.

19. *Atlanta Constitution*, October 24, 1919.

20. Reprinted in the *Dallas Express*, April 30, 1921.

21. *Brooklyn Daily Eagle*, August 26, 1937.

22. *Nevada State Journal* (Reno, Nevada), August 28, 1937.

23. "Do We Believe in the 'Fall of Man'?" *Literary Digest*, November 20, 1920, 36–37.

24. *Indianapolis News*, July 10, 1920. Picture of Lloyd George singing in *The Sun and the New York Herald*, August 29, 1920.

25. The Associated Press story was picked up by many papers. See, for example, *Fort Wayne Sentinel*, October 17, 1921.

26. *The Age*, November 13, 1920.

27. *The Commoner*, April 1921, 5–8.

28. John Steinbeck, *Working Days: The Journals of "The Grapes of Wrath," 1938–1941*, ed. Robert DeMott (New York: Viking, 1989), 65; see also 161.

29. Steinbeck to Elizabeth Otis, September 10, 1938 and undated, in Elaine Steinbeck and Robert Wallsten, eds., *Steinbeck: A Life in Letters* (New York: Viking, 1975), 171, 173.

30. Steinbeck to Pascal Covici, January 1, 1939, in Steinbeck and Wallsten, *Steinbeck: A Life in Letters*, 174.

31. Harry Valentine, ed., *John Steinbeck: A Collection of Books & Manuscripts*, foreword by John R. Payne (Santa Barbara: Bradford Morrow Booksellers, 1980), entry 132.

32. John Steinbeck, *The Grapes of Wrath*, with an introduction and notes by Robert DeMott (New York: Penguin, 2006), 150–51, 345, 349.

33. *Winnipeg Tribune*, May 20, 1939.

34. Saul D. Alinsky, *Reveille for Radicals* (New York: Vintage Books, 1989; Chicago: University of Chicago, 1946), 191.

35. Beatrice Kaufman and Joseph Hennessey, eds., *The Letters of Alexander Woollcott* (New York: Viking, 1944), 217–18.

36. Thomas Fensch, ed., *Conversations with John Steinbeck* (Jackson: University Press of Mississippi, 1988), 6. The article appeared on April 23, 1937.

37. Fensch, *Conversations*, 33.

38. Steinbeck to Elizabeth Otis and Annie Laurie Williams, March 19, 1937, in Steinbeck and Wallsten, *Steinbeck: A Life in Letters*, 138.

39. Roy Simmonds, "The Reception of *The Grapes of Wrath* in Britain: A Chronological Survey of Contemporary Reviews," in John Ditsky, ed., *Critical Essays on Steinbeck's "The Grapes of Wrath"* (Boston: G. K. Hall, 1989), 74–75.

40. Alexander Woollcott, "Shouts and Murmurs," *New Yorker*, February 6, 1932, 30, 32. See the introductory biographical sketch in Kaufman and Hennessey, *Letters of Alexander Woollcott*, vii–xxii.

41. United Press story in the *San Bernardino County Sun*, July 5, 1941.

42. *San Bernardino County Sun*, March 30, 1942.

43. William L. Bird Jr., *"Better Living": Advertising, Media, and the New Vocabulary of Business Leadership, 1935–1955* (Evanston, IL: Northwestern University Press, 1999), 66–118.

44. "Woollcott Speaking: The Battle Hymn of the Republic," Julia Ward Howe Papers Concerning the *Battle Hymn of the Republic*, 1897–1906 (MS Am 2195), Houghton Library, Harvard University.

45. "Hymn from the Night," Julia Ward Howe Papers Concerning the *Battle Hymn of the Republic*.

46. https://www.oldtimeradiodownloads.com/drama/the-cavalcade-of-america/hymn-from-the-night-1944-09-18.

47. *Morning Herald* (Hagerstown, Maryland), January 2, 1942.

48. Edward Randolph Welles, "Pardon—Power—Peace: An Historic Sermon," *Living Church*, February 4, 1942, 12–13.

49. "The Presidency: Conference, In Church & Out," *Time*, January 12, 1942, 11.

50. Celia Sandys, *Chasing Churchill: The Travels of Winston Churchill* (New York: Carroll & Graf, 2004), 146–47.

51. "The Presidency: Conference, In Church & Out," 11.

52. Available at the Imperial War Museum website, http://www.iwm.org.uk/collections/item/object/1060021454.

53. Full text of the prayer and a pdf of the original typed copy available at http://www.fdrlibrary.marist.edu/aboutfdr/d-day.html.

54. *Newsweek*, June 19, 1944, 36, 38.

55. *Los Angeles Times*, June 6, 1944.

56. "Roxy, New York," *Billboard*, August 12, 1944, 25.

57. From the United Press story in, for example, the *Evening News* (Harrisburg, Pennsylvania), April 17, 1945.

8. Exotic Medley

1. Pauline Maier, *American Scripture: Making the Declaration of Independence* (New York: Knopf, 1997), ix–xxi. See the helpful overview of the history of the National Archives building at https://www.archives.gov/about/history/building.html.

2. See, for example, *Democrat and Chronicle* (Rochester, New York), September 17, 1947; *Berkshire Eagle* (Pittsfield, Massachusetts), April 23, 1947.

3. *Chicago Tribune*, February 8, 1942.

4. *Pittsburgh Press*, February 17, 1947; *New York Times*, February 18, 1947.

5. See Kevin M. Kruse, *One Nation under God: How Corporate America Invented Christian America* (New York: Basic Books, 2015); Bruce Feiler, *America's Prophet: Moses and the American Story* (New York: William Morrow, 2009), 208–40.

6. *Free Russia*, July 1891, 1. See also Jane E. Good, "America and the Russian Revolutionary Movement, 1888–1905," *Russian Review* 41, no. 3 (July 1982): 273–87.

7. "Society of American Friends of Freedom: Protest against the Russian Extradition Treaty," *American Advocate of Peace*, May 1893, 103–4.

8. See the comprehensive list of over 400 hymnals that include the "Battle Hymn" at hymnary.org.

9. Elisabeth Elliot, *Shadow of the Almighty: The Life & Testament of Jim Elliot* (San Francisco: HarperSanFrancisco, 1989), 142; originally published in 1958.

10. Billy Graham, "Will God Spare America?," in *America's Hour of Decision* (Wheaton, IL: Van Kampen Press, 1951), 119.

11. Carl F. H. Henry, "The Marvel of the Rose Bowl," in *America's Hour of Decision*, 98–99.

12. *America's Hour of Decision*, 5.

13. *America's Hour of Decision*, 65.

14. Jonathan M. Bryant, *How Curious a Land: Conflict and Change in Greene County, Georgia, 1850–1885* (Chapel Hill: University of North Carolina Press, 1996), 90.

15. See the advertisement in the *Independent* (Long Beach, California), August 13, 1964, and the article about a local showing in the *Las Vegas Optic* (Las Vegas, New Mexico), December 26, 1969.

16. Video available at http://billygraham.org/video/russian-army-choir-at-1992-moscow-crusade/. The *Washington Post* story was reprinted in the *Reading Eagle*, October 31, 1992.

17. Richard Drew, "Runner-Up Can Be Winner," *Independent Star-News*, November 6, 1966.

18. Drew, "Runner-Up Can Be Winner."

19. Anita Bryant, *Mine Eyes Have Seen the Glory* (Old Tappan, NJ: Fleming H. Revell, 1970), 105.

20. Bryant, 105.

21. Bryant, 106–10.

22. Italics in original.

23. Bryant, 101–12. Italics in original.

24. For details of the controversy, see the report in the *Independent Press-Telegram* (Long Beach, California), June 5, 1977.

25. Brian McNaught, "Why Bother with Gay Rights?," *The Humanist* 37 (September–October 1977): 34–36.

26. See Beecher's *A Plea for the West* (Cincinnati: Truman & Smith, 1835).

27. Video available at https://www.youtube.com/watch?v=kJcN9zbDs-g.

28. James Keller, *Make Each Day Count: A Christopher Thought for Every Day of the Year* (Garden City, NY: Hanover House, 1955), 56.

29. Biographical and publishing details come from Thomas Lask, "Papal Fiction," *New York Times*, March 18, 1979; John Leonard, "Books of the Times," *New York Times*, April 12, 1979; Francis X. Murphy, "The First American Pope," *New York Times*, April 15, 1979; Edmund Fuller, "Bold Novel about the First American Pontiff," *Wall Street Journal*, April 16, 1979; Carol Lawson, "Behind the Best Sellers," *New York Times*, June 3, 1979; Bruce Weber, "Walter Murphy, Author and Princeton Political Scientist, Dies at 80," *New York Times*, May 1, 2010; Stan Katz, "Walter F. Murphy, a Hero of War, and of Scholarship," *Chronicle of Higher Education*, July 30, 2010; and Justice Samuel Alito's foreword to the new edition of *Vicar of Christ* (New Orleans: Quid Pro Books, 2014).

30. Sotirios Barber, "Walter Murphy and the Public Spirit" (unpublished paper), http://lapa.princeton.edu/hosteddocs/APSA_Law_and_Courts.pdf.

31. Thomas Lask, "Papal Fiction," *New York Times*, March 18, 1979.

32. Walter F. Murphy, *The Vicar of Christ*, 35th anniversary edition with a foreword by Justice Samuel Alito (New Orleans: Quid Pro Books, 2014), 304–6.

33. Murphy, 524.

34. Murphy, 524–25.

35. Full video available at http://www.c-span.org/video/?204880-1/arrival-ceremony-pope.

36. Laura Bush, *Spoken from the Heart* (New York: Scribner, 2010), 409.

37. http://www.rushlimbaugh.com/daily/2013/04/25/remembering_the_day_president_george_w_bush_welcomed_pope_benedict_with_the_battle_hymn_of_the_republic.

38. http://blog.adw.org/2010/11/the-battle-hymn-of-the-republic-as-bible-hymn-of-the-republic/.

39. *The Unitarian*, May 1890, 253–54.

40. Julia Ward Howe Papers, 1790–1951 (MS Am 2214), Houghton Library, Harvard University.

41. See "America's Promise," at https://www.lds.org/ensign/1979/09/americas-promise?lang=eng.

42. David W. Stowe, *How Sweet the Sound: Music in the Spiritual Lives of Americans* (Cambridge, MA: Harvard University Press, 2004), 88–89.

43. Michael Hicks, *The Mormon Tabernacle Choir: A Biography* (Urbana: University of Illinois Press, 2015), 114–16.

44. "'Battle Hymn' Sets Precedent as Pop Single," *Billboard*, September 14, 1959, 2.

45. "Her Hymn Is Pop Hit," *Life*, October 5, 1959, 133.

46. For the instances cited here, see W. F. Crafts, "The Temperance Ribbons," *Christian Union*, July 31, 1878, 84; "Some Notable Women," *Weekly Wisconsin* (Milwaukee) March 7, 1891; Frances Willard, *Glimpses of Fifty Years: The Autobiography of an American Woman* (Chicago: H. J. Smith, 1889); "Words Spoken at the Exercises at the Chicago Normal School, March 5, 1902," *Elementary School Teacher and Course of Study* 3, no. 10 (June 1902): 723; "New Battle Hymn of the Republic," *Democrat and Chronicle* (Rochester, New York), February 8, 1899; and the editorial in the *Decatur Herald* (Decatur, Illinois), January 12, 1965.

47. *New York Times*, August 22, 2010.

48. *New York Times*, July 24, 1962.

49. *Chicago Tribune*, January 8, 1965.

50. Hicks, *Mormon Tabernacle Choir*, 116, 121, 124, 131–32, 144, 147.

9. A Severed Nation

1. Program available in the Papers of Julia Ward Howe, 1857–1961, A-24 (M-133), Reel 6, #19, Schlesinger Library, Radcliffe Institute, Harvard University.

2. *Washington Post*, November 19, 1961.

3. *Indianapolis Star*, November 26, 1963.

4. *Detroit Free Press*, November 25, 1963.

5. "Tributes to President," British Pathé, http://www.britishpathe.com/video/tributes-to-president.

6. *Life*, February 12, 1965, 38; *Life*, February 5, 1965, 68.

7. *Corsicana Daily Sun* (Corsicana, Texas), January 30, 1965, 1, 4.

8. Graham Greene, "Nightmare Republic," *Sunday Telegraph* (London), September 29, 1963; *New Republic*, November 16, 1963.

9. Graham Greene, *The Comedians* (New York: Viking Press, 1981).

10. Greene, *The Comedians*, 229.

11. Edmund Wilson, *Patriotic Gore: Studies in the Literature of the American Civil War* (New York: W. W. Norton, 1994), 91–98.

12. Wilson, 96.

13. See Richard M. Gamble, *In Search of the City on a Hill: The Making and Unmaking of an American Myth* (London: Continuum, 2012), 132–37.

14. Daniel J. Boorstin, ed., *An American Primer* (New York: Penguin/Meridian Classics, 1985), xiii.

15. Boorstin, 402, 404.

16. Robert N. Bellah, "Civil Religion in America," *Daedalus* 134, no. 4 (2005): 40–55; originally published in 1967.

17. Bellah, 40.

18. Bellah, 49.

19. Bellah, 54.

20. Robert N. Bellah, *The Broken Covenant: American Civil Religion in Time of Trial*, 2nd ed. (Chicago: University of Chicago Press, 1992), 53; originally published in 1975.

21. Ernest Lee Tuveson, *Redeemer Nation: The Idea of America's Millennial Role* (Chicago: University of Chicago Press, 1968), vii–viii.

22. Tuveson, 197.

23. Tuveson, 199–202.

24. Tuveson, 198.

25. Gary Williams, *The Hungry Heart: The Literary Emergence of Julia Ward Howe* (Amherst: University of Massachusetts Press, 1999), 267–68n57.

26. James A. Grimshaw Jr., ed., *Cleanth Brooks and Robert Penn Warren: A Literary Correspondence* (Columbia: University of Missouri Press, 1998), 297, 321, for letters about the project from 1960s and 1970s.

27. Cleanth Brooks, R. W. B. Lewis, and Robert Penn Warren, eds., *American Literature: The Makers and the Making, Book B: 1826–1861* (New York: St. Martin's Press, 1973), 1158–62.

28. Brooks, Lewis, and Warren, 1160.

29. Brooks, Lewis, and Warren, 1160.

30. Brooks, Lewis, and Warren, 1161.

31. Brooks, Lewis, and Warren, 1162.

32. Cleanth Brooks, *On the Prejudices, Predilections, and Firm Beliefs of William Faulkner* (Baton Rouge: Louisiana State University Press, 1987), 151.

33. M. E. Bradford, "The Rhetoric for Continuing Revolution," in *A Better Guide Than Reason: Federalists & Anti-Federalists*, with a new introduction by Russell Kirk (New Brunswick, NJ: Transaction, 1994), 194–200.

34. Wendell Berry, "American Imagination and the Civil War," *Sewanee Review* 115, no. 4 (2007): 587–602; quotations at 591 and 595. This Berry essay also shows the influence of Wilson's *Patriotic Gore*.

35. Berry, 595.

36. Edgar Lee Masters, "Sexsmith the Dentist," from his *Spoon River Anthology*; cummings's "Memorabilia"; Pound, Canto 20 of the *Pisan Cantos*; Dunbar-Nelson's play, first performed by her schoolchildren in Wilmington, Delaware, and then published in W. E. B. DuBois's *The Crisis*, April 1918, 271–75; David Mamet, *American Buffalo* (New York: Grove Press, 1976), first performed in Chicago in 1975.

37. John Updike, *Self-Consciousness: Memoirs* (New York: Alfred A. Knopf, 2006), 79–80. See also Sukbhir Singh, " 'Back on to the Life Wagon': An Interview with John Updike," *Irish Journal of American Studies* 5 (1996): 77–91.

38. Updike, *Self-Consciousness*, 103.

39. James A. Schiff, "The Pocket Nothing Else Will Fill," in James Yerkes, ed., *John Updike and Religion: The Sense of the Sacred and the Motions of Grace* (Grand Rapids, MI: Eerdmans, 1999), 58–59.

40. Photo and story distributed by UPI. See, for example, the *Corvallis Gazette-Times* (Corvallis, Oregon), March 1, 1960.

41. *Palm Beach Post* (West Palm Beach, Florida), March 7, 1960.

42. Herbert Mitgang, "Her Song Goes Marching On," *New York Times*, January 28, 1962.

43. Full text and audio available at https://kinginstitute.stanford.edu/king-papers/documents/birth-new-nation-sermon-delivered-dexter-avenue-baptist-church.

44. https://kinginstitute.stanford.edu/our-god-marching.

45. https://kinginstitute.stanford.edu/king-papers/documents/ive-been-mountaintop-address-delivered-bishop-charles-mason-temple.

46. Video available at https://www.youtube.com/watch?v=TcYOHNWZ3jQ.

47. Full video available at http://www.c-span.org/video/?166032-1/british-memorial-service.

48. Richard Wightman Fox, *Reinhold Niebuhr: A Biography* (San Francisco: Harper & Row, 1987), 219.

Epilogue

1. *New York Times*, April 11, 1903; *Indianapolis Journal*, June 7, 1903.

2. Excerpt from Maud Howe Elliott's diary, February 17, 1932, Julia Ward Howe Papers Concerning the *Battle Hymn of the Republic*, 1897–1906 (MS Am 2195), Houghton Library, Harvard University.

3. *Los Angeles Times*, February 18, 1932.

4. See Woollcott's syndicated column in the *Miami News*, March 22, 1942.

5. This account of the Freedom Train is drawn widely from the folder "American Freedom Train (1)" in Box 64 of the John Marsh Files at the Gerald R. Ford Presidential Library, Grand Rapids, Michigan, and from www.freedomtrain.org.

6. *Pittsburgh Press*, March 9, 1977.

7. "Magee, David B.," in Donald C. Dickinson, *Dictionary of American Antiquarian Bookdealers* (Westport, CT: Greenwood Press, 1998), 137–38.

8. *Daily Herald* (Provo, Utah), March 8, 1970.

9. See Harold Holzer, "Collecting's First Family," *Americana*, March–April, 1980, 41–47.

10. Christie's press release, October 6, 2005.

11. http://www.christies.com/lotfinder/books-manuscripts/howe-julia-ward-autograph-manuscript-signed-5636282-details.aspx.

12. Noah Charney, "Critics Call It Evangelical Propaganda; Can the Museum of the Bible Convert Them?," *Washington Post*, September 4, 2015.

13. "Battle Hymn of the Republic Returns to Its Birthplace," https://www.museumofthebible.org/news/battle-hymn-republic-returns-its-birthplace.

14. Frederick Nietzsche, "On the Uses and Disadvantages of History for Life," in *Untimely Meditations*, trans. R. J. Hollingdale with an introduction by J. P. Stern (Cambridge: Cambridge University Press, 1983), 62.

15. Ernest Renan, "What Is a Nation?" (lecture delivered at the Sorbonne, March 11, 1882). A modern translation is available in Ernest Renan, *What Is a Nation? And Other Political Writings*, trans. M. F. N. Giglioli, with a foreword by Dick Howard (New York: Columbia University Press, 2018).

16. J. Peter Burkholder, *All Made of Tunes: Charles Ives and the Uses of Musical Borrowing* (New Haven, CT: Yale University Press, 1995), 376–79.

17. George Santayana, "The Genteel Tradition in American Philosophy," in Douglas L. Wilson, ed., *The Genteel Tradition: Nine Essays by George Santayana* (Cambridge, MA: Harvard University Press, 1967), 54.

18. John Lukacs, *Historical Consciousness: The Remembered Past* (New Brunswick, NJ: Transaction, 1994), xxxvi, 126, 148, 377.

19. H. L. Mencken, *A Book of Prefaces*, 2nd rev. ed. (New York: Alfred A. Knopf, 1917), 216.

INDEX

201.7209 Gamble, Richard M.
GAM
        A fiery gospel.

$28.95

DATE			